what Matters MOST

"*What Matters Most* is an engaging theological reflection on the important work of introducing—or reintroducing—young people to a vital spiritual life in Christ. Leonard DeLorenzo takes on the courageous task of challenging the prevailing cultural ethos that encourages youth to value accomplishment, achievement, and scholastic metrics over faithfulness to the Gospel's call to listen, remember, respond, and sacrifice."

Rev. Mark L. Poorman, C.S.C.
President
University of Portland

"Leonard DeLorenzo sheds profound light onto how faith is rooted in ways of being in the world that are often at variance with the grasshopper habits of digital natives. He beautifully demonstrates how a Christian culture, with its way of seeing the world, is necessary to liberate us from the anxious narratives of our time and glimpse God's way of being, which we are constantly invited to share. I am grateful for this book. It has taught me much."

Rev. Timothy Radcliffe, O.P.
Author of *Take the Plunge*

"I *love* what Lenny DeLorenzo wrote! Love it. I need to reread this book every single year to remind myself how to minister to young people well and why it's important to do so. His personal witness, masterful insights, crucial and compelling questions, and practical explanations make *What Matters Most* an essential text for anyone who works with and loves young people today."

Katie Prejean McGrady
Catholic speaker and author of *Follow*

"This book is a must-read for those who work with young Catholics and struggle to help them find the depths of God in their overscheduled lives. Leonard DeLorenzo urges us to seek and embrace silence for ourselves and his thought-compelling stories remind us to dwell in the presence of God every day as we accompany young people along their paths of vocational discernment."

Katherine Angulo
Associate Director of Youth Ministry
Archdiocese of Atlanta

"Raising kids just got a little easier. Thanks to *What Matters Most*, parents and faith formation ministers have a map for the difficult journey of raising Catholic children in the midst of a confusing world. Leonard DeLorenzo invites us to look to Mary as the perfect role model for choosing to live as disciples. You will be encouraged and experience a spiritual deepening because of his excellent work!"

Michael St. Pierre
Executive Director
Catholic Campus Ministry Association

"*What Matters Most* is both radically simple and profoundly challenging. It portrays our work in the formation of young people today—tomorrow's saints—as daunting but doable. The ultimate goal is clearly, positively, and often *beautifully* defined."

Adam Kronk
Head of School
La Lumiere School

what Matters MOST

Empowering Young Catholics for Life's Big Decisions

LEONARD J. DeLORENZO

AVE MARIA PRESS AVE Notre Dame, Indiana

© 2018 by Leonard J. DeLorenzo

All rights reserved. No part of this book may be used or reproduced in any manner whatsoever, except in the case of reprints in the context of reviews, without written permission from Ave Maria Press®, Inc., P.O. Box 428, Notre Dame, IN 46556, 1-800-282-1865.

Founded in 1865, Ave Maria Press is a ministry of the United States Province of Holy Cross.

www.avemariapress.com

Paperback: ISBN-13 978-1-59471-807-6

E-book: ISBN-13 978-1-59471-808-3

Cover and text design by Andy Wagoner.

Printed and bound in the United States of America.

Library of Congress Cataloging-in-Publication Data is available.

Dedicated to our children:

Caleb Elijah, Felicity Thérèse,
Josiah Xavier, Isaac James, and
Gianna Magdalene

Contents

Preface

I received a call in the spring of 2016 from the president of my high school alma mater. He phoned to tell me that I would be inducted into the school's Ring of Honor. I was shocked to learn I would receive this honor, and that I was shocked is itself somewhat shocking.

I don't remember how or when I started to desire honors as a child but I do know that it became second nature to me: receiving praise as a way to measure myself and draw the admiration of others. I was already rather comfortable with this desire when I visited my high school for the first time as an eighth-grader and I saw the student body president stand in a place of honor to address us prospective students and our parents. I desired that honor, and four years later, I stood in his place. The same thing happened when I saw the captain of the varsity soccer team and the valedictorian and the senior class award winners: I glimpsed honor, and I desired it. So I was doubly shocked when I learned I was chosen for this new honor because I didn't expect it—even though it was just the sort of thing I usually desired.

I am grateful for being shocked in both senses. My gratitude runs deep, all the way back to when I was fourteen years old and was enrolled in a school that goes by the name "Mater Dei." From that day to now, I have spent every day of my life associated with an institution that bears the name of Our Lady—first as a high school student in Southern California, and then for the rest of my schooling, and now in my work at another place dedicated to Mary in northern Indiana, the University of Notre Dame. For someone like me who has always been so much in danger of cultivating ambition for my own honor and glory, my saving grace is the fact that Mary, Mater Dei, Notre Dame, Our Lady, has taken me under her mantle.

For Mary, her honor is always her mission. I learned that first at Mater Dei High School, though I did not fully know it at the time. I learned that the honor of accomplishment includes the grace of acknowledging support, and those who have supported me from then to now are many.

I learned that the honor of leadership includes the grace of remaining with others in their suffering, as when I was asked to help carry the coffin of an underclassman, Samsun Phan, who died in an accident when I was senior. Leadership then meant not only carrying his body and speaking of him at his funeral Mass, but also going to sit with his mother, in her home, grieving at the loss of her only child. The honor was all mine, and yet it was not for my own glory.

I learned that the honor of distinction includes the grace of being humbled. I learned that from one of my best friends, Bryan Zech, who came straight over to congratulate me with a sincere smile on his face when I—rather than he—was chosen as class valedictorian. The truth is that Bryan was always smarter and was frankly more deserving of the honor than I was, but the selection committee did not choose the best and most accomplished student in this case. He honored me with his humility and friendship. Ever since he died just a few years after finishing law school, I find that what I remember most is that smile and the time he congratulated me. It is a memory wrapped in the mystery of who he was and who he is: he smiled so easily and so freely, and he could laugh like a child, even with all his brilliance and composure. The generosity of his friendship was truly a gift for which I should have said "thank you" more sincerely. The real honor now would be to live more gratefully, in truth.

I have great love for Mater Dei not just for what it does, but for what it is—for whose it is—and for who it has called me to be, patiently but firmly. Even while I was becoming ever more comfortable "hankering for praise" for myself, as St. Augustine puts it, I was also secretly being schooled in that hard and saving discipline of channeling and redirecting ambition, directing my desire away from the lust to be admired and toward the willingness to admire others. Far from the valedictorian, I am still a novice in this.

So yes, I did see the irony in being inducted into Mater Dei's Ring of Honor, which I considered a very great honor indeed. It was just the sort of thing I would have always wanted for all the wrong reasons. But I have learned that the true measure of my gratitude is the degree to which I lavish honor on others, for their glory, in love. To say "thank you" means communicating two things at once: my sincerity and my pledge to live into the honor I have received.

Gratitude, after all, is truth telling. Learning how to really say "thank you" is liberating, because it sets me free from the control of my own ambition, my own concern for status, my own secret desire to be praised. Thank you, Bryan. Thank you, Samsun and Mrs. Phan. Thank you, Mater Dei. Thank you, Mother of God.

During a class discussion recently, a student of mine said, "I feel like we are taught to be ambitious but we are not taught how to listen to the voice of God." I know exactly what he means. This is why the education that Mary provides is a saving grace: she teaches us how to listen to the voice of God—patiently, humbly, and also courageously. Mary leads us to what matters most.

This book is about listening and acting. This book is about helping young people find their way into the freedom of the Gospel with the courage of a Christian disciple. That means, therefore, that this book is also about helping adults—like myself—who are charged with raising and educating young people. It is our mission to form them in such a way that they might encounter the Word of God and muster the courage to respond, with conviction and a sense of responsibility, especially in the face of life's big decisions. I suppose this is all a pedagogy of gratitude: learning how to recognize a gift for what it is and then saying "thank you," both with sincerity and with the pledge of yourself. In the Christian lexicon, we might identify this as the call to missionary discipleship or the art of vocational discernment.

This is a book about Christian formation in both subtle and explicit ways. I want to diagnose some of the most stubborn impediments to freedom in our modern lives and to propose what we might do about these impediments. At the same time, this is not my own private opinion—a set of my own ideas offered to you, my reader—although I am of course responsible for what I write. Instead, this book keeps at its heart the person of Mary, who shows us what discipleship is and who nurtures disciples into sanctity. Her vocational discernment—her missionary discipleship—is the keynote.

And who might you be, dear reader? You might be a parent concerned with or at least questioning how to raise your own children toward holiness. Or, you are someone who might someday be a parent, and all of this is also intended for you because, as I will emphasize, the formation for parenthood must begin well before we ever receive the first positive pregnancy test or adoption match.

You might be a Catholic educator, thinking about what you teach, how you teach, and the environments in which you educate your students. You might be a young adult who is at once in the throes of your own vocational discernment while simultaneously on the threshold of having others asking *you* for mentoring and guidance. You might be a campus or parish minister, or even a theologian with pastoral concerns, who would be willing to ask "How do we make it easier for young people to be Catholic?"

It is good news indeed that the bishops from around the world are considering the topic of young people, faith, and vocational discernment at their 2018 general synod. To that end, my own place of work—the McGrath Institute for Church Life—has convened a preparatory conference to explore the very question I just posed above. Whether at the Vatican or in your home, parish, school, or diocese, what is absolutely true is that taking seriously the responsibility of forming young people in faith means that we absolutely cannot focus on one age group alone. Rather, we must take something like a continuum approach to Christian formation, where we ask what we hope for our young people to become in twenty years and then move toward those ends. We do not form teenagers to be faith-filled teenagers, but to be faith-filled adults. Adult faith formation does not begin in adulthood but in childhood. In a very real sense, investing in our young people today is investing in the young people they themselves will form and evangelize. As such, there is an irreducible cultural focus to this book right alongside the personal focus, with the hope that we can work together to think about how we evangelize through the cultures we form, even while working to evangelize, catechize, guide, and support the persons charged to our care right now.

This particular book builds in some ways from the two books I wrote previously, one on the theology of the Communion of Saints (*Work of Love: A Theological Reconstruction of the Communion of Saints*, UND Press, 2017) and one on the craft of telling stories of grace (*Witness: Learning to Tell the Stories of Grace That Illumine Our Lives*, Ave Maria Press, 2016). It is not at all necessary that you read those books before reading this one, but I do want to acknowledge that what I have written here would not have been possible without the study of the theology of holiness and communion in the first title, or without the explorations into the mystery of grace and demanding task of storytelling in the second. I cite those two books throughout this one just to highlight some of the thoughts that I am building on here. It is also the case, therefore, that every word of gratitude that I expressed in the acknowledgments for those two books is carried over into this book. Upon the foundation of the generosities and gifts of many have I learned to think, speak, pray, and write. Where I still fail is due largely to my own ineptitude as a student of the great cloud of witnesses who have surrounded me.

In Gratitude

I am becoming increasingly aware of the fact that nothing comes from nowhere, including and especially "my own" thoughts. This growing realization is due, in part, to combing back through what has somehow become nearly two decades of notes about many of the topics that emerge in this book. These notes are evidence of how, when, and with whom ideas and convictions that have long since settled into my mind and heart were once new to me and came to me from, with, or alongside others in particular places and at particular times. I simply cannot account for all of this, both because of my sheer lack of memory and the sheer enormity of the task. All the same, I would like to offer a short catalogue of gratitude for the places where and the people with whom I spent time while the words in this book were being written, beginning in fall of 2016.

In October of 2016, I had the great privilege of leading a group of sixteen college students on a pilgrimage to Malta. Alongside my fellow pilgrims, I was moved by the Marian faith of Malta. This faith was embodied in the members of the Society of Christian Doctrine, whose simplicity, intentionality, and directness in lives dedicated to fraternity, prayer, meekness, and catechizing young people were as beautiful as they were persuasive. The inimitable Ruth Lasseter was our liaison to the Maltese and the Society; Ruth is generous and caring beyond all reckoning—I am grateful for her friendship and for all those to whom she introduced me in the spirit of friendship.

The students in the courses I taught in fall 2016, spring 2017, and summer 2017 are very much present in these pages, and some of them are really present since they were kind enough to allow me to include excerpts from their own writing in this book. Sometimes, reading my students' work astounds me and teaches me more than I think I teach them. This is especially true of the three Church Life Interns with whom my colleagues and I worked during the 2016–17 school year: Alexandra Viegut, Andrew Miles, and Madeline Lewis. It was a gift to first guide them and then follow them into creatively reimagining the beauty of the Church's life.

Between the latter part of 2016 and the summer of 2017, I was given the opportunity to speak at the National Conference on Catholic Youth Ministry, the Gulf Coast Faith Formation Conference, the Los Angeles Religious Education Congress, and the National Association for Lay Ministry Conference. In each venue I was challenged to articulate my thoughts clearly, to listen attentively to the interests and questions of pastoral ministers and educators, and to consider over and over again what is most urgent, most pressing, and most relevant. In the course of preparing these presentations, fielding questions, and learning from those who joined these sessions, insights that made their way into this book were forming.

The same is true of the opportunities given to me to speak at parish communities of St. Irenaeus in Park Forest, Illinois, and St. Joseph in South Bend, Indiana, where we focused on mercy, character, and St. Joseph during the Lenten season. From a distance, I joined the Lakes Catholic Parish of the Diocese of Broken Bay, Australia, with whom I designed evangelization workshops focusing on the practice of crafting stories of grace, both through video lectures and reflection resources. The fruit of that work was then transferred to the Diocese of Lafayette-in-Indiana, where I was invited to lead these workshops in person. A visit to the Archdiocese of Atlanta with my colleagues Tim O'Malley and Brett Robinson provided an opportunity to explore the pressing needs of young adults and new possibilities for both the cultural support and personal efforts intended to strengthen the bonds to and within the Church during this critical stage of life. Finally, Our Lady of Fatima Catholic Church in Spokane, Washington, hosted me for the better part of a week to lead a parish mission. I am especially mindful of how my days in the peaceful Spokane home of Tammy and Dwaine Plummer afforded me time in quiet, with easy access to wooded trails and the night sky free of light pollution. I do not know how exactly to account for the benefit of those gifts, but I do know that the finishing touches for chapter 2, along with some of the key movements of chapter 5, somehow materialized in between the natural wonders of eastern Washington, the tabernacle sanctuary of the parish, and the prayers that arose naturally from my heart during those days spent with good people. Thank you to Fr. Terry Johnson, Peter Mueller, Fr. Rex Curry, Amy Daniels, Damellys Sacriste, Katherine Angulo, Paul Sifuentes, and Deacon Dan Glatt for inviting me into your communities of faith.

I attended two funeral Masses during the time I was writing this book, both of which were in my home parish. The first was for Joe Lazarra, one of the best men I have ever known, whose own words of prayer appear at the end of chapter 2. The second was for Julia Ameduri, a longtime parishioner and owner of the best and most popular pizzeria in South Bend. When you are trying to write about things that matter, mourning and praying for those who made their own lives matter in all the most important ways is a great gift because none of this is merely theoretical and not a bit of it is hypothetical. Joe and Julia were gifts to our parish and our community; I miss them, but I hope for them. Even more, I hope in them for me and am grateful to be in communion with them and with those who love them.

All the while, I have been blessed to work with incredible people day in and day out, beginning with my unfailingly supportive boss, John Cavadini. I am also incredibly grateful for the time I spent designing and teaching a course with my now longtime colleague, Megan Shepherd, on the topic of "Tensions in Vocational Discernment," out of which the initial ideas for this book arose. I have also learned much from my onetime teacher and now colleague and friend, Vittorio Montemaggi, who has a rare gift for friendship and whose own writing does not just include but indeed embodies gratitude. Vittorio has made gratitude into a theological category.

The first person to read an entire draft of this book was Kathryn Thompson, while Brett Robinson generously read portions of the manuscript in process, as did Claire Fyrvquist and Adam Kronk. The gift of their time and insights is not lost on me. The staff at Ave Maria Press is also due my immense gratitude. They are patient, professional, and dedicated people who not only know their business but also believe in their mission. Tom Grady was the first person with whom I talked about this book, and from there, Eileen Ponder has been my editing partner; she has made this book immeasurably better than it would have been otherwise.

I began to lay this foundation of gratitude—incomplete as it is and must remain—with an expression of gratitude for Mater Dei High School, my first Marian home. To my general thanks, I want to add my particular appreciation to Helen Steves, who has showered me with motherly care since I was fourteen years old, caring for me as her own. I am but one of a great many who lay claim to that high honor. I am likewise grateful to Steve and Ellen Viau, Patrick Murphy, Frances

Clare, Martin Stringer, Laurie Rollinson, Cindy Egan, the late Carol Ann LaRosa, and Margery Fischer, who was my first theology teacher.

Above all, I thank my wife and constant companion, Lisa. She is the mirror who shows me both who I am and who I am not yet but hope to become. She allows me to be that mirror for her, however bristly I am at times in my mannerisms and moods. She shows me who Mary is in the way that she loves and believes—that is, she shows me what it looks like to give a home to the Word of God. It would be fitting to dedicate this book to Lisa, but since I already dedicated one to her—and since this book considers Mary, who herself found all her joy in her beloved son—I will honor my wife with gratitude by dedicating this book to our children—Caleb Elijah, Felicity Thérèse, Josiah Xavier, Isaac James, and Gianna Magdalene—with whom we are well pleased.

January 1, 2018
Solemnity of Mary, Mother of God

1. From My Daughter to the Blessed Mother

And I'll walk slow, I'll walk slow.
Take my hand, help me on my way.

—Mumford and Sons

One Sunday I was tucking in my then five-year-old daughter when she started talking about a boy in a wheelchair whom we had seen earlier in the day. It was obvious to her that the wheelchair was permanent rather than temporary, and she wanted to know why he was in that chair. I explained, as best I could, that the muscles in his arms and legs worked differently than hers and mine and, as a result, he could not walk on his own. He used the wheelchair to get around, and that's how his family was able to take him to the park by our house. My daughter thought for a second and then said that it must be hard for him not to be able to walk; I said that it probably was. Looking at the photo of St. Thérèse of Lisieux hanging next to her bed, I asked her if she wanted to ask St. Thérèse to pray for that boy. She said, "No. I want to pray *with* St. Thérèse for him."

St. Thérèse found my daughter first. Sure, my wife and I gave her "Thérèse" as a middle name, but that didn't cause or guarantee the attraction. I think the photos started it—photos like the ones that now surround her bed. In every photo, Thérèse exudes a youthful exuberance mixed with mature confidence. Thérèse caught my daughter's eye as a small, small child because of the way Thérèse looked at her through those

1

photos. Thérèse has the look of someone who is free and who is brave, and those eyes captivated my daughter's young imagination. The look of that saint showed my daughter the kind of eyes she wanted to have: eyes that are alert, bold, compassionate, confident. That night was one of the many times I have been struck by my daughter's own eyes, how they are open to other people, how she is willing to see what they are going through, how she remembers them, and how she wants to respond, to do something for them.

Parents have moments like this, when the beauty of their own children surprises them, delights them, inspires them, and even intimidates them. There is a lot of pressure involved in raising kids—not just about doing all the little things right but, more grandly, about knowing if we are setting them on the right course for the long run. What I saw with my own eyes that night—and what I heard—was like a flash or a blast of clarity: *this* is what I want for my children; *this* is who they ought to be. They should see others and remember them; they should care about what others are going through; they should be bold in wanting to do something for others, know how to do it, and take the giant leap into *actually* making it happen. My children should be free, and they should be brave, and they should know what matters most. My daughter learned all that from looking at a saint looking at her, and I learned something fundamental about parenting in the light of that saint who shows me what I ought to want for my children.

A very wise teacher once taught me that we should "always begin with the end in mind." As I have grown older, I have come to see that this is not really a revolutionary idea, but it is still absolutely fundamental. Expecting too little, aiming for the wrong goals, or having only a vague sense of what "completion" looks like will doom scientific experiments, business deals, and construction projects alike. It will also seriously hamper pastoral strategies or, even, the complex efforts of parenting, mentoring, and educating in faith. Prior to coming up with strategies or approaches, plans or proposals for how to form young people in faith, we must "always begin with the end in mind"—in other words: What are we preparing them for? What do we want them to become? Who do we hope for them to be? In the most direct terms, the end to which all of Christian formation tends is the formation of saints. That is what matters most.

Saints are complete disciples: they have received the love of God in Christ to the extent that they live only in, from, and for that love. Saints are therefore defined by charity—they receive it and they give it; it is their lifeblood. They have been cured of sin—of selfishness—making them free to share the love of God with others. For a saint, there is no such thing as a "private" good because they consider the good of others as their own. As a parent, St. Thérèse shows me what the completion of my children's formation looks like: to desire the good of another in Christ. As a theologian, the saints teach me how everything we learn about God must begin in prayer and return to prayer, guiding us into a life of charity, which is the only way that we can truly know the love of God in truth. Those who have mentored me in Christian discipleship over the years have taught me that mentoring others means guiding them toward what it means to be a saint: to be prayerful and charitable, to be humble and bold, and to set our hearts first of all on the love of God in Christ so we might become fully ourselves in him.

In my roles as parent, theologian, and mentor, the saints have shown me what matters most, and they reveal the end to which Christian formation aims. The life of the saint is the life of true freedom, and the journey of discipleship is about learning what it means to be free. In the chapters that follow, we will focus on some of the most prevalent obstacles to freedom in modern life while also reimagining how to form young people for the true freedom of a Christian. This means that we will be exploring the Church's sacred duty of accompanying young people in faith and through vocational discernment—toward *who* they are called to be and, therefore, *what* they might do. In other words, we will explore how we empower young Catholics for life's big decisions.

This all begins, though, with the love of God in Christ, who makes the saints who they are. While we will chart a course for forming young Catholics throughout this book, we first have to get our bearings—and those bearings come to us through the saints, through scripture, and principally, in Jesus Christ. In this opening chapter, then, we will heed who Christ shows himself to be, in and through scripture, before focusing on the first disciple, who is also the mother of all the saints: Mary. From Christ through Mary, I will suggest that we can understand "the end" to which we form young people from discipleship into sainthood as making them ever more capable of both hearing for themselves and asking of others one simple question: "What are you going through?"

The Question at the End Is the Divine Question

"What are you going through?"[1] The whole mystery of the Christian life is wrapped up in this question. It is so important that we might as well orient all of our efforts in formation and education toward enabling each and every person to intently hear this question in his or her own life, to directly ask this question of others, and to personally commit to all the consequences of both listening to and speaking these words. Those who live in Christ are capable of considering and responding to this question time and again, and they delight in it. Christian maturity, then, is measured according to how fully we each allow this question to shape who we are becoming. This is not a measure that we invent on our own but, rather, one that we inherit because God asks us this question first.

Drawing near to two disciples as they walked seven miles from Jerusalem to Emmaus on the first morning of the Resurrection, Jesus asks the troubled travelers, *What are you discussing as you walk along?* (Lk 24:17). They are discussing what had happened in recent days, how the one to whom they had dedicated their lives had been put to death, how their hope died with him, how they were downcast and sorrowful, but also how they were strangely confused by the nonsensical news they received of an empty tomb and an angelic announcement of new life. The irony is remarkable as they tell their story to the only person who has absolutely no need of an account of the things that have taken place. But Jesus asks, and he listens.

Only after listening does Jesus tell them who the messiah really is— the one they were really hoping for, in the secret depths of their hearts and well beyond the limits of their imaginations. They thought they knew the scriptures, but he himself is the light by which they can see what they were not capable of seeing before. And though Jesus is the one who knows fully, he still gives them yet another opportunity to speak; and they use that opportunity to invite him inside, to dine with them. It is there, inside their home, that he takes the bread, blesses it, breaks it, and gives it to them, making himself known to them as the one they always desired but never fully knew. Their eyes had been prevented from seeing him because they were blinded by their own expectations, they had hoped in the wrong things, and their imaginations were too small to see what God had been doing in those days—and so they were doomed to suffer. But they came to know him, Jesus—their love, their hope—as the one who asked them what they were going through, who let them invite him in, who took their bread to bless and break and share as the gift of himself. It would not have been enough for Jesus to broadcast an announcement of the saving mysteries of those sacred days because the whole point is that he himself is the Word of God who asks humanity wounded by sin, "What are you going through?" And he listens by entering in; he heals by sharing in that pain; and he blesses by making that wounded old thing something new in his love.

This single episode is the Gospel, whole and entire. The Good News is that God asks us "What are you going through?"—and he listens, he understands, and he does something about it, *in person*. This does not mean, of course, that we always have the right idea about what we are going through—after all, the Word that created heaven and earth rightly exercises the authority to call us "foolish" from time to time (see Luke 24:25). But even then the Lord gives us the chance to speak, to put into our own words what we are going through. Apparently, it matters to God that we speak and, even more, God is willing to listen. On the authority of Jesus and all the scriptures that, as one, testify to who he is as God-with-us, we come to recognize that God *always* listens to what we are going through, *always* sympathizes with our weakness, and *always* acts on our behalf (see Hebrews 4:14–16).

The question "What are you going through?" contains the whole mystery of Christian life because, first and foremost, God asks this question of us. We might very well ask "Why?" but the only response we will receive is something like, "This is simply who God is." When God reveals his name to Moses in Exodus 3, he reveals himself to be the one who has *seen the affliction of my people* and who *heard their cry* and *knows their sufferings* and has *come down to deliver them*, to bring them to *a land flowing with milk and honey* (Ex 3:7–9; cf. 3:14–17, *Revised Standard Version*). When Moses hears the divine name of YHWH, what he hears is often translated as "I am who am" or, alternatively, "I will be who I will be," which amounts to God saying, "What I do tells you who I am."[2] The disciples traveling from Jerusalem to Emmaus encountered the fulfillment of what the Israelites first glimpsed in the journey from Egypt to Canaan: God listens, God knows, God acts . . . *in person.* This is who Jesus is: the listening, sympathizing, active Word of God made flesh (see John 1:14).[3]

Love of God and Love of Neighbor

When Jesus himself responds to the question about what commandment is most important of all, it is worth bearing in mind just who God reveals himself to be when we hear Jesus say that *you shall love the Lord your God with all your heart, with all your soul, with all your mind, and with all your strength* (Mk 12:30). Remembering who God shows himself to be tells us who we are loving when we love God: we are loving the one who listens to us, knows us, and acts for us. Loving God means loving the one who loves us, always.

But Jesus does not stop there. He was only asked which commandment was first of all, and yet he goes on to tie a second commandment to it: *You shall love your neighbor as yourself* (Mk 12:31a). In the first breath, Jesus instructs us to love the one who does nothing but love us, who shows us that this is simply who he is as God. In the second breath, though, we are commanded to love those who may very well *not* love us, who may even at times despise us, and who certainly are not as consistent or reliable in character as the God whom Jesus teaches us to call Father. Nothing, it seems, could be more sensible than loving God and nothing potentially more hazardous than loving our neighbor.

What binds these two commandments together as one is that single, central question: "What are you going through?" The one who loves God without reserve will know himself or herself as nothing other and nothing less than the one whom God cares for, fully and personally. It means to know Jesus for who he is, for who he is *for you*—the one who makes the God of Abraham, the God of Isaac, and the God of Jacob into the one whose very name means "I am the one who saves you."[4] To love God wholeheartedly means to love the one who makes you whole, and if you are safe in the love of this God, what is there to fear?[5] Seen from this perspective, the courage necessary to hazard the love of neighbor is born in the love of God.

This all suggests that love of neighbor is the fruit or consequence of the love of God—and this is not false—but there is more to say about this because love of God is not something that is first mastered before love of neighbor is attempted. This is because, first, when I encounter Jesus as the disciples on the road to Emmaus did—as the Word of God drawing near to ask "What are you going through?"—I am not encountering the Savior who comes to me alone. Rather, I am encountering the one who comes first to the *whole of humanity*, to the *whole human race*, to heal and sanctify *us*. Even on the individual level, the God who hears me, sympathizes with me, and acts for me is the same God who hears, sympathizes with, and acts for others. Loving God necessarily means recognizing "what God is doing in the lives of others."[6]

Second, if we remember whom we love when we set out to love God, we recognize that loving God means allowing the *way* God loves to persuade us. God takes us seriously: what we say, how we suffer, what we need—all of that matters to God. The manner in which Jesus acts with the disciples on their way to Emmaus is characteristic of the divine way of love: "not to overwhelm with external power, but to give freedom, to offer and elicit love . . . to knock gently at the doors of our hearts and slowly open our eyes if we open our doors to him."[7]

The hazardousness of loving our neighbor is itself already contained in the love of God for us—that is, God hazards *neighborly* love for us. The first part of the great commandment that Jesus announces in Mark

12 is the command for us to recognize the hazardousness of God's love for us and to be grateful, while the second part of that command is for us to *go and do likewise* by loving our neighbor as God loves us (see Luke 10:37). If we were to think of the Parable of the Good Samaritan in these terms, we would come to see that Jesus himself is the Good Samaritan first, the one who hazards the love of the wounded one and claims him as his neighbor in mercy. Only afterward and by that very love do we—who were first *half dead* when he found us (Lk 10:30)—receive the freedom as well as the duty to love others with the recklessness of those who are safe in the love of God.[8] In short, we show our trust in God's providential care in and through our risk of love for others.[9]

St. Catherine of Siena understood the inextricable connection between Jesus' command to love God and love neighbor in her contemplation of Matthew 25:14–46. In the depth of her prayer, Catherine heard the Lord speak these words to her:

> I love you without being loved. Whatever love you have for me you owe me, so you love me not gratuitously but only out of duty, while I love you not out of duty but gratuitously. So you cannot give me the kind of love I ask of you. This is why I have put you among your neighbors: so that you can do for them what you cannot do for me—that is, love them without any concern for thanks and without looking for any profit yourself. And whatever you do for them I will consider done for me.[10]

In the action of love of neighbor, we learn to live in the love of Christ because in Christ, God took us as *his* neighbor and accepted all the consequences of asking the question of compassion that turns strangers into neighbors: "What are you going through?"[11]

I claim that this question—"What are you going through?"—presents the mystery of Christian life because in it, love of God links to love of neighbor. This union is realized in the person of Jesus Christ, and it is the harmoniousness of his charity that the saints enjoy. The call to discipleship that resounds first from the baptismal waters and bubbles up all the way to the completion of our communion with God and union with one another in the heavenly kingdom echoes forth each time we allow this question to be spoken to us and each time we dare to speak it to others. We can measure progress in discipleship on the way to sanctity according to our willingness and capacity to listen to and speak this question of compassion.

Every Christian's distinctive vocation—that is, the particular shape his or her discipleship takes—is a personal expression of the concern for "the other" that this question captures in its eloquent terseness. The complete Christian—the saint—is the one who holds nothing back from the love of God, and in the freedom of that love gives everything for the good of one's neighbor. This is what St. Thérèse preached to my daughter through her eyes, the same beauty that I witnessed in my daughter—who saw, remembered and, in her small way, loved the young boy in the wheelchair who was heading to the park.

The Sweet Command of Christian Ministry

When God the Father says, "What are you going through?" in his only begotten Son—the Word made flesh—we are healed and made free. As we learn to say this to one another, we become holy as the Spirit makes us one in Christ. But as we are all too aware, we often fail to hear God's Word spoken to us and we fail to open our ears to hear what others are going through. This is not simply a lack of will, because there are all kinds of other obstacles that get in the way of hearing the Word of God and hearing our neighbors, and therefore of acting from God for love of our neighbors. We need to be skillful in recognizing what these obstacles are, especially in our modern world. We must think both faithfully and creatively about how to respond to these obstacles in favor of accompanying young people into the freedom of faith and the courage of missionary discipleship. The end we should have in mind is forming young people to be free and brave as saints, capable of asking that one, all-demanding question: "What are you going through?" And the way in which parents, educators, ministers, and mentors lead them toward that end is to mediate Jesus' simple command: *Be opened!* (Mk 7:34).

By the power of those words, Jesus allowed the deaf to hear and the mute to speak.

Those who accompany young people and maturing disciples are called to cooperate with Christ's work—we help them to be open. We carve out for them the time and space to hear, we form them in the dispositions to listen, and we nurture in them the abilities to respond. All of this is a matter of freedom: the task of freeing young people from what prevents their openness, the task of directing them in what it means to be free, and the task of preparing them to take responsibility for their freedom—that is, to empower them.

According to St. Luke, the disciples of Jesus *are those who hear the word of God and act on it* (Lk 8:21; cf. 11:28; Jn 15:14; Jas 1:22). A disciple is open, he listens, and he responds. It is the Word of God who takes the initiative, the same Word who perceives what is closed and deaf and listless and commands it to open up. Learning to live by this Word is the art of the Christian life.

The personal, particular shape this discipleship takes in the life of each Christian is his or her vocation, in the fullest sense of the term.[12] Every vocation is situated in a specific historical moment, amid certain preexisting conditions like abilities and limitations, opportunities and necessities, and even language and customs.[13] More significantly, though, every authentic Christian vocation in every age and under every historical condition is ordered to Christ's own mission and identity, which he expresses in his prayer to the Father: *that they may all be one* (Jn 17:20, RSV). These words open up the meaning and mission of all human life: to seek communion with God and the unity of the entire human race—that we may share all things in common, by the love of God who has come to share all things with us (see Acts 2:44–47; 4:32–35).[14] This means that every vocation is ordered to the life of the Church, a life *hidden with Christ in God* (Col 3:3).

As the sign and instrument of Christ's love in the world, the Church's responsibility in every age is to form the faithful in Christ's mission and identity. Like every generation before us, this responsibility faces its own distinct challenges in the different ways in which all of us—but perhaps especially young people—are *not* open, are *not* prepared to listen, and are *not* equipped to respond to the Word of God. Today, we have our own forms of deafness and our own impurities of speech. We are blind in our own ways to the work of God and to the needs of others. Those of us who are parents, educators, ministers, and mentors share in the delightful duty of first recognizing these forms of incapacitation—whether cultural or personal—and then echoing Jesus' sweet, skillful, and strong command to *be opened.*

Mary: Model and Mother

We are created to be open to the Word of God, and yet we close up; we are made to be open to our neighbors, and yet we resist. Through the ministry of the Church—in liturgy and sacrament, in proclamation and teaching, in the missions of mercy, in family life—we meet Jesus Christ, who unites us in himself to one another and to the God he calls Father, opening us up to his Word and remembering us to our neighbors. The Church gives the space for hearing the Word of God and acting on it, the time for receiving and for giving, and the ritual movements that train our hearts and minds—along with our hands—for following the path of discipleship to our final end as saints in full communion.

The Church is like a mother who tends to her children: guiding them, teaching them, comforting them, empowering them. Even more, the Church *in person* is a mother who, in and as herself, is the perfect harmony of hearing the Word of God and acting on it: Mary, Mother of God. The Blessed Mother is at one and the same time the model of discipleship and the mother of all the saints: she is free and she is brave, she receives and she gives, she holds the Son of God and she holds the ones he loves. All the saints resemble their mother, who faithfully and creatively acts in response to the Word of God for the life of the world. The union of love of God and love of neighbor takes flesh in her.[15]

Since we must "always begin with the end in mind," and since we must also reimagine the ways in which we empower young people for the fullness of discerning which life choices will draw them toward the fullness of Christian discipleship, we should look to Mary. She never fails to see us in her son so that in her, we find both the model of vocational discernment and the mother who teaches us what it means to be open to God and how to do it. What I will set out to do for the rest of this chapter, then, is to gaze upon Mary as she hears the Word of God and acts on it. I will focus primarily on the Annunciation narrative in the first chapter of Luke's gospel, paying close attention to what the scriptural testimony itself reveals about the fullness of freedom and courage that is hidden within Mary's seemingly simple "yes" to God. What at first glance seems like Mary's passivity is, when properly contemplated, the freest and bravest activity of which human beings are capable. We will see how the Blessed Mother models for us and teaches us what is true discernment of God's call and how to respond to it. In her witness, we are instructed in the priority of listening, the potency of signs, the power of prophecy, and the privilege of sacrifice. Mary will teach us how to take up this sacred duty of patiently but deliberately forming disciples to be saints, especially as we minister to young Catholics. Under her maternal care, we learn how to really say and really hear, "What are you going through?"

The Priority of Listening in Mary's Pondering

Mary's freedom begins not in speaking but in being spoken to, not first in a manner of doing but in a way of receiving. In the Annunciation narrative, the major speaking role belongs to the angel while Mary utters just two lines, the second of which begins her full act of creative love. In order to eventually apprehend the freedom and the courage hidden within Mary's *fiat*, we have to pay attention to how she receives the words that are spoken to her in the Annunciation (nb: It is best to read the remainder of this chapter with a Bible open beside you).

In the Annunciation narrative, the angel speaks three times (see Luke 1:28, 30b–33, and 35–37). After each instance, the focus shifts to Mary, with her words in verse 38 being the most well known and, in fact, the culmination of the whole narrative. But Mary's previous two responses show us more about *how* she received the angel's delivery of the divine announcement, and this *how* is the crucial precondition for *what* she freely and bravely says at the end of the narrative.

The first way that she receives is in silence (v. 29) and the second is with a question (v. 34). The only way to fully grasp what is going on here is to do what the evangelist Luke wants us to do when we read this narrative: juxtapose it with the episode that comes immediately before this one, in which the same angel appears to Zechariah, the father of John the Baptist. The narrative of the announcement of the conception of John the Baptist closely resembles the narrative of the announcement of Jesus' conception, which is precisely what makes the subtle differences between the two narratives all the more important. As with Mary, there are two moments when the *how* of Zechariah's reception is featured.

The first moment occurs in verse 12 as the angel suddenly appears: *And Zechariah was troubled when he saw him, and fear fell upon him* (Lk 1:12, RSV).[16] Notice how similar this is to what is said of Mary after the angel's initial greeting in verse 29: *But she was greatly troubled at the saying, and considered in her mind what sort of greeting this might be.* What is similar is that they are both "troubled," and what is different is that fear falls upon Zechariah while Mary considers the greeting in her mind.[17] We should notice this initial difference between Zechariah, for whom the appearance evinces fear, and Mary, who takes in what is troubling her to consider it, or, to put it more simply, to try to figure out what is going on. It is also worth imagining what someone does when stricken with fear: the person tends to recoil, jumping back into a defensive posture. Mary's initial posture as described by "considered" (or elsewhere, "wondered") is not like preparing to strike back but rather preparing to contemplate.

The stronger distinction between the two figures comes with the first words that they utter in their respective narratives. Zechariah says, *How shall I know this?* (v. 18), while Mary says, *How can this be?* (v. 34). Again, these sound similar, but notice how the center of attention shifts from one question to the other. In Zechariah's question, the focus is on himself—How can *I* know this?—whereas in Mary's question, the focus is on what is happening—How can *this* be? Zechariah wants knowledge—that is, he wants proof to ease his curious and doubtful mind.[18] Mary wants to understand—she has given the benefit of the doubt to the messenger and is trying to catch up to what has been proclaimed to her. Mary is willing to grant that the announcement is true, and she is preparing herself for collaboration. Zechariah places himself in opposition to the announcement because the one thing he takes as certain is the impossibility of conceiving a child, being a man advanced in years whose marriage is marked by infertility. In short, Zechariah challenges the angel while Mary takes on the challenge of seeking to understand.[19]

This distinction in their postures and initial responses to the angel's announcement leads to the radical disparity between how the angel continues his announcement to Zechariah (vv. 19–20) and to Mary (vv. 35–37). The angel had already told Zechariah how this would all happen—namely, that his wife, Elizabeth, would bear him a son, meaning that the two of them would conceive this son together. Zechariah's accusatory question back to the angel came after he had already received more information than Mary had when she responded, so he should have been in a better position to trust. Since even with more information Zechariah was still unwilling to trust and wonder, since Zechariah fails to recognize the precedent for what the angel is announcing (as we will explore in the next section), and since his speech back to the angel is the product of fear, the angel strikes Zechariah mute. Indeed, this is a form of punishment but, seen from another angle, it is also an act of mercy. Mary, who is willing to listen, is already ready to receive the new thing the Lord is doing; Zechariah, who cannot or will not listen attentively, must remain in silence without speech so that the only thing he can do is the very thing he needs to do: listen. Only after learning how to listen will he be able to speak well.[20]

Mary never gets a full explanation—the angel's response to her question is filled with mystery. *The holy Spirit will come upon you and the power of the Most High will overshadow you* (v. 35), thus indicating that the presence of God will descend upon her like it descended upon

Mount Sinai, where the Lord met his people Israel and from which the work of constructing the tabernacle commenced (see Exodus 24:15, 33:9, 40:35; cf. 1 Kgs 8:10; 2 Chr 5:13; Is 6:4; Ezr 44:4; Rv 15:8).[21] The whole event is shrouded in mystery, a mystery into which Mary herself is being drawn. The manner by which she allows herself to be drawn into this mystery is by opening herself as the one who considers, who wonders, or, more pointedly, who "ponders." The question *How can this be?* never leaves her; rather, she makes a habit of asking this question, sitting with the work of God in her midst, and waiting upon understanding.

For the rest of the Lukan infancy narrative, Mary's pondering builds as a central theme. When the shepherds come to the manger and make known to Mary and Joseph the announcement of great joy they received from the angel (Lk 2:8–20), we are told that *all who heard it wondered* (v. 18) but Mary is singled out as the one *who kept all these things, pondering them in her heart* (v. 19).[22] When Mary and Joseph present the infant Jesus in the Temple (Lk 2:22–38), they both marvel at Simeon's proclamation of fulfillment regarding the child, but again Mary is singled out—this time by Simeon's own words—as the one for whom *a sword will pierce through your own soul* (v. 35). Here again, the marveling and wondering goes deeper, right to Mary's core where she keeps these mysteries regarding her son. Then again, at the very conclusion of Luke's infancy narrative, we are given one last image of Mary as the one who ponders. When Mary and Joseph return to the Temple to find preteen Jesus after being separated from him for three days (Lk 2:41–51), they do not understand what he tells them but *his mother kept all these things in her heart* (v. 51). In context, this last note of pondering is not just in regard to the words that Jesus spoke to them that day in the Temple but also and especially about the mystery of his conception, his birth, the angelic proclamations pertaining to him, and his obedience to them (v. 51). In short, Mary is the one who never ceases to welcome the mystery of her son; who permits herself to be troubled and to wait on understanding; who allows him to be revealed rather than forcing interpretation; and who gives a home for the wonder of divine love to transform the flesh in which he dwells.

The Potency of Signs in Mary's Memory

Because Mary ponders, she has time to remember. Think again about Zechariah's response: in his astonishment at the angel's appearance and message, he recoils in fear and then strikes like a serpent with a question that basically says, "prove it to me." The slight difference between his question and Mary's drives him far apart from her disposition of pondering, which becomes a defining characteristic of Jesus' mother. Zechariah fills the air with his own interpretation—a question stuck in his own way of looking at things. Since he will not wait and seek to understand but rather demands to know, he does not grow to recognize what is going on. More precisely, he does not take the time to remember and so he misses the sign that would indicate that this indeed is the Lord who is working in a way similar to how the Lord has worked before. The great irony is that the sign that Zechariah misses is the very thing on which he is fixated: his age and marital infertility.

Because Mary ponders, she does not miss what Zechariah misses; rather, she remembers. In the third and final portion of the angel's address—the portion that follows her question *How can this be?* (v. 34)—the very last thing that the angel tells her is the first thing he told Zechariah: *And behold, your kinswoman Elizabeth in her old age has also conceived a son; and this is the sixth month with her who was called barren. For with God nothing will be impossible* (vv. 36–37). Her cousin Elizabeth's pregnancy is the sign, but why exactly does that pregnancy matter so much? It matters because by that pregnancy, a whole history is being evoked and, moreover, something radically new is now beginning to happen. This sign, however, is only meaningful for one who remembers the history of salvation.

For someone reading the Gospel of Luke for the first time, it might seem like Luke himself has pretty bad manners. This is because the first thing he does after greeting his reader (which is cordial enough) is to introduce two of his main characters—Zechariah and Elizabeth—which also seems cordial enough, until the seventh verse of his first chapter. In that verse, after identifying Zechariah as a priest and his wife as the descendent of priests, both of whom were righteous and faithful, he does not just mention that they were both *advanced in years* but makes a pointed remark about Elizabeth herself: *Elizabeth was barren.*[23] That really puts a fine point on it, so much so that it is difficult to imagine anyone with any sense of common decency ever introducing anyone in such a manner. Yet the angel who appears to Mary identifies Elizabeth as *the one who was called barren* because the truth is that Elizabeth's barrenness is incomparably significant since it is out of her barrenness that the child John will be born. That is remarkable in its own right, but it is even more remarkable because of the one to whom Elizabeth is directly connected in virtue of this most unlikely of events: Abraham's wife, Sarah.[24]

In Genesis 18:1–15, three visitors are passing by the Terebinths of Mamre in the heat of the day, when Abraham welcomes them into his tent and offers them hospitality. After Abraham places a meal before them, the visitors ask about his wife Sarah and then tell Abraham— within earshot of Sarah—that by the time they return in the spring, Sarah will have a son. Sarah, of course, laughs, because *Abraham and Sarah were old, advanced in age* (v. 11), which is exactly what Luke says of Zechariah and Elizabeth. But if we thought that Luke lacked manners in drawing our attention to Elizabeth's barrenness, his elocution does not quite compare to the directness of what we read at the end of this verse about Abraham and Sarah: *Sarah had stopped having her womanly periods* (v. 11b). In no uncertain terms, we are being told that it is physically impossible by course of nature for Sarah to conceive and bear a child. She is indeed *barren*, and when she does eventually conceive and bear Isaac, she becomes, paradoxically, "the barren mother."

For those with even passing familiarity with the Book of Genesis and this central character of Abraham with his wife Sarah, the importance of that particular child cannot be overstated. While he was still called Abram of Ur and living in Haran, the Lord called Abram to go into the land of Canaan where he would become the father of a great nation (Gn 11:31–12:9). This promise is everything. But of course, no nation springs from this man—in fact, he and his wife cannot even bear one child who would start their lineage. The Lord persists with his promise, though, and even intensifies it: *Lift up your eyes . . . all the land which you see I will give to you and to your descendants forever. I will make your descendants as the dust of the earth* (Gn 13:14, 15–16, RSV). Yet, not even one child. The Lord presses further, saying, *Fear not, Abram, I am your shield; your reward shall be very great* (15:1, RSV); words to which Abram understandably responds, *O Lord, what will you give me, for I continue childless* (15:2, RSV). Rather than softening his promise, the Lord intensifies it again: *Look toward heaven, and number the stars, if you are able to number them. . . . So shall your descendants be* (15:5, RSV). And again, when Abram is ninety-nine years old, the Lord pledges to make a covenant with him and changes his name to Abraham, promising that *I will make you exceedingly fruitful; and I will make nations of you, and kings shall come forth from you. . . . And I will give to you, and to your descendants after you . . . all the land of Canaan, for an everlasting possession; and I will be their God* (Gn 17:6, 8; cf. 17:19, RSV).

All this time, as the Lord doubles-down again and again on his promise, putting more and more weight on the importance of Abraham and Sarah bearing at least one child, Sarah's barrenness becomes more pronounced and more troublesome. *Now Sar'ai, Abram's wife, bore him no children* (16:1). *Then Abraham fell on his face and laughed, and said to himself, "Shall a child be born to a man who is a hundred years old? Shall Sarah, who is ninety years old, bear a child?"* (17:17, RSV). She, who, again, is pointedly noted to have *stopped having her womanly periods* (18:11) is marked by an emptiness reminiscent of the void out of which God calls creation (Gn 1:1–2). Sarah laughs at the visitors' announcement of her forthcoming pregnancy because she knows, better than anyone, that barrenness is her defining characteristic in regard to the Lord's promise. Because she cannot conceive, the promise cannot be fulfilled. Yet she does conceive, for one reason and one reason only, which is to answer this question: *Is anything too marvelous for the Lord to do?* (18:14). No, nothing is too marvelous for God.

This is the history that Zechariah forgets and that Mary remembers. When Mary hears the last part of the angel's announcement—*this is the sixth month with her who was called barren. For with God nothing will be impossible* (Lk 1:36–37, RSV)—she recognizes that the Lord who worked wonders for Sarah to fulfill his promise to found the nation of Israel from their father Abraham is now working wonders for Elizabeth to complete that history. There were others who resembled Sarah in some respects earlier—Rebekah (Gn 25:21), Rachel (Gn 30:22–23), Samson's mother (Jgs 13), Hannah (1 Sm 1)—but only Elizabeth fits the barren mother motif that began with Sarah.[25] Because she ponders, Mary has time to remember, and because she remembers the history of salvation, Mary reads the sign of Elizabeth as the Lord speaking to her.

This sign of Elizabeth's pregnancy, which has ramifications for the whole of Israel, is also part of the divine communication to Mary, *personally*. In recognizing the marks of Sarah in Elizabeth, she recognizes the continuity of the narrative of salvation: God who was at work *then* is the same God who is at work *now*; as Sarah was the beginning, Elizabeth is the culmination. Here again, though, noticing the resemblance makes the differences all the more important. Mary herself is receiving an announcement of an uncommon pregnancy, and in that respect she is like Sarah and Elizabeth and all who stand in their line. But unlike Sarah and Elizabeth, Mary is not *old* and she is not *barren*. Whereas Sarah and Elizabeth had each passed beyond their childbearing years, Mary is now just beginning hers. Elizabeth is the sign that with Mary, something new is beginning, and she knows it (see Luke 1:54–55).[26] By the time she utters her "yes," the Lord has spoken to Mary through her memory that what began with Abraham is being fulfilled through her in a previously unimaginable way.[27]

The Power of Prophecy in Mary's Speech

Mary cultivates a listening disposition, and as she listens, she remembers the history of salvation that is now being extended and completed through her. She recalls the ways in which God worked in the history of Israel, and she therefore recognizes that the same God who worked in the past is at work now, in a way that is both continuous with and variant from how God worked previously. In sum, Mary hears the angel's announcement as the Word of God moving in her midst, and because she knows this to be God's Word and is willing to trust in it, she yields not only to God's initiative but also to God's standards for measuring value. What she hears from the angel takes the typical way in which the value of things is measured in the world and turns it upside down. When Mary does speak, then, her words flow along the tide of divine wisdom—that is, her words are prophetic.

Mary is a student of God's Word. Like a good student, she adapts herself to what she hears rather adapting what she hears to suit her own preferences. As the angel delivers the divine lesson, she receives it whole and entire, not simply as a set of facts but even more as a way of understanding. The angel tells her that she will bear a son, that his name will be "Jesus," that he will be great, and further, that he shall be called the "Most High," that he will occupy David's throne, that the household of Jacob will be his domain, and that his kingdom will have no end (vv. 31–33). This name "Jesus" points to the identity of her son while also definitively interpreting the whole history of salvation. Whatever true greatness is will appear in him: look to him to learn greatness. The one named "Jesus" will be both her son and the *Son of the Most High*, and for Luke "Most High" means God (see 1:35, 76; Acts 7:48; 16:17; cf. Luke 6:35) as it does for the demoniac later in his gospel (see Luke 8:28; cf. Mark 1:24). Whoever God is will be made known in this one who becomes Mary's son. The promised messiah who will reestablish the united monarchy of David will be found in this one named "Jesus," and all the hopes of the children Jacob—that is, Israel—will be realized in him. This name—"Jesus"—takes the name that God revealed to Moses and unveils the final degree of the intensity of intimacy in that name, since, in Hebrew, this name means "God saves." Here is God, the Savior—*in person*.[28] In the span of a few words, the divine lesson that the angel delivers is the dawning light that reveals the full meaning of all the scriptures: here, under the name of "Jesus," is all the power of God—the greatest power, the incomparable power—made present, in the flesh.[29]

The angel has spoken in terms of power, and yet what is being revealed here is the true meaning of power, which looks quite a lot like power's undoing. The name "Jesus" is not power as the world measures power, but as God measures it (see Philippians 2:9–11). Whereas the typical form of measuring power in the world moves from the top down, the measure that is being revealed in the lesson given to Mary is power from the bottom up. She does not hear "power" and assume her own interpretation; instead, she receives the Word of God as a son and learns from him what power is. When she sings her Magnificat to her cousin Elizabeth, we begin to hear all that her "yes" to the angel entailed. She says "yes" to the Lord's greatness and the way he looks with mercy upon her lowliness (vv. 46–50); "yes" to his strength that does not submit to the arrogant but rather confounds them (v. 51); "yes" to responding to people on the basis of need rather than on the basis of prestige and strength (v. 52); "yes" to filling up those who are empty and to emptying those who fill up themselves at the expense of others (v. 53); and "yes" to the one who remembers his people in mercy, fulfilling his promise to Abraham by loving his descendants (vv. 54–55). In saying "yes" to this child named "Jesus," Mary says "yes" to the revolution of perspective that God is working in the world, a revolution that will mean the rise of those made low and the fall of those made high according to the unjust measures manufactured through skewed social structures and covetous hearts alike (see Luke 2:34–35). In saying "yes" to "Jesus," Mary says "yes" to God's interpretation, God's perspective.

Peeking ahead to the beginning of Luke 3 allows us to see just how topsy-turvy things get through the inauguration of God's "power" in "Jesus." In setting the stage for the social conditions of the time, Luke names the prominent ones who hold power over this little sliver of land on the eastern bank of the Mediterranean: Tiberius Caesar, Pontius Pilate, Herod, Philip, Lysanius, Annas, and Caiaphas (vv. 1–2). This is a litany of the towering mountains of power overshadowing the plains and valleys of the land and its people. These are the powerful ones, the ones who control and measure power, the ones who are caught up in conflicts of power, whose self-interest sways the movements of their subjects, whose hidden interests exert influence, whose possessiveness is potent even when ineffectual, who exercise political might and religious manipulation, who constitute the forces of the day, and whose primary concern is to hold on to what they have, to never lose, and, if possible, to get what they do not yet control, whether by overt or covert means.[30]

It is precisely into this situation and among these figures—the symbols of the world's power in their time and place—that *the word of God came to John the son of Zechariah in the desert* (Lk 3:2). And what does this *word of God* speak through Zechariah? Only what the prophet Isaiah had foretold: that the low things—valleys—shall be filled in, that the high things—mountains—shall be made low, that the crooked things shall be made straight, that the rough things shall be made smooth, for the Lord's salvation is coming to human flesh, here and now (Lk 3:4–6).[31] What are the high things, the crooked things, the rough things? Luke just named them: Tiberius Caesar, Pontius Pilate, Herod, Philip, Lysanius, Annas, and Caiaphas. Their way of measuring is coming to an end; God's way of measuring is coming into fashion, not by exerting even more power in the way they exert power but, rather, by refusing to play their game, by exercising the power to walk away from the possibility of controlling others, and by granting freedom. John the Baptist not only announces this, but he also does it: when Jesus arrives, John blesses him and walks away. Jesus himself reveals this as the divine way in the desert of temptation (Lk 4:1–13) and then ultimately in the garden of the final temptation (Lk 22:39–46). All of this was already hidden in Mary's "yes" and heralded in her prophetic speech (Lk 1:38, 46–55). When she speaks, she speaks according to what she hears, and what she hears is God's way of doing things in and through her son.

The Privilege of Sacrifice in Mary's Fiat

Mary does not control events; she controls her response. In the *fiat* she offers in response to all that the angel has declared, Mary's "yes" means at once that she yields to the Word of God and that she wills for this to be. She chooses to wait upon the Word of God. Not only will her *let it be* later be found on her son's lips in the Garden of Gethsemane—*not my will but yours be done* (Lk 22:42)[32]—but also we hear in her words the timeless echo of the very Word by which God called the world into being: *let there be light*, or, in Latin, *fiat lux* (Gn 1:3). After listening to the angel, Mary orders into being that which is-not-yet. Her "yes" is a genuine act of creation that harmonizes with God calling the world into existence and Jesus accepting in full the identity of the Father's only Son.

Mary accepts the power to create in response to God's Word and so she also accepts the responsibility for doing so. The meeting of this power and responsibility is her privilege to sacrifice. This seems an odd "privilege" unless we learn from Mary, who learned from the Word of God what the meaning of true freedom is. True freedom involves the possibility of each of us taking responsibility for being someone, to accept the cost of our decisions, and to follow through on what we promise. In all its depth, Mary's free decision to accept the Word of God made flesh as her son involves accepting that she will not control him but rather love him, and like all love but this love most of all, loving will be costly. When the *power of the Most High* overshadows her (1:35), she says *let it be* though she cannot see everything that genuine act of freedom will entail. In fact, her lack of control over the events accentuates the full degree of freedom she exercises: she is free to trust in the Lord with a trust that does not rest on any other safeguard or assurance. In the darkness of her uncertainty, her faith says: *let there be light.*

The only thing that Mary is promised is a child (1:31). As discussed above, in saying "yes" to him, she is saying "yes" to all that he will be and all that will come about through him. From what we know of any mother, we can easily imagine how Mary was filled with expectations and hopes of what her son would be. He was an obedient child, who lived and learned from his mother and from Joseph (see Luke 2:51), though even from the start Mary knew—in some way exceeding her understanding—that her heart would break for him (see again Luke 1:34–35). If we step out of the Lukan arc for a moment and set our gaze on the Passion narrative of John's gospel, we glimpse in one breathtaking glance the depth of Mary's sorrow—that is, the full cost of the responsibility for freely loving her child.

In the Gospel of John, Jesus' mother and the beloved disciple stand with Mary Magdalene and others at the foot of the Cross. The synoptic gospels say that the disciples who witness the crucifixion are watching from afar (see Mark 15:40–41; Matthew 27:55–56; Luke 23:49), but here alone in John's gospel, those who love Jesus much are close to him as he suffers. Looking down to them, Jesus gives his mother to the care of his beloved disciple and he gives his beloved disciple to the care of his mother. To her, the beloved disciple will be a son; to the beloved disciple, Mary will be mother. All the while, Jesus hangs upon the Cross and voices his suffering in the words *I thirst* (Jn 19:28). He is reciting Psalm 69, taking up as his own the words of the psalmist: *My throat is parched . . . I looked for compassion, but there was none, for comforters, but found none* (vv. 4, 21). And so here stands Mary, who was promised a son, watching her son suffer, hearing her son cry out for the compassion that will not come, and having her son instruct her to love another as son in his place. She receives a child at the foot of the Cross, but this is not the child that she expected—that child dies.

Commenting on Giovanni Bellini's painting of the *Madonna on the Meadow* in which a young Mary sits ponderously upon a field gazing meditatively upon the infant Jesus asleep on her lap, Timothy Verdon writes that

> the sadness of the mother suggests her acceptance of her Son's intention to offer himself in sacrifice. Her interiority serves indeed to treasure and ponder her Son's will, and her humility consists in seconding it. Her prayer is an adherence to this divine plan so absolute that the young woman's legs cannot support her weight, and Mary sinks into the dust. Prayer is thus the capacity to inhabit someone else's suffering.[33]

What kind of freedom is this? What power? In saying "yes" to her son, Mary already says "yes" to a future she cannot control, to suffering that is sure to come, to a plan that is not her own design. She entrusts herself to the Word of God, and she accepts responsibility for this choice. She sacrifices her own expectations, which she holds loosely. She sacrifices her own comfort. She sacrifices the confines of her heart to make room for the condition of another—for God's own Son, no less. And, in the end, she sacrifices the finality of her own decision, refusing to stick to what she might have thought she had agreed to and welcoming instead the call to become mother to the one whom the Word-made-flesh gives to her. We cannot fully grasp the power of her *fiat*; we can only marvel at it. What freedom, what bravery!

Returning to the Lukan arc, we see just what the expansion of Mary's "yes" came to include. Gathered together in the upper room after Jesus ascends to the right hand of the Father, the apostles and *some women* and the "brothers" of Jesus *devoted themselves with one accord to prayer* (Acts 1:13–14). And right in their midst, gathered with them, is *Mary the mother of Jesus*. Here is the mother whom Jesus had given to his beloved disciple, and here is the community of the beloved to whom Jesus had given his own mother. It is upon this community—the twelve who reconfigure the tribes of Israel and who draw into one body all those who *hear the word of God and act on it*—that the Holy Spirit falls and the Church is born. She whose "yes" gave the Word of God a place to dwell among us stretches her "yes" to gather up those whom her son loves. Her "yes" brings her beyond the boundaries of whatever expectations she might have had as she relies with unfailing confidence on the Word of God to whom she has entrusted herself. Mary's "yes" is not without pain, and yet it is filled with her own freedom to commit herself to her mission, to become ever more capable of it, and to follow through.

Mary's Way to Missionary Discipleship

If we return to the disciples on their way to Emmaus after contemplating the mystery of Mary's freedom and bravery as presented from the beginning of Luke's gospel, we will see that those disciples were led from their own deafness into Mary's openness, from their own muteness into Mary's speech, and from their own confusion into Mary's wonder. To begin with, they spoke too much and in the wrong way, so they had to learn to listen just as Zechariah did before them. When Jesus calls those disciples *foolish*, he silences them, rendering them mute in order to instruct them how to hear and receive him. In the space of that silence, they take on new memories—in particular, their memories are reconfigured in the light of Jesus' Resurrection, in which he himself teaches them (see Luke 24:27). In response to their new willingness to welcome the stranger (24:28–29), Jesus opens their eyes, curing them of the lingering effects of what they had wanted to see—that is, a messiah with power that would outcompete the other powers of their day—and allowing them to see what God is doing in their midst, in God's very own fashion—that is, redeeming and raising up the lowly by serving their needs, in person. Jesus reveals their hunger to them by breaking bread for them, and they recognize him and themselves and the truth all at once. The fruit of this proclamation of the Word and this offering of bread at the hands of the Lord is that they sacrifice their old expectations—*but we were hoping that he would be the one to redeem Israel* (Lk 24:21)—and *set out at once* with the freedom of a new mission, to *recount what had taken place* (24:33, 35). Their words burst forth like Zechariah's canticle, as their untied tongues now dance with delight to proclaim what the Lord did for them, this new and marvelous thing that the Most High is doing in their risen Savior.

This is how disciples are formed and how disciples become saints: by learning to receive and respond to Jesus as Mary does. In her pondering, memory, prophecy, and sacrifice, Mary is free to love and is capable of it from the start. She gives a home to the Word of God, who draws near and shares in our humanity through her to ask us in the most intimate way, "What are you going through?" As we learn to hear these words, we discover a compassion that exceeds our understanding. It is a gift so precious that we ought to sell everything else for the sake of it, holding on to nothing else in order to trust in the value of this one gift. Remarkably, God allows and commissions those whom he has called to form and heal and empower others. This is the mystery of discipleship—of hearing the Word of God and acting on it—which first becomes full in the patient, trusting, bold, and liberating action of Mary, who says *let it be.* Mary is the model for disciples and the mother of the saints who claims us as her children by holding us close to her beloved son, nurturing us all into the freedom and courage of hearing what she hears and saying what she says.

2. Pondering and the Meaning of Time

No further acceleration is
possible this side of the light barrier.

—Marshall McLuhan

I don't set an alarm clock for the morning. I don't need to: I have children. I cannot rely on my young children for consistent wakeup since nothing about their days is regulated by appointed times. It is my older children who provide this consistency. In the midst of their grammar school years, they are dialed in to the prescribed schedule of school days. They set alarms, they rise, they stir, and so then do I.

It would not be much of a stretch to say that our mornings move like clockwork. Give or take six or seven minutes, we are out the door at the same time every day, heading off to school by the appointed hour. Before that, all the procedures of the morning are executed in pretty much the same order, each day. By the time the kids hop out of the car, they are somewhere between three and ten minutes from the commencement of the well-regimented daily schedule of their school. They walk up the stairs to the right, I pull away from the curb slightly to the left, and we each head into a schedule appropriate to and designated by the places where we spend most of our daylight hours.

Meanwhile, back in our house, my wife buzzes in the predictably unpredictable schedule of a home under the rule of younger children who have not yet crossed into the common order that will wrap around them in the kindergarten classroom. We will all meet her back home at our appointed times, but *not* to detach from moving with the demands of a schedule. The kids now have places to be and things to do: soccer practices, gymnastics, music lessons, various check-ups and check-ins for this, that, or the other thing. This all means, of course, that my wife and I also have schedules to keep, which, as most parents learn, really means that our kids' schedules largely determine our schedules. The schedule overflows into weekends, where activities congregate and fester, ordering the days of the "end" of the week to the rhythms of the week itself. Saturday becomes something like an extended version of Wednesday evening. Sunday is like a second Saturday, or else a pre-Monday: a whole day to either finish up the tasks of the previous week or start up the tasks of the following week.

All the while the clock ticks: sleeping hours, waking hours, bells and alarms and reminders. And with each tick, the next thing is drawing nearer and then the next thing and the one after. Bedtime is the last appointment of every day, one last task for which we *desperately* try to be on time in a day that is ordered by tasks rushing toward us. One after another, these events have caused us to move quickly and expeditiously in an effort to be on time.

What parent hasn't complained not so much about running a schedule but rather being *run by* a schedule? What child in our typical modern lifestyles hasn't felt the effects of this, even if they haven't named it in quite the same way? In our moments of delirious exhaustion or dizzying exasperation, we might even ask a question such as, "What is this all for?" There are all kinds of vague and implicit reasons we might give for why, if all goes according to plan, our days and nights run like clockwork:

"to make our children well-rounded";

"to help them to thrive";

"to give them opportunities to find their passions";

"just trying to make ends meet";

"doing my best to get ahead"; and so on.

It sometimes seems like the only constant is that time is passing and that there just doesn't seem to be enough of it. *This*, then *this*, then *this*, then *this* . . . try be on time. We have made time a "thing" and yielded ourselves to this "thing," as though it has power all its own. Over and over again, we just feel like we don't have time. That's because time has us.

Taking Time with Time

As we saw in the last chapter, Zechariah did not have time for the angel's message. Actually, more to the point, he didn't give the angel his time or, maybe more to the point still, Zechariah just was not capable of giving time. In that very first moment of the angel's address, Mary "considered" while Zechariah was "overcome with fear." In other words, Mary gave time to this unscheduled encounter while Zechariah recoiled from the interruption: he wanted to *know* how to make this new concept fit with what he was doing and how he already saw things. Rather than pausing, he just reacted, and in the speed of his reaction, he failed to notice the context that Mary learned to see.

In each of the next four chapters, we will explore one of the four marks of Mary's discernment, beginning now with her *pondering*. We are going to think about what it means to *have* time and to *give* time while also thinking about how most of us have become accustomed to *not* having time and feeling *unable* to give it. We are going to take a step back to see how we have been trained to chop up time and to see time as an impersonal, constantly moving stream in which we are being moved, leaving us to feel stretched, under the looming threat of our own insignificance. What I am going to argue is that the problem is not with the practical need to order and measure time, but rather with falling out of touch with what time is really for. We are going to talk a little bit about clocks, a little bit about patience, a little bit about digital media feeds, a little bit about educational settings and families, and ultimately about the third commandment: *Keep holy the Sabbath* (Ex 20:8–11; Dt 5:12–15).

I want to "take time with time" because as we have already seen with Mary, true Christian discernment depends on taking the time for deep listening. I call her listening "deep" because the kind of listening necessary for discernment allows a message, a call, *the word* to move past the defenses of your stylized "self" and touch the tissues of your heart. Deep listening allows the subtle intricacies and implications of what you encounter to slowly unravel as you ponder what you take in. Pondering allows your imagination to move around what you receive, seeing it from different angles or listening to different tones, like when you learn to recognize how different instruments and recurring movements are contributing to the work of a single symphony. The greatest defense that each of us puts up against deep listening is our own preferred way of interpreting things, on our own terms. Sometimes, this preferred way is nothing more than what we have become accustomed to. The deep listening of pondering is the discipline of waiting to understand. This discipline is the beginning of the process—the art—of discernment.

Deep listening does not just happen. It is quite obvious that it did not just happen for Zechariah, who was forced to learn how to listen, but it is also true that it did not just happen for Mary. She was ready to listen because she was well practiced in taking time—or, rather, of giving time. If we want to learn just how much discipline and training is hidden within Mary's disposition to consider and then more deeply to ponder, which made all the difference in contrast to Zechariah's fear, then we ought to think about the ways in which our own skittishness, our own habits of dispersing our attention, or own predispositions to reactionary responses make us much more like the one who needs to be struck mute than the one who was ready to begin discerning. We do not need to psychologize Zechariah—all we need to know is what we are told: he was fearful. If we examine ourselves, we may see the many, often hidden ways in which this predisposition to fear rather than trust emerges. Like Zechariah, we are often impenetrable because we are inattentive: we have lost the ability to give time and so we need to recover that capacity.

Odd as it may sound, discernment really begins well before there is anything to discern—in other words, the beginning is not the beginning. Mary shows us how we ought to be when the *Word of God* comes to us; Zechariah shows us how we usually are. Zechariah became like Mary, and those of us who are like him need to develop her capacity for pondering. It is all a matter of time.

The Beginnings of Time

Fear not! I am not going to propose that we stop keeping track of time. That would be patently ridiculous and, even worse, impractical. I tend to appreciate, for example, that when I show up to the classroom to lecture, my students meet me there at the same time. I penalize them if they do not keep the appointment. Keeping track of time allows us to start and end things together, even if, like any teacher, I do wish my students would remember that class is over *when I say it's over* rather than the very moment the clock ticks to a certain time.

I do not want to focus as much on how timekeeping helps us order our days but rather on how we have detached the order of timekeeping from the very order that makes it meaningful. It is not so much *that* we measure time that is at issue as it is *how* and *why* we measure time that matters. The condition in which we find ourselves in the modern world of feeling like time is running us is a major symptom of the loss of Sabbath rest. Before we get to the Sabbath—a rather long time from now—let us think about why we started measuring time the way we do and what the consequences of these measurements are in modern life.

School days, work days, banking hours, show times, tip-offs, face-offs, kickoffs, first pitches, tee times, doctors' appointments . . . all these and many more are set to the regular periodic intervals that a single piece of technology measures in a standard and universal manner: the clock. The invention of the clock was not the beginning of human beings' measurement of time. Rather, the clock's invention is the beginning of the abstract measurement of time.

Go ahead and stare at an analog clock (rather than a digital one) and ask yourself: "What is it keeping track of?" I think you're bound to say "time," and if not that then "seconds" or "minutes" or "hours," which are all measures of time and therefore just ways of speaking about it. At the real risk of making this all too philosophical, we could ask "What is time?" It has become its own thing, as if it is just there, and what we have learned to do is chop it up so we can count its pieces as they pass by.[1] Our notion of "time" is not set to the rising and setting of the sun or the seasons of agrarian life or heartbeats; instead, we measure all these things to the one stable thing in modern life: time as the clock measures it.

If we try to discover where the pressing need that gave rise to the invention of the clock emerged, we will find ourselves, at some point or other, looking into the early stages of monastic life. The monastery was established as a sanctuary of order in the midst of the disorder of what was then "modern life" during the last days of the Roman Empire. Monasteries established a rhythm to life that was not subject to the fluctuations of worldly events, where powers in conflict generated unending instability. Each day in the monastery was set to a rhythm of prayer according to the canonical hours—that is, each day was ordered to seven periods of prayer, and the beginning and conclusion of this set of prayers was the measure of one day. What was needed for keeping these hours was a signal to the community to gather for each session of prayer, and this signal was the striking of a bell.

Unless the rhythm of the community was to be set to the best guesses or whimsy of the bell ringer, the bell ringer himself needed some way to space out the intervals of prayer and therefore regulate the movements of monastic life. The desire to organize days and nights according to this regular rhythm was the basic inspiration that led to the invention of the mechanical clock, which was designed to run on its own.[2] Once the mechanical clock started running, the bell ringer followed its lead, and eventually the bells were just programmed to synch with a clock.

Developing a functioning clock was useful to a monastic community, for "the clock is not merely a means of keeping track of the hours, but of synchronizing the actions of men."[3] That is precisely the point of the monastic community: synchronizing the actions of monks with periods of prayer. But imagine, if you will, what the sound of those bells eventually came to mean for the surrounding countryside and urban settings that grew up around these monasteries. The tolling of the bells offered regular divisions to sleeping and waking hours that were otherwise either unmeasured or, at best, loosely organized into discrete periods. It is only practical—and even quite wise—to utilize the order that those bells suggested, breaking the day into the periods the bells announced.

But now consider the potential problem: within the walls of the monastery, those bells are calls to prayer. Outside the walls, where the monastery's rule does not reach, those bells may draw its hearers to prayer, but not necessarily. And of course, as we might imagine, these measurements of time that are deemed useful will rather swiftly be detached from their original and ultimate meaning, especially for the sake of commerce. Sacred time becomes secular time.[4]

I have told this story rather quickly and without a lot of detail because what I want us to grasp is the phenomenon of dissociating the discipline of measuring time from the reason for measuring it so precisely in the first place. It is almost just an accident of history that such a great impulse for accurately measuring time emerged in a distinctly religious context in the West, but this coincidence will prove not so coincidental by the time we return to this idea of the monastic measurement of time at the end of this chapter. What is important for us now is that we, who almost cannot imagine time any other way, are the inheritors of this radical innovation that is symbolized in the clocks that sit in just about every room into which we walk, clocks that are strapped to our wrists, clocks that are regulating the devices in our pockets, the clock that is staring at me from the top corner of my computer screen, and the clock that both you and I probably have running in our heads right now. We cannot help but think of time as a "series of units of equal duration" that allow us to measure and set our activities on its terms, rather than measuring time by our activities.[5]

If time is its own entity, then either time has no meaning or we have to supply it with meaning. The logic of the digital age is nothing if not an overwhelming proposal about the meaning of time. In fact, this proposal is so overwhelming that we typically cannot see what is being proposed. We just absorb it. And this has everything to do with how we are training our young.

The Logic of the Internet and Streaming Time

I hate to break your concentration, but I would like you, if possible, to open up a web browser. Type a single letter into the address bar at the

top of the page. What happens? Most likely, a host of possible web destinations is presented to you. If you keep typing, those suggestions will
change, perhaps even narrow. Now think about what just happened. You
went online, and immediately the possibilities for moving around came
rushing toward you. There are lots of possibilities, *endless* possibilities.
Things like predictive text and web histories are making it easier and easier to seize one of those options, and from whatever option you choose,
lots of other options will be presented to you. It is right there from the
beginning and on every page of the Internet: the possibility of moving
somewhere else, seemingly instantaneously. That is point number one.

Consider another point: If you were to open any social media site,
what might you see? You are probably going to see some kind of stream,
which we may call a "feed." And what is entering the feed, for you to
eat? Snippet, snippet, snippet, snippet. Snippets of what? The sky's the
limit. If you are on Instagram, you might encounter photos of just about
anything. If you are on Twitter, you'll find brief messages about any
number of things. And if you are on Facebook, you'll see long and short
messages, big and small photos, videos, news reports, fake news, spon-
sored posts, and direct and indirect communications about anything and
everything. The point is not what you find on social media; the point is
that you are being fed.[6] The very instant that something appears at the
top of the feed, you are already trained to expect the message or image
that will come next to bump it downward. It is just a matter of time.

Here is my third and last point about the Internet, at least for now:
If you think about what the Internet is asking you do with your eyes,
how would you describe it? As you might imagine, I have given this
some thought—so here is my answer: my eyes are being trained to scan
and move. It's in the address bar, it's there in hyperlinks on webpages,
it's in sidebars with videos and images and ads, it's there on every social
media site: the abundant, copious, ever-increasing opportunity to look,
look elsewhere, look somewhere again, and all the while always already
be anticipating that something else to look at will suddenly appear in
some way.[7]

Let's wrap up these three points together. First, the Internet is itself built on the premise that possibilities should be endless and that access should become ever more readily available.[8] Every technological advancement that touches in some way on how the Internet functions (whether in algorithms, computer processing, connectivity, etc.) is meant to make the whole experience faster and more efficient, and to get us moving. In fact, predicting where we are going to want to move even before we really think about it is part of the plan. Second, as more and more images come into our field of vision—delivered there ever more expeditiously—the greater the reward we receive for having learned to move quickly. There is more out there, more coming, and so if we move quickly, we will reap the reward of finding more. *Seek and ye shall find*, so hurry up and seek.[9] We end up wanting to be interrupted because interruptions bring new information. And then third, the more we do all of this, the better we get at it. Skim and move, skim and move, skim and move. It is sort of like dancing: the more you practice a routine, the lighter your feet will feel and the more effortlessly and gracefully you will float through the choreography.[10]

What about a smartphone? For the most part, the smartphone has just cut out the web browser and the address bar (though these are still in there), so we are even closer to the multiplicity of possible destinations now popping out at us as icons. Every time we touch a smartphone, we are already touching this whole web of connections. And if by chance our phones are not connected at the moment, we might find ourselves wandering around aimlessly looking for meaning . . . and by that, I mean a WiFi signal.[11]

What does this all have to do with time, Christian discipleship and vocational discernment? In our digital age—which is not going away—we are formed more strongly but more subtly than ever before to actually see "time" flying by us. There is far more than we can possibly comprehend appearing before our eyes, so we are trained to interpret as quickly as possible—glancing, judging, moving. Even when we stay in one place—on one page, in one thread, with one conversation—isn't there some persistent fear lurking somewhere inside of us that we should be somewhere else? Shouldn't we get going—if not with our feet or even our eyes, at least with our thoughts? This is what it feels like to live within an "ecosystem of interruption technologies."[12]

If this is what happens online, what happens when those habits and preoccupations and skills that we are being trained to learn there follow us into our off-line lives? Like the sounds of the bell billowing from the monastery, the way we are instructed to measure time on the net echoes far outside its walls. In fact, more and more, it feels like the Internet does not have any walls, not only because everything is becoming "smart" (which means digitally connected) and "social" (which means digitally sharable) but also because our thoughts are drawn back to digital space even when we are not plugged in. It is as if we are immersed in a totally new kind of human environment.[13]

What would it be like to have more and more of our lives run according to this logic of the Internet, which is getting stronger and more efficient all the time? I suppose it would be just like being run by a schedule—one thing after another coming toward us, forcing us to hustle and bustle to keep up with it all, rushing from one activity to the next, and sometimes just feeling numb as it all flies by. I sometimes find myself sort of just waiting for something to pop up in my inbox even though I have many other things to do. It is like I feel the need to have my schedule dictated to me by the next interruption.

In our digital world, being overscheduled and being ever more tech savvy are far from unrelated. One did not necessarily cause the other but, rather, they are mutually reinforcing phenomena. There is a lot coming at us, the pace is quickening, and time is not on our side.

Now . . . This

Neil Postman shrewdly diagnosed the very dynamic I have just described five years before Tim Berners-Lee invented the World Wide Web. Postman was writing about television. Television is not the same thing now that it was in 1985, and part of what has changed is that segments of television programs are now routinely chopped up into smaller bits for quick consumption, while each individual viewer has the authority to set his own private viewing schedule with the help of streaming services, DVRs, and on-demand functionality. What Postman saw in the nightly news, though, was enough for him to grasp what was already happening to media and therefore how the viewing public was being trained to take in information. He recognized that the content of the information was not at all the most important thing; the most important thing was that any and all information—no matter how unrelated or decontextualized—was being streamed together, in one continuous feed. To Postman, it only took two words to signal this paradigmatic shift: *Now . . . this.*

> "Now . . . this" is commonly used on radio and television newscasts to indicate that what one has just heard or seen has no relevance to what one is about to hear or see, or possibly to anything one is ever likely to hear or see. The phrase is a means of acknowledging the fact that the world as mapped by the speeded up electronic media has no order or meaning and is not to be taken seriously. There is no murder so brutal, no earthquake so devastating, no political blunder so costly— for that matter, no ball score so tantalizing or weather report so threatening—that it cannot be erased from our minds by a newscaster saying, "Now . . . this." The newscaster means that you have thought long enough on the previous matter (approximately forty-five seconds), that you must not be morbidly preoccupied with it (let us say, for ninety seconds), and that you must now give your attention to another fragment or a commercial.[14]

Nightly news does not hold the same prominent place in the public sphere that it did in America in the 1980s. Yet, if you look on a "news" website—say CNN or Fox or the Huffington Post—you can easily see what Postman is talking about. The words "Now . . . this" are no longer spoken, they are merely assumed. This same thing is true of an Instagram feed, or a Twitter feed, or a Facebook feed, or what might appear through Snapchat or even Tinder. Or think about commercials: one commercial advertisement has nothing at all to do with the next one since each is its own little mini-drama. In the digital age, our eyes comprehend what our ears used to: "Now . . . this."

Postman argues that "Now . . . this" operates in television because television brings together two previous inventions in a seamless way: telegraph and photography. The telegraph annihilated the proportions of space: information could move from one place to a very, very distant place at incredible speed. Information was no longer limited to the speed at which a human being could move—by foot, by horse, by train—but now would begin to approach the speed of light, which borders on instantaneity. The photograph captures an image and makes it a discrete object, disassociating it from its context.[15] Put these two things together, and you have the possibility of context-less objects capable of moving at the speed of light. Snippet, snippet, snippet, snippet. An image could be everywhere and nowhere at the same time, and so too, therefore, could those who receive these images.

While this should sound bizarre, it actually sounds like a pretty apt description of what happens now. What is really bizarre is that this way of the world now seems natural.[16] How else would I keep up with the news? How else would I communicate with people I do not see every day? How else would I stay connected? As Maggie Jackson argues, simultaneity is redefining our notion of *time*, while virtual is shattering our notion of *space*, and perpetual movement is reconfiguring our relationship to *place*.[17] The experience of being everywhere and nowhere all the time through digital space is changing our conception of what it means to live in this world.

This touches on a deeper thesis in Postman's work and my own argument, which goes beyond television and the Internet and frenetic daily schedules. Here is that thesis: the default way in which we are now trained to view the world is as a series of disjointed images and idiosyncratic events, a bunch of stuff that either does not have any context or is waiting for us to give it our own. We are trained to become data consumers and data producers, image consumers and image producers, efficient multitaskers who grow our own bandwidth in order to handle more and more volume.[18] It is amazing what human beings can do, but what I just described is not nearly enough to account for the Christian view of a human being.

The only coherence that is offered to this barrage of information and appointments is that more is coming. The stream—the feed—is the only consistent context, if we may call it that. If all these many things are going to find any other context than merely the fact that they are part of a feed, then we have to take up the task of giving these things our own context. Over time, a child's daily and weekly schedule becomes a profile: *my project of becoming fully myself.*[19] In social media space, this looks like a self-curated, algorithmically aided, individualized feed, where my preferences, actions, and predictive behaviors shape the environment in which I find myself. No two social media feeds are the same, and that is by design. The new environment that the logic of the Internet creates—an environment that spreads outward into non-digital space, especially as more and more non-digital space is mingled with digital portals in the "Internet of things"—demands a new rubric for what it means to survive and to thrive. The key to that rubric is multitasking: doing multiple things all of the time, and the more you can do at once, the better. As your eyes dart from place to place, so must your fingers (your "digits") as well as your thoughts.

The Thrill of the Chase

There is a certain sense of exhilaration to all of this and even something like a feeling of liberation. It seems like anything is possible and that you are bound by nothing. You can be connected to anything and anyone at any time while you craft your own project out of these endless opportunities because there is always more coming. This is the meaning of time in modern life: more is coming, so hurry up and make something.

In an Apple ad called "Your Verse," sweeping landscapes mix with mystical music, as the voice of Robin Williams from *Dead Poet's Society* guides the narration through lines from Walt Whitman's *Leaves of Grass.* After less than two minutes of pulsating visual imagery that matches and accentuates the power of the poetry, the ad arrives at Whitman's crucial line that then leads directly into Apple's own pointed charge to the consumer: "that the powerful play goes on and you may contribute a verse. . . . What will your verse be?"[20]

This is one of the most invigorating ads I have ever seen. Everything is possible, and I only get one shot. My life is what I make it and, in the end, it is up to me. That "powerful play" is that everything is moving, building, happening and "my verse" is my opportunity—my one and only opportunity—to catch up, to step up, to show up and make something of myself, to contribute before it is too late.

The choice and opportunity is in my hands (with an iPad Air, of course), which makes the whole deal so appealing: I am in control, and I can make something of myself. At the same time, though, we can already feel the hidden downside to this tantalizing promise of a peak experience: I am on the clock. The pressure is on to achieve, to create, to prove myself and count for something. "The powerful play" will go on *whether or not* I "contribute a verse." I could matter, but I do not necessarily matter. I *could* fade away; I *could* count for nothing.

If this all seems a rather dramatic take on a ninety-one-second advertisement, it certainly is. But those ninety-one seconds of rapidity establish a microcosm—a whole cosmos in miniature—of the notions of time, space, and place as rendered in the modern world. It also makes a claim, therefore, on what it means to be a human being, at least the kind of human being worthy of aspiration. In this vision, we start from the position of not yet being enough with the possibility of becoming enough. And that is the perfect recipe for inducing anxiety.

To Be Overcome

To be anxious is to be *overcome with fear*. It is not necessarily fear of something in particular but, rather, anxiety here is the persistent state of being fearful. By one popular definition, anxiety is fear without an object.[21]

If we take Apple's "Your Verse" as an apt metaphor for the vision presented in the increasingly digital world, then what we end up with is something like the inverse image of Psalm 139. In that hymn, the psalmist marvels at the inescapability of *being known* in and through his

Creator, with whom it is *impossible* to be *unknown*. There is nowhere the psalmist could go or even imagine where his Creator would not already know him.

In Apple's counter-psalm that follows Whitman's poem, the consumer's starting point is the condition of *being unknown* with the possibility of *becoming knowable*, at least for a time. That starting point situates the consumer in a condition of worry—persistent, unbreakable worry whenever he is *not* making himself known and therefore knowable. To become significant is a perpetual task, and sometimes it is just easier to do nothing at all.[22]

This is what it is like to live in a world of broken narrative. In the "Your Verse" universe, every individual moment requires a new narrative of meaning. *You* have to make the narrative. The rapidity of what you perceive to be separate and disconnected snippets forces you into reactionary responses—reactions in the eye, in the fingers, in the mind, in speech. That this is happening is virtually imperceptible because it is just so overwhelming. With each new moment (and every moment is equal in duration) you are stepping into a cloud of unknowability: the state of being unknown and therefore having to make yourself known. This is really a *pseudo*-narrative of disjointed moments and fragmented identities. Such is the condition of the modern-day Zechariah who is as yet unable to listen.

In the next chapter, we will examine the importance of recovering a coherent narrative, which has to do with Mary's *remembering* (read: drawing pieces together as she recalls what happened before). Our issue here is with the ecosystem of interruption and the perpetual state of distraction, which the constant feed of images, the constant demands of a multitasking schedule, and the constant stream of time exacerbate. I am not a psychologist or a medical professional, and so I do not want to presume to speak authoritatively on anxiety disorders. But I have spent the past nineteen years on a college campus, and what has become abundantly clear to me is that at this point, the majority of college students spend at least a good portion of their time in some state of anxiety, whether or not they have a diagnosable condition. What is equally clear is that the *more* accomplished these young people are, the *more* adept they are at multitasking, and the *more* they are plugged in and connected, the *greater* their sense of not being enough, of not counting enough, of not doing enough seems to be. They know how to do a lot of things and their scores on most metrics are record-breaking, but the one thing they cannot seem to do is rest. Stay still. Remain focused. Wait. And it's not just them. They are the mirror and the barometer of where modern life is now and where it is going.[23]

Mary was not *overcome with fear* but rather allowed *the power of the Most High to overshadow* her (Lk 1:35). The new thing that had come to her *did* surprise her and even confuse or "agitate" her. But she did not give in to the temptation to react hastily; she did not try to fit this new thing into her own self-generated context; she did not show the signs of having to quickly interpret so as to move on to the next thing. She did not worry about announcing her own identity or making herself known. Instead, she took time to listen. She considered, and eventually she pondered: resting, focusing, waiting.

Mary shows us where we ought to be and where we ought to lead others in order to begin the process of discernment. What Mary was already capable of is what Zechariah had to become capable of during his period of silence. He had to learn to slow down and pay attention.

Turning Point: Strategic Patience

Up to this point, the picture I have painted might seem pretty bleak and rather overwhelming. It seems that we are staring at a tidal wave of immediacy and rapidity and multitasking and persistent worry. We cannot undo the digital age and we cannot just cocoon ourselves or our young people from the world in which we live. It might seem like there is nothing we can do but just hold on and try to resist the scattering of our attention and the saturation of time for as long as we can, knowing that eventually we will be overcome. If this were indeed our only recourse, then we would be generally powerless. But we are not powerless, and there is a way for us to respond, especially in our efforts to form young people to be free and to be brave, to become capable of true vocational discernment and missionary discipleship, to be empowered for life's big decisions. We have to reclaim the power of patience, and to do that, we need to create spaces where patience can be learned and acquired as a skill. Everything turns on patience, the very thing on which Mary's own response pivots.

Before talking about why patience is power, I first want to talk about creating spaces that cultivate patience. As I mentioned above, the one thing that college students seem largely incapable of doing these days is resting. By and large, they have great difficulty staying in one place, sticking to one task, holding their attention on one thing for a sustained period of time. I sympathize with this because I have trouble with it, too. Like them, I have been trained to multitask, to shift my focus, to gaze and interpret quickly, to accomplish and accomplish and accomplish and move along. What I have attempted to show in the earlier parts of this chapter is that we are becoming what our environment is training us to become. If we are going to become something other than what just about everything around us leads us to do and to be, I suppose we could try to just will ourselves into a different way of being by "intention," but I think we will quickly find ourselves either exhausted or failing, or both. What we need are not just intentional *people* but intentional *spaces*. Small cultures, if you will, in which the qualities that we desire and want to see are encouraged—even *forced*—so that it is easier for people to be patient, attentive, composed.

One of these "small cultures" is the culture of the classroom. What Jennifer Roberts—an art historian at Harvard—says about the intentionality of the educational spaces into which she wants to lead her students is instructive:

> I want to . . . [create] opportunities for students to engage in deceleration, patience, and immersive attention. I would argue that these are the kind of practices that now most need to be actively engineered by faculty, because they simply are no longer available "in nature," as it were. Every external pressure, social and technological, is pushing students in the other direction, toward immediacy, rapidity, and spontaneity. I want to give them the permission and the structures to slow down.[24]

This short paragraph has been hugely influential on my own teaching philosophy and, in particular, in how I think about the spaces I create for my students and what I ask them to do with their time in my courses. It occurred to me that in and through the spaces I create for them, I can prompt them to disperse their attention or focus their attention. I can seek to appease their oftentimes incessant desire to be amused—a desire I share when I myself am in the position of student—or I can help guide them toward the difficult discipline of concentration. I can scatter their attention and satisfy that scattering with a lot of stimuli, or I can try to help them move toward the "details and orders and relationships that take time to perceive."[25] In short, I can quicken the pace or I can slow down the pace. I was born in northern New Jersey and raised in Southern California, so the urge to quicken the pace is "second nature" to me. But what my students and I actually need is quite the opposite.

One way in which I cultivate the classroom as a space for attentiveness is to intentionally separate the physical classroom space from other points of connection. In a college setting, this means actually forbidding the use of personal technological devices in the classroom—not just while class in session, but before and after class as well. Once my students and I walk through the door to the room where it happens, we know we have entered a space where we are going to pay attention to the content of the lesson, to our own thoughts, and to what one another says. To this end, I now include a paragraph on all my syllabi that states this firm policy. Moreover, I spend a bit of time on the first day of class talking about this policy and also stating, in no uncertain terms, what is almost certainly going to happen to them in just about every class session, which is that at some point or other they will likely get *bored*. I do not set out to make my classes boring, but I do want the classroom space to be free of the easy exits we often rush toward when we start to lose interest in something, according to our own preferences. Indeed, they will find it hard to pay attention. They will have to discover ways to stay focused, to listen to one another, and, worst of all, to listen to me. This struggle is exactly what I want them to experience. If they have to fight to stay focused in the space of my classroom, they will build up some of the strength and resources necessary for paying attention in any setting: while reading, while talking with friends, while on a date, while attending to the mundane aspects of life.[26]

Distraction is the condition of being pulled apart or pulled off course; it is like being derailed or taken "off track."[27] Most of the world in which we live is becoming more and more an echo chamber of distractions within an ecosystem of interruptions. There is always a quick way to get our attention out of the jam of any situation. This is why we need to teach attention not only in order to learn various subject matters better, but also as its own skill.[28] In a deep way, we cannot teach anything more important to our students than *how* to pay attention. This lesson will take different forms in different settings and situations. As educators, we teach them how to pay attention, we create the environments in which they can do it, and then we help them to actually do it while also holding them accountable to the task. We also have to stay focused ourselves.

Simone Weil argues that "the development of the faculty of attention forms the real object and almost the sole interest of studies."[29] That is a remarkably strong claim and one that gets even stronger as Weil connects this ability to pay attention that school studies sharpens to the capacity for prayer itself, which she says consists almost entirely of ordering "all the attention of which the soul is capable toward God."[30] She notes that "something in the soul has a far more violent repugnance to true attention than the flesh has for bodily fatigue,"[31] and on this point she is in perfect agreement with St. Teresa of Avila, who thinks that for most of us our souls—our interests, our affections, our desires—are heading off in all directions within us like a bunch of wild horses.[32] Teresa's course of treatment for her sisters who want to pray but do not know how to pray is to guide them gently, tenderly, but also deliberately through the prayer of recollection. This prayer is nothing other than the regular and persistent practice of remaining still, allowing your thoughts to be pulled together, and focusing your whole self on the presence of the Lord. As you first become quiet, all of the various concerns and preoccupations dart around in your head and heart, but the whole point of the practice of prayer as Teresa teaches it is to take time to slowly learn how to be in one place at one time, with singular focus.[33] As Weil and Roberts attest in their own respective ways, the classroom is a space where this ability can be cultivated.

Seen from this perspective, almost any exercise in patience is both formative and necessary. When I taught a course on theology and art with my friend Bridget Hoyt, who is a curator in our university's museum, we took this challenge of *forcing* our students to pay attention very seriously. We knew it would be painful for them because attentiveness is always painful—it costs you something—and it is even more painful for those who are out of practice. But some pain is necessary to heal us and make us grow, and in and through our particular course, that is precisely the opportunity we wanted to give our students.

One of the ways we inflicted this healing pain was to require each student to spend three hours—three *dreaded* hours—with a single and rather simple piece of art . . . all by themselves. The whole point was to practice paying attention to what is there, while waves of boredom were inevitable. The students had to take notes on what they were seeing, on what questions started to arise after looking for a long time, on what they started to recognize and at what point they recognized it, and on what they had to revise through continued observation. In the end, dread turned into some form of delight, though I don't want to oversell that point. Some noted that the time was peaceful, the practice almost meditative, and the slow discovery of initially unseen elements or patterns quite rewarding. The pain of attentiveness touched on the fire of desire: they actually enjoyed learning to see, waiting to interpret, coming to understand rather than presuming to already know or being in a rush "to get to the point" and figure things out. They actually enjoyed being in a completely different flow from the rapid pace of the rest of their lives. If Roberts is right—and I think she is—that the conditions for deceleration and slow-learning are no longer available "in nature" for us, then the virtue of "strategic patience" has to be intentionally developed, even assigned and required.[34]

I know that teaching in a college setting is not the same as teaching in high school, middle school, or grammar school. For those who teach in the other settings, smartphones in the classroom might not be the most pressing issue and asking a student to spend even one hour in front of a piece of art is more likely to elicit calls from less than understanding parents than notes of appreciation from their children. I also know, however, what it is like to teach at an institution that sets a pace that is *not at all* conducive to the "deceleration, patience, and immersive attention" that I am emphasizing here. I cannot change the larger culture in which I am asked to teach, which, in this case, is my own *Catholic* institution. What I can do is try to shape the smaller culture over which I do have authority—the culture of my classroom, the culture of my course—in such way that my students recognize an alternative to how they are being urged to move in just about every other aspect of their lives.[35] True, my courses are in some sense one more thing my students have to attend to and balance in their already overloaded schedules, but if I can strategically teach *patience* as I teach my subject matter—in the very *way* I teach my subject matter—then I can hope that my own little "counter-culture" will resonate with the desire for integration and commitment that I know exists within each of my students, just as it exists in me. This is something like a "mustard seed" approach.

In our schools and in our parishes, we need to look around at the spaces we are creating and what they are inviting people to do, assessing how those spaces are inviting people to interact and in what manner. We also need to assess the manner in which we are asking our students to learn. Walk through a mall or an airport and you will see the ways in which those spaces incite people to move and desire—namely, to buzz around and split their attention, fluttering from one shiny item to the next. In those spaces, it is like everything that pops out to you on the Internet or through your smartphone has been broadcast from virtual to physical space. That kind of space may feel inevitable, but it certainly is not. We can, should, and must create other kinds of spaces, spaces that value slowing down, paying attention, and learning how to be patient. These are the spaces where time becomes a gift rather than the enemy.

The Primacy of Patience

When we ask the question about why patience is so important anyway, we find ourselves looking directly into the depths of God's own love and at the primary space of formation: the space of the family. In his post-synodal apostolic exhortation on the family, Pope Francis presents the space of the family—in the home—as, first of all, a place where the benefit of time is given. This understanding emerges from a scriptural meditation on the meaning of "love."

In the fourth chapter of *Amoris Laetitia*, Francis sets our gaze on what is certainly the most overused reading in the history of Christian weddings: 1 Corinthians 13. This hymn is so familiar that it is easy to forget to marvel at it or even take it seriously. To most of us, it now sounds about as thrilling as a greeting card. Perhaps that is why it is especially fitting for contemplating family life, which it is also easy to forget to marvel at or even take seriously. Francis doubles-down on the seemingly unremarkable nature of love and the family by offering a thoughtful and instructive reading of this hymn in order to unearth the neglected richness of the overused and under-considered meaning of "love." By reading Paul closely, Francis discerns that the first two attributes of love that the hymn mentions—love is "patient" and "kind"—are the source of the redemption of time that grows from within the life of the family itself.[36]

The Greek term translated in English as "patience" is, as Francis notes, *makrothyméi*, which is itself the term that is used to translate the Hebrew term *'erek 'appayim*, as found in Exodus 34:6. When this term is used in Exodus, it states a divine attribute: *The* LORD *passed before [Moses], and proclaimed, "The* LORD, *the* LORD, *a God merciful and gracious, slow to anger* ['erek 'appayim], *and abounding in mercy and faithfulness"* (RSV, cf. Nm 14:18, Wis 11:23, 12:2, 15:1; Ps 86:15, 145:8). When Paul begins to speak of "love" he is therefore not simply translating a term from Hebrew into Greek; he is actually translating a divine attribute into human life. In the one who practices love as being "slow to anger," divine love is taking flesh. In the case of Exodus 34, God reveals himself as the one who is "slow to anger" in being patient with sinners—actually, a sinful nation—and who therefore leaves open the possibility of repentance. In other words, God gives sinners the gift of time. Depending on how we look at it—and we need to look at it both ways—God's patience is on the one hand the withholding of the just power to strike at sinners by allowing them to immediately feel the full effect of their own sin, while on the other hand, God's patience is the revelation of true power in being absolutely free from the compulsion of the situation in order to wait upon future possibilities, in hope.[37]

Patience is therefore the first and most important exercise for those who love; patience is how you show your love. Patience is the power to restrain yourself in opportunities to assert dominance—even when the circumstances seem to justify such a move—for the sake of waiting for and waiting with the other person for whom the possibilities for change and growth always abound. As Francis reads Paul, the patience of love is proper to a creature who, in humility, is called to "recognize that other people also have a right to live in this world, just as they are . . . even when he or she acts differently than I would like."[38] Patience is the option for the *other person's good*, for their sake. In the space of family life—in the space of the home—patience creates space for other people to be. And as we know all too well, sometimes the patience we extend to others is actually the gift of time we ourselves need in order to grow and change, to take on a different perspective or just get over ourselves. Learning how to do this with those with whom we share the space of daily life—often in close quarters—is the training necessary for practicing patience anywhere else in the world, in any other situation and with any other company. Patience is a prerequisite of really asking a question like "What are you going through?" and meaning it.

The other half of the opening pair in Paul's hymn then describes the proactive complement to patience. This next word, "kind," is only used here in the whole of the Bible: in Greek, *chrestéuetai*. The root word, *chrestos*, denotes a good person—that is, "one who shows his goodness by his deeds."[39] By linking this with patience, Paul is instructing the church at Corinth—and the rest of us—that while you wait on the other person and give them the gift of time, you are not simply meant to leave the other person to his or her own devices. Rather, you must discern how you might help them and act upon their needs. The time that you give to the other person—that space for them *to be* and to grow—is therefore shaped, as much as possible, to nourishing and nurturing them. They are given time as a gift to become freer and more alive, with "kindness" that helps them along the way. It is absolutely true that nature—including human nature—abhors a vacuum. There is no such thing as completely neutral space. Following "patience" with "kindness" means giving the space for others—as well as the space for our relationship with them—a positive charge. (Working out exactly what this means is more or less the task of the next two chapters.)

This pairing of "patience" and "kindness" then puts everything else into place. By giving the gift of time and allowing that time to be beneficial to the other person, you avoid "jealousy" that makes you regret the other person's good fortune; "boastfulness" and "arrogance" that puff you up and make you into a pushy know-it-all; "rudeness" that reinforces preexisting negative attitudes; "irritableness" that grows from hidden indignations; and "resentfulness" that obsessively keeps count of wrongs and refuses to give the other person the possibility of an open future.[40] "In other words," Francis writes, it is in this practice of love within the family that we learn to "rejoice at the good of others when we see their dignity and value their abilities and good works."[41] If you practice love in this way as, primarily, "patience" and "kindness," you become capable of "bearing all things" because you see other people in a wider context, "believing all things" because you are habitually open rather than habitually distrustful, "hoping all things" because you realize that oftentimes your expectations will go unmet, and "enduring all things" because you acquire a stable disposition for seeking good.[42]

On the authority of St. Paul, then, it is completely warranted to claim that the development of a holy character—as growing into the likeness of God (Gn 1:26–27)—always, always, always begins with patience. To fail in patience is to become enslaved to compulsion, the shifting forces of mood, and, above all, fear. Without patience you are easily overcome with fear. But patience is not some mere thing that is just there, within you. It does not just "happen"—it must be developed and practiced, now more than ever. To turn again to Jennifer Roberts, we can think about the primacy of patience and the difficult, necessary task of teaching it:

> The virtue of patience was originally associated with forbearance or sufferance. It was about conforming oneself to the need to wait for things. But now that, generally, one need *not* wait for things [and we might add one is *expected* not to wait], patience becomes an active and positive cognitive state. Where patience once indicated a lack of control, now it is a form of control over the tempo of contemporary life that otherwise controls us. Patience no longer connotes disempowerment—perhaps now patience is power.[43]

In ways that we can no longer really imagine, people of previous centuries had no choice but to wait for a lot of things, to exercise patience. In our present day when all the "natural" reasons for having to exercise patience are being taken away, we have to make a choice for patience. It is easier than ever to entertain and to amuse ourselves, to escape from each other when we are sitting in the same room together or even at the same table, and so we must now opt for patience if we are going to have it. We need to reclaim this power—the power Mary had when the divine love took flesh in her. Even more, we need to teach this power to our young. If we truly want to form disciples who are free and brave, capable of taking up the cost of love and living out the mission of the Gospel through their very lives, then it is absolutely necessary that we give them the opportunity to slow down, to pay attention, to wait.

Educational spaces can and should play a part in cultivating strategic patience through regular practices of attentiveness, to which we may well add the liturgical spaces in which we slowly learn how to move according to a different pace through repeated practice.[44] But the prime training ground for renewing the capacity for patience always lies with the family, where love is first learned. Patience begins at home. Only with patience will our young people—and we ourselves—be liberated from the bondage of rapidly moving time, where more and more just keeps coming at us without any break for rest.

This need for rest is not new, even though our conditions today are unique in certain respects. The deeply human need to break from the otherwise hurly-burly pace of commodified, abstract time is written right into the fabric of creation itself, as part of its "natural," created order. This order, which corresponds to the true meaning of time, is secured and revealed in the third commandment given to Moses and fulfilled in Jesus Christ: *Keep holy the Sabbath* (Ex 20:8–11; Dt 5:12–15).

Changing Times

It took a long time for us to get to the most important topic of this whole chapter. It was tempting to try to get here sooner, but perhaps we will come to see that taking time to build to this moment gave us the opportunity to move around the message we are receiving, seeing it from different angles and listening to different tones. This final point is fairly simple, and yet from this simple point springs the whole approach to building up the capacities for vocational discernment and forming missionary disciples in our modern age. The point is that we need to recommit to keeping Sunday separate from the rest of the week. Actually, the point is even stronger than that: we need to allow Sunday to reorder the meaning of time itself, as God intends.

When we thought about why the needs for keeping track of time the way we do began, we found ourselves looking at the rhythms of life in the monastery, which are ordered to the canonical hours of prayer. As the bells of the monastery sounded outward into the surrounding areas, those measures of time that the bells marked were taken up for other purposes, so that the ultimate reason why time was being measured in the first place was effectively forgotten. Maybe if a master timekeeper came down from the monastery to teach those of us in the modern age what the true meaning of time is, we could learn how to reclaim time as a gift rather than being subject to its demands like an unrelenting burden. Fortunately, God always provides for us through saints whom he raises to respond to the direst needs of each particular era. And for us, in our need, one of the saints who shows God's direct response—a saint through whom God's own patience with us works—is none other than the father of the saint who has been teaching my own daughter what it means to be free and brave. This saint is the father of Thérèse of Lisieux: St. Louis Martin, the clockmaker.

Louis Martin was born in 1823 as the Industrial Revolution was settling into its enduring form, and he died in 1894 just as Frederick Winslow Taylor was developing the systematic measurement of time that fit the demands of such a "revolution." Louis's life thus spanned the period in which the very notions of time that have become most familiar to us were crystallizing. If we see Louis against the backdrop of "Taylorism," by which the jobs in a factory—and later in all areas of commerce—were broken down into their most elemental parts and orchestrated to maximal efficiency for "productivity" and therefore profit, we come to see Louis as the true revolutionary whose creativity in Gospel living springs from the discipline of keeping time in a different order.[45] He lived with this order of time in the midst of the secular world because his attempt to leave the secular world failed—thank God.

Louis Martin failed to advance in the first vocation he pursued: the vowed religious life. He was the well-schooled and well-mannered son of a soldier who wanted to apply the discipline that came naturally to him within the walls of the monastery. Inside those walls, he would be able to practice careful work ordered to the rhythms of prayer over long years of attentive focus and habituation. When he went to make his application to the monastery, though, he was sent away because he did not know Latin. He returned home and spent the next several months studying the language diligently with a tutor, but eventually he had to abandon his studies due to illness. This man who sought to retreat to the monastery to live according to its rule was forced to permanently return to the active life where he would take up the other craft in which he had apprenticed: clockmaking.[46]

Louis did not abandon his ideals when the setting for his vocation changed. Within the rhythm of the world, Louis allowed his workshop to become a form of the monastic retreat he once sought within the walls that he hoped would take him away from the world's movement. As he worked at fine-tuning his craft of clockmaking, he kept as the central gear of all his work the *refrain from work* that he practiced every Sunday—the Christian Sabbath.

Despite the best business practices of his day, the customs of his competitors, and the expectations of his customers, Louis closed his shop on Sundays. On this day, he abstained from engaging in any commerce whatsoever, freeing himself from the law of competition from which his "competitors" never broke. Louis was capable of calling his own work "good" because his work did not control him. He rested. He practiced leisure. He took time. He walked through the countryside and observed the movements of nature. He walked through town and observed the movements of the poor.[47] He spent time with his children and showed them what it means to make yourself available, to hand over your time, and to give your attention freely and generously. He prayed.

His craft of clockmaking called for "close application, a long apprenticeship, and repeated experiments in practical workmanship."[48] In his workshop, he studied how the patient work of a craftsman, if undertaken in an environment conducive to steady intention, can produce seemingly simple products that hide untold complexities, like a clock. By his practice of Sabbath rest, Louis ordered his family's life according to the simple but essential discipline of keeping Sunday separate, refusing to allow it to become just like every other day. Under the tutelage of their father—the master timekeeper—Louis's family learned to speak of time in terms of liturgical feasts, where one child then the next became the central figure in the family's celebration: first communions celebrated alongside birthdays and feast days alike. Their apparent simplicity kept hidden the untold complexities of their maturing holiness. In the midst of a world that was becoming more unbreakably addicted to commerce and expediency with each passing day, the Martin family observed the liturgical cycle—a different rhythm for time—that preserves the dignity of creation, and the dignity of those commanded to *keep holy the Sabbath.*[49]

Louis carried within his own steady discipline what the sound of the monastery's bells themselves could not guarantee: that the original and ultimate meaning guiding the measurement of time is the return to prayer. Prayer is the leisure of resting in God's own rest, which is natural to creation and therefore *good* for us, even *very good*. Sunday is what prevents us from feeling like we have to always be preoccupied with creating our own meaning, ensuring our own significance, competing against everyone and everything else for space and time. When Sunday is observed, we intentionally return to being creatures rather than pretending to carry the burden of the Creator. Sunday is *God's* time.

Louis did not order Sunday according to the demands of the other days of the week; he ordered the other days of the week according to his primary duty of Sunday. *Sunday always came first.* He did not practice Sunday only when it was possible; rather, he determined what was possible for the other days of the week according to the time Sunday gave to them—in other words, Sunday dictated that the number of days for work in any given week was, at most, six. Because he practiced the priority of Sabbath rest, he learned how to find joy in his days of work precisely because his work was not everything. He was formed into a more observant, more patient, more considerate person *because* he regularly practiced this rest.

Everything about our lives seems to push against breaking from the rhythm of the week to make Sunday different. When all other time on the schedule is full, it seems that we need to make use of Sunday to get more done—or just to keep pace. That is because we have allowed time to get out of order. We allow the six days to tell us what Sunday can mean instead of allowing Sunday to tell us what the other six days can mean.

For example, since the kids in our town are in other sports leagues that practice and play on weeknights and on Saturdays, our Catholic schools hold their league games on Sundays. It is the only way to fit the games in. But what are we fitting in? We are fitting in one more thing to do, one more activity like the other activities, one more piece of the profile, one more instance of "Now . . . this." We have allowed the overflowing possibilities of the six days to tell us what Sunday should mean.

As another example, I know from experience that when we do stay at home, it is just easier to zone out and lock in to whatever is passing over the television waves, through Netflix, on social media sites. The temptation to just quickly look at email is so strong that the only way to get the thought out of my mind is to power off my phone and computer on Saturday night and put them in the top corner of my closet. Though I am not in the office, there is the persistent temptation to allow Sunday to be littered with more of the same, just under a different guise.

Here is what I believe is the non-negotiable key to becoming capable of Mary's pondering *especially* in our present age: prioritizing Sabbath rest. It must truly be non-negotiable. To be very direct: we need to shut off all of the gadgets and clear the schedule. Sunday must be what I hope my classrooms will be: a space for focus and attentiveness, for patience and consideration, for prayer. We *will* miss out on things, our kids *will* miss out on things, but that is part of the pain of attention and the balm of rest. That is what happens when Sunday orders time. I could try to dress up this point in fancier attire, but this is just the naked truth.[50]

Sunday must once again become the day set apart from being *overcome* so that we may *consider* and eventually learn to *ponder*.

What exactly does it mean to *rest* and be at *leisure* in this time that is a break from the otherwise frenetic pace of life? Our focus will shift to that question in the next chapter, where we begin to explore what patience, waiting, considering, *pondering* give us time for—that is, *remembering*, or learning to see the context. In the chapter after that, we will focus on the actions—the speech—that this recognition of context draws out of us, before turning in the last full chapter to contemplating the importance of sacrifice in this whole process of discernment.

Before we take up the second mark of Mary's free and brave discernment, though, maybe we should listen to just one "snippet" from Louis's ninth and youngest child, as she testifies to learning more about her own vocation at the age of thirteen or fourteen:

> One Sunday, looking at a picture of Our Lord on the Cross, I
> was struck by the blood flowing from one of the divine hands.
> I felt a great pang of sorrow when thinking this blood was

falling to the ground without anyone's hastening to gather it up. I was resolved to remain in spirit at the foot of the Cross and to receive the divine dew. I understood I was then to pour it out upon souls. The cry of Jesus on the Cross sounded continually in my heart: "*I thirst!*" These words ignited within me an unknown and very living fire. I wanted to give my Beloved to drink and I felt myself consumed with a *thirst for souls.*[51]

It is so easy to get caught up in the drama of Thérèse's vision that it becomes equally easy to forget or even marvel at the first thing that she says: she pondered the passion *one Sunday*. The skeptic will see this as a coincidence, and the expert planner will see it as virtually insignificant, but what they each miss is that Sunday was anything but coincidental or insignificant for Louis the clockmaker, who was quite intentional about preserving that day for himself and his family. They were in the habit of giving their undivided attention to the Lord that day.

3. Memory and the Authority of Hidden Assumptions

God gave us our memory so we
might have roses in December.

—J. M. Barrie

"Is this heaven?"

"No, it's Iowa."

If you are reading these words, it is highly probable that you, like me, have not been to heaven, though you may have been to Iowa at some point. Iowa is lovely, but I can't imagine mistaking it for heaven. Maybe that's because I don't really know what to look for.

When Ray Kinsella built his own little piece of heaven in the movie *Field of Dreams*, he followed the seemingly nonsensical promise that turning his plowshares into baseball bats and his crop rows into foul lines would draw some untold company. Even as he was building this destination for dreamers, the prophecy within the film—eventually spoken in the only voice that should ever deliver prophecy: that of James Earl Jones—reveals that the dream is really for something other than the field itself. The thing that matters is not the place at the journey's end but rather to enjoy what you find there—*that's* how you might come to find something like heaven in the middle of Iowa:

> People will come, Ray. They'll come to Iowa for reasons they
> can't even fathom. They'll turn into your driveway, not know-
> ing for sure why they're doing it. They'll arrive at your door,
> as innocent as children, longing for the past. "Of course, we
> won't mind if you look around," you'll say. "It's only twenty
> dollars per person." And they'll pass over the money without
> even thinking about it, for it is money they have and peace
> they lack. And they'll walk off to the bleachers and sit in
> their short-sleeves on a perfect afternoon, and find they have
> reserved seats somewhere along the baselines where they sat
> when they were children, and cheered their heroes. And they'll
> watch the game, and it'll be as if they'd dipped themselves in
> magic waters. The memories will be so thick, they'll have to
> brush them away from their faces. People will come, Ray.[1]

I love the little throwaway line near the end of that monologue
where the sublime experience of this game—on this field—is described
as bringing the pilgrims enjoyment so wonderful that "it'll be as if they'd
dipped themselves in magic waters." That is a shorthand way of indicating a transformation. The destination is one thing, yet who the wayfarers
become as they arrive is something else. In the original book on which
this film is based—a book that has somewhat bizarre religious over-
tones—W. P. Kinsella wrote this particular line in the following manner: "It will be as if they have knelt in front of a faith healer, or dipped
themselves in magic waters where a saint once rose like a serpent and
cast benedictions to the wind like peach petals."[2] Those must be pretty
remarkable waters if someone emerges from them with all the violent
thrust of a serpent but with the desire to bestow blessings as gently as
flowers on the breeze. Perhaps something significant is lost in the film
when the image of a "saint" is left out. Who else but a saint could capture the radical nature of a serpent who learns to bless rather than curse?

Imagine trying to teach a serpent to redirect all his instincts toward
a new end. I imagine you would have to do nothing less than make him
forget all his former actions and instincts before teaching him how to
use the same power for a new action, one which is quite the opposite

of his former one. That is what it would be like for a soldier to wholly recast the power of his own efforts in favor of a new purpose—you know, like St. Ignatius of Loyola, who was first broken of his own ambition in order to be re-formed for a new purpose. (St. Paul also comes to mind.) In service of that new end, Ignatius exercised no less passion than he did on the battlefield, but now when he arose like a serpent it was to build up rather than strike down.

I doubt that Kinsella (the author) knew that he was indeed describing an actual saint when he used the contrasting images of serpents and benedictions to capture the kind of transformation that those who learned to enjoy the fruits of the field would undergo. When he was a child, St. Juan Diego would have received a traditional lecture from his father in which he was told "not to rise like a serpent and shoot anger against the people, instead receive them in love."[3] When that child grew into a man, he fulfilled and exceeded his father's instruction when, at Our Lady's own instruction, he rose up before Bishop Zumarraga to let petals fall from his *tilma*. St. Juan Diego is himself Kinsella's seemingly odd image of one who embodies all the power of a striking serpent in order to bless rather than to curse. Juan had to be given the courage of a soldier while Ignatius had to be given the meekness of a peasant. In either case, the union of opposites—"the bold peasant" and "the meek soldier"—is no less peculiar than a serpent offering benediction, which, again, is so anomalous that only something like magic could explain it.

This is all pretty loaded imagery for a story about a baseball field in the middle of Iowa. That's because *Field of Dreams* isn't about a baseball field; it is about something like a taste of heaven. More to the point, it is about enjoying rather than merely arriving; remembering rather than merely observing. For Kinsella, the saints of baseball that he imagines are not made by coming to the Iowa field; they are made by *enjoying* the game they find there. Iowa is not heaven because heaven is not a goal, and heaven is not a goal because gaining admission is not the point. *Enjoying* heaven is the point.

Saints are not just people who end up in heaven; saints are people who *enjoy* heaven—in fact, they love it there. This means that the matter of heaven has to do with the sort of person you become and, therefore, it is a matter of transformation. Indeed, Christian discipleship is about who you become when the mission God gives you shapes your identity, and the transformation by which disciples become saints always entails the gift of a new memory.

In the last chapter, we examined the issue of losing ourselves to time through the pace of schedules and the rapidity of the digital world. I argued that the recommitment to the observance of Sabbath rest is essential to breaking from the overwhelming nature of the modern world, where we do not have time to ponder or even consider. But slowing down and relearning how to be patient is not enough, even though that is about as far as most popular books analyzing the conditions and effects of the technological world and digital cultures take us.[4] That's because Christianity is about more than *not* being a certain way. Christianity makes a positive and definitive claim on what is the truth of the human person and the intended end to which we are called.[5]

From the very beginning of this book, I have placed the saints as the icons of both holiness and humanity, who show us who we are and what we are to become, in Christ.[6] Mary is the mother of the saints and the perfect model of Christian discipleship not because she *avoids* being a certain way but because she is free and brave to be herself in Christ. Yes, she takes time and she ponders, but the space that her patience opens up is not an empty space. Rather, in the space she enters into through the time she gives for receiving the angel's message, Mary activates a definite memory, she is identified concretely, and she is located within a narrative. Patience and attentiveness alone may only yield to us the awareness of what narratives, scripts, or "codes" are guiding our lives. To enter more deeply into the radical adventure of vocational discernment, though, we must now address how assumed narratives and unarticulated desires shape our vision of ourselves, one another, and the world in which we live. All of this will show that what is at stake is not only where we end up or what we end up doing, but also who we become and learn to love. This has everything to do with how we are forming, educating, and training our young people and how we can better set the conditions conducive to them learning what matters most in growing as disciples of Jesus Christ.

Bathing in Heavenly Bliss

If the aim of Christian discipleship is to become saints who enjoy heaven, then we ought to move from the baseball diamond that was Kinsella's image of heaven to saying something about the reality itself. What is it that saints have learned to enjoy? Bl. John Henry Newman had a way of speaking of heaven that made it seem rather unenjoyable, at least at first glance. In one of his better-known sermons, he describes heaven like this:

> Heaven then is not like this world; I will say what it is much more like—*a church*. For in a place of worship no language of this world is heard; there are no schemes brought forward for temporal objects, great or small; no information how to strengthen our worldly interests, extend our influence, or establish our credit. These things indeed may be right in their way, so that we do not set our hearts upon them; still (I repeat), it is certain that we hear nothing of them in a church. Here we hear solely and entirely of *God*.[7]

For most of us—myself included—spending eternity in a church sounds pretty terrible. If heaven is like a church, then maybe it is rather like baseball: it's tedious, it's repetitive, and it takes forever. That, in fact, is precisely Newman's point. We tend to conceive of heaven on our own terms, but we would do well to practice reconceiving of ourselves in the God-given terms of heaven.[8] The language of this world is often the language of suspicion and duplicity, under which we hide our private motives and agendas. The schemes of this world are typically directed toward our own self-promotion or comfort. And the credit we seek to accrue in this world is often weighted in the laudations we earn or even the laudations we trick others into conferring upon us. Who could relax and enjoy themselves in a place like that? You would constantly have to be on your guard, and there would always be some lingering suspicion about other people. If even one dubious, selfish person exists in a city, then the integrity of the whole city is compromised. And so God says, *nothing unclean shall enter [the heavenly city], nor anyone who practices abominations or falsehood, but only those who are written in the Lamb's book of life* (Rv 21:27, RSV). If heaven is to be the perfect city in God's own image, then the corrupted language, the dubious schemes, and the competitive ambitions of this world must be driven out.

A church—rightly conceived—is a place free of the games of duplicity and manipulation because it practices its participants in another game altogether: that of learning to enjoy a place where the good we do not earn is given and where we delight in sharing that good with others. That place, in full, *is* heaven. In the world, we often practice springing our energies in poisonous maneuvers to either subtly or not-so-subtly advance ourselves even at the expense of other people. In a church, we practice taking the good of others as our own good. The energy expended might be comparable, but the purpose is not. In a church, the mighty learn how to wield their might in favor of the meek, and the meek learn how to boldly lead the mighty in benediction.

Newman is preaching that in a church we learn to take on a new bodily memory that is fit to the conditions of heaven—we practice *enjoying* that way of being in the choreography of life eternal. Only once our memories are cleansed of past grievances (everything we hold against each other, rightly or wrongly), shame (the guilt under which we hide ourselves), and worldly ambition (our stubborn habit of seeking our own private good first), may our memories be restored to new life in forgiveness, gratitude, and charity. Newman, in another sermon, encourages us to seek memories redeemed in mercy:

> Let us thankfully commemorate the many mercies He has vouchsafed to us in times past, the many sins He has not remembered, the many dangers He has averted, the many prayers He has answered, the many mistakes He has corrected, the many warnings, the many lessons, the much light, the abounding comfort which He has from time to time given. Let us dwell upon times and seasons, times of trouble, times

of joy, times of trial, times of refreshment. How he did cherish us as his children![9]

There is a lot to remember there, and remembering all of that would take all of our energy, all of the time. This activity would be so engaging that we would hand over all we think we've earned and all we think we're due as if it were "pass[ing] over money without even thinking about it" in order to enjoy the peace we once lacked. Money, here, stands for all that worldly ambition procures and giving that up is precisely the admission price for the heavenliness of a "perfect afternoon."[10]

But think about what it would be like to forget all those worldly maneuvers in order to move fluidly with the maneuvers of heaven. This would mean not forgetting the lives we have led but, rather, remembering our lives and one another in light of mercy. It would take something like "magic waters" to form us in this redeemed memory. Of course, that is the image W. P. Kinsella used for describing the change that comes over those wayfarers who enjoy the field of dreams, but, well before him, it was also how the poet Dante imagined the process of transformation necessary for those on the threshold of heaven as they actually become capable of heaven.

At the top of the Mountain of Purgatory—that place of transformation in the *Commedia*—Dante imagines two boundaries of water on either side of the Earthly Paradise (which is not heaven itself but rather heaven's threshold, or earth restored to its created goodness). In truth, the two bodies of water are the same river that flows "from God's own will,"[11] but on one side of the Earthly Paradise it is called Lethe and on the other side it is called Eunoe. The River Lethe is a river of forgetfulness: as if by magic it "take[s] the memory of sin away."[12] These waters wash away all the prideful, envious, wrathful, slothful, covetous, gluttonous, and lustful urges and habits, leaving the one who emerges from the waters without memory. Every memory is taken away from the one who plunges into these waters because all of his memories—like that of a serpent for whom the instinct to strike with venom flows in every part of himself—were tinged with aspects of the sins that plagued him. To be without memory, though, is not to be yourself, and to become yourself is the whole point of the purgatorial journey. Therefore, on the other side of the Earthly Paradise, the River Eunoe flows to restore the memory of "all good done."[13] All that power expended upon ulterior motives, slanderous thoughts and deeds, furtive games of rivalry, and actions muddled with undue self-regard—all of *that* power is restored and released for a holistic purpose: to praise the One who blesses and to serve the good of others. On the far bank of Eunoe, the saint emerges with the power of a rising serpent speaking benedictions that are as fragrant, delicate, and comforting as petals on the wind.

Now consider what a tragedy it would be to spend all your energy trying to "get to heaven" only to hate it there when you arrive. This is Dante's predicament when he arrives at the threshold of heaven only to discover himself too sorrowful, too attached, too guarded to receive the joy prepared for him.[14] Those "magic waters" make him ready.[15]

What if you loved your "twenty dollars" so much that you just couldn't part with it for the sake of gaining admission to unending joy, on God's terms? What if you nursed a grudge so deeply that you wouldn't let it go? What if you were so obsessed with being better than others that you just couldn't stand a place where you're supposed to admire everyone else? What if you were so accustomed to chasing after goals and achievements that you were incapable of permitting yourself to *enjoy* what you spent all your time seeking? What if you demanded that heaven be what you want rather than learning to want what heaven is? Léon Bloy once famously penned that "life only holds one tragedy: not to have been a saint." That sounds right, but maybe another way of saying the same thing is to say that the lone tragedy is getting to where you always wanted to be and not enjoying it. What Kinsella, Newman, and Dante recognize is that changing the means changes the ends we realize; in other words, what we practice desiring affects what we become capable of enjoying.

What We Are Training Our Young People to Enjoy, or Not

In looking to heaven as the furthest horizon for the Christian disciple, we see that "getting there" is not the main point. The main point is becoming the kind of person who *enjoys* and even *loves* what heaven is, as God's own city. When "getting in" is the main thing that matters, we overlook the importance of how we journey and that, in the end, changes who we are and what we are capable of enjoying when we get where we want to go. Rather than some abstruse theory, this dynamic speaks to a most practical concern—it is about who we practice becoming. This is so practical that this way of thinking about heaven permits us to analyze and measure all other manners of formation—whether explicitly religious or not—according to this same dynamic of the way of journeying (the means) shaping what we become capable of enjoying, or not (the ends). Therefore, when we think of how young people are measuring and designing themselves—as well as the ways in which we are grooming them—we can begin to see just how significant are the habits, values, and dispositions they develop in pursuit of what has become a primary goal for all activities and efforts relating to American childhood: college admissions.

The connection between the desire for heaven and the desire for the "college of my dreams" is that both are occasions for establishing a sort of destination obsession. It seems that what matters most about heaven is that "I get there" in the end, and what matters most for the first eighteen years of life for many young people—especially in the United States—is that "I get into the school of my dreams," or maybe just get in somewhere. Sometimes the concern for getting kids admitted to college begins for parents as early as shortly after the first positive pregnancy test or adoption match. The most prestigious colleges and universities have only become more selective, with competition for the coveted spots in the next freshmen class intensifying year after year. Not everyone plays the college admissions game, but the cultural standards for whom we generally consider as the successful young people is at least implicitly and oftentimes quite explicitly calibrated to the standards of admissibility.

Somewhere lurking in the imaginations of American teens and preteens is the great test at which everything about them will be present even though they will be physically absent. In some mysterious room hidden behind closed doors, their profiles will be delivered, weighed, and summarily judged. The verdict will be clear: admit or non-admit. Perhaps the jury will continue their deliberations for a few extra excruciating weeks or months under the cover of "wait list," but eventually each candidate will hear either what he or she desperately wanted to hear or desperately feared hearing. Whatever goes on in that room where it happens will remain shrouded in mystery before, during, and after the college admissions process unfolds. Hence, the students immerse themselves in making the profile to be judged in their absence as complete, sparkling, outstanding, impressive, distinctive, and compelling as possible.[16] And they will not be alone in concerning themselves with the project of their own admissibility: parents, guidance counselors, and the whole elementary and secondary school system will join them. "College preparatory" is the code name for modern American childhood.

When getting into college—especially the "right college"—is *the* goal, then there is a tendency to evaluate and measure everything else according to that desired end. We train children and teens to cultivate ambition toward that end, to measure themselves according to admissibility, and to compete with one another for position and ranking. For those in the most prestigious and selective colleges, the ambitious, achievement-driven, metrics-obsessed, comparison-laden, goal-oriented behaviors that they all *had to* cultivate in order to get into their "dream schools" are the very same habits that prevent them from *enjoying* college as a place of learning and growth. When these students get to college, they just keep doing the same things they have always done, except now in a new venue—they've become accustomed to pursuing accomplishments and calculating their worth by inverse comparison to the merits of others. They just keep chasing after the next big goal or, as is becoming more and more common, they run out of steam and breakdowns of varying degrees of severity occur. In short, their capacity to learn in order to grow, to venture even at the risk of failure, and to allow themselves to be seen as *in process* rather than *finished products* is dulled precisely because of how "the system" shaped them in order to achieve admission in the first place.

As part of a five-part series in the *New York Times*, William Fitzsimmons, Dean of Admissions and Financial Aid at Harvard, responded candidly to the question of a mother concerned about what she described as "pressured and stressed teenagers who have been on a long march toward college that began at birth." Here is the two-part exchange:

> (*NYT* reader, Colleen Smith): I once attended a preschool admissions tour where a parent actually asked how many of the preschool's graduates had attended Ivy League colleges. My daughter is now in third grade and participates in only one extracurricular activity because she values free time and wants to play. Nonetheless, when I cross paths with my daughter's overscheduled, horse-jumping, violin-playing peers, I can't help but wonder whether my choice to let my girl play will eventually leave her wanting in the eyes of an admissions committee.
>
> (William Fitzsimmons): Students begin their sports, music, dance, and educational enrichment classes at remarkably young ages. The "specialists". . . do indeed hone their crafts relentlessly and, at times, joylessly for many years.
>
> Colleges are often blamed for this, but college is only one stop on the way through the fast lane to the proverbial brass ring. The "right" graduate school, the "right" sequence of steps in every profession—all leading to the outsized rewards of "The Winner Take All Society."
>
> . . . It is common to encounter even the most successful students, who have won all the "prizes," stepping back and wondering if it was all worth it. Professionals in their thirties and forties . . . sometimes give the impression that they are dazed survivors of some bewildering lifelong boot camp. Some say they ended up in their professions because of someone else's expectations, or that they simply drifted into it without pausing to think whether they really loved their work. Often they say they missed their youth entirely, never living in the present, always pursuing some ill-defined goal.[17]

Whether you are a parent who either consciously or subconsciously engineers your kid's childhood in view of the prospect of college admissions, or whether you are, like Smith, opting for more undesignated time for your child, it is not hard to identify with the subtext of her observation. She is confessing that the standards for measuring the wisdom of parenting and the value of childhood are often made in reference to the looming judgment of college admissions, both for those who "play the game" and for those who do not. For those who play, there is the pressure of getting every piece right; for those who do not play, there is the threat of getting the whole thing wrong. Fitzsimmons's response is no less telling since he observes that this generalized college admissions' anxiety is actually part of a larger cultural issue of "never living in the present, always pursuing some ill-defined goal." During childhood, that ill-defined goal is college, but what happens when students get to college is that the habit of chasing and seeking and measuring themselves against some remote and oftentimes vague standard on the horizon does not go away—it just shifts from college to something else.

The problem is not with the destination itself but with the script running underneath the journey.

The Sour Taste of Dreams

I happen to teach at a "dream school." For many of the students who enroll in undergraduate studies at the University of Notre Dame, this is exactly where they always wanted to go. For others, Notre Dame was one of several very competitive schools to which they applied and, for one reason or another, this is where they ended up (and though no one at Notre Dame will readily admit it, for some of these students Notre Dame was a respectable "backup school"). Moreover, somewhere north of 80 percent of the student body is Catholic.[18] It is probably fair to say that no one ends up at Notre Dame by accident—the students who matriculate in a place like Notre Dame accomplished a lot before they ever stepped foot on campus. They did well in the classroom, they performed well on standardized tests, they were engaged in extracurricular activities, and they held leadership positions. In short, they rose to the challenge of college admissions, and they "won the game." When we look at them, we see what we have come to value through the college admissions process, which is itself a reflection of what we have come to value in our society more broadly, as Fitzsimmons hinted at above.

In light of this, I want to include some of these students' voices in this discussion about desire, college admissions, and the cultural script running underneath it all. I did not go searching for the short stories I share; rather, these are the stories that just came to me in the courses I taught most recently. All of these testimonies have to do with the relationship between the pursuit of college and who the students discover themselves to be in the college setting.

Testimonial 1: The Memories of Who I Have Been

> Throughout high school, I accumulated A's like the rich man in Luke's gospel accumulated the grain from his harvest (see Luke 12:13–21). As the seeds that had been planted at the very start of my education bloomed, I reaped the fruits of the harvest of my intellect. I collected each honor and accolade, each high test score and good grade, building up an impressive résumé full of my achievements, storing them all for the future goal of applying to college.
>
> College admissions were on my mind from the time I started high school. My college-prep school was filled with people like me: we were all headed to college, and many of us were striving for admission to some of the best schools in the country. The environment demanded excellence, encouraging my desire, and reinforcing the pressure to perform exceptionally well.
>
> Like many of my peers when it came to the college admissions process, I not only played the game; I crushed it. I joined more clubs than I had interest in attending, as padding for my résumé. I decided that I would earn a GPA above 100, on a 100-point scale, through getting high grades in weighted Honors and AP classes. . . .

My intensity continued through to my senior year. I edited my college application essay to perfection, crafting it into a masterpiece. I even applied to some very prestigious schools that I had no interest in attending, because that was what people with my grades and test scores were expected and encouraged to do.[19]

Since this is part of a larger reflection, it is important to note that this was written as a prayer to God in the model of Augustine's *Confessions*. What this student ultimately "confesses" is that the firm footing of identity was accomplishments rather than God—in other words, the image of success stood in place of the image of God. The "confession"—first of all as "praise" and then, within that larger context, of "sin"—has to do with the ways in which re-creation was needed and is now occurring in this person's life, where a sense of God's call is replacing the lust for success. Even still, elsewhere in the reflection the student confesses that, "even as I worked on writing this confession, at one point I burst out in frustration to a friend, 'I want to get an *A*!'"

Testimonial 2: The Whispers of Who I Wanted to Be

The second excerpt is from a different student writing for the same assignment. The student begins by recalling how the overriding concern of much of her childhood and teenage years were related to receiving praise from others, being affirmed for her accomplishments, and being regarded as "excellent," especially when compared to others. She remembers trips she took to Notre Dame's Grotto as a young girl and the feeling of awe she experienced there. Now that she returns to that beloved place as an undergraduate student who set her heart long ago at winning that designation, she finds herself questioning what plan she had been following all those years and who she is now that she's finally "arrived":

In that future I had seen glinting in the lights of the candles at the Grotto during my visits as a prospective student—I came expecting that future of my own creation. Where was the girl I thought I was? The girl who confidently marches into

unfamiliar situations without a glance behind for her inse-
curities? Who can give and give of herself to school, friends,
church, socializing, and still have something left over for herself? Who trusts and loves and laughs brazenly? Who is herself, unequivocally and consistently? She was there, I came to
realize. She was the trap I set for myself and "the bonds" I had
"forged for [myself]" (*Confessions* III.16). She was the voice
in my ear that whispered, "You are not enough. You are not
wanted; you are not loved. Look at everyone else—see how
easily they glide through life. See how many boys are enam-
ored. If you are not this, you are not perfect. If you are not
perfect, you are not anything."

What was first semester like? I felt as if I was thirsting
and drowning at the same time. Panicked, frantically running
to the same well within myself every moment to discover it
empty, empty, empty. Yet, simultaneously, finding myself
unable to drag myself there, to choke down the muck of
my own inhibitions, to gag and drown in the loneliness and
despair that inhabited my soul. I searched ceaselessly for that
perfection on my own terms, for the validation of *my* vision
of myself. Me, my, mine . . .

I listened as my friends told me about their new boy-
friends and their wonderful new friends and I tried—desperately—to keep the quivering waver out of my voice because,
what would they think? Would they see the broken, messy,
so-carefully-kept-under-wraps Abby? No, I couldn't allow
that to happen. Because if they saw her, if they knew about
her, then the perfect, happy, put-together Abby would be
eclipsed by the shadow of the other. And then, suddenly, all
that would remain of me would be the broken shell. This was
where I lost sight of you, God. This was the moment when
my soul turned away and I stepped away from our dialogue.
You were with me in the anxiety-induced depression, in the
comparing and contrasting, and in the constant streams of
*thinking thoughts analyzing improving driving try harder work
harder be better be perfect*. I left you behind, however, when

> I let hope drift from my heart and descended, of my own
> volition, into that lion's den of despair.[20]

For someone who has spent considerable time and energy preparing an image of a polished and perfected person who would be deemed
worthy in the eyes of others, showing signs of weakness, vulnerability,
and incompletion is a terrifying prospect.

Testimonial 3: The Vision of Who I Am Becoming

The third and final excerpt comes from a student writing a different
assignment in another course. What this student tells us is that right in
the forms of desiring that are written into the assumed path of success in
a high-achieving environment is the real potential of changing not only
what someone wants but also how they want and who they see themselves becoming. In the midst of this short excerpt, the shift from chasing
after college admissions to chasing after the next horizon is disclosed:

> I have certainly become more career-driven during my years
> in college, and now, as a junior, I've begun to persuade myself
> to distance myself from friends, from religion, and from other
> relationships that take time and effort, because the only thing
> that will matter at the end of college is my GPA and whatever
> graduate program I am accepted to. As a result, I have made
> myself vulnerable to letting ambition control my life, and
> have even become miserable in fulfilling my "dreams" and
> "goals." I've lost the true goals behind acquiring an educa-
> tion—goals that seemed so clear when I first began my Notre
> Dame journey. I feel that I am no longer the same person
> who wrote about wanting to get to know God as the answer
> to the question, "Why are you applying to Notre Dame?"[21]

The long-ingrained habits of achieving, striving, and advancing that
made this student, like the ones before, a desirable candidate for college admissions in the first place did not suddenly vanish once college
began. In fact, those habits were reinforced and the ways of desiring were

strengthened. These students were exactly what their selective institution of higher education said it wanted them to be:

> World-class pianists. Well-rounded senior class leaders. Dedicated artists. Our most competitive applicants are more than just students—they are creative intellectuals, passionate people with multiple interests. Above all else, they are involved— in the classroom, in the community, and in the relentless pursuit of truth.[22]

What is troublesome here is not just this student's feeling of disorientation but also that this student happens to hit all the marks that we want to see in those graduating from top-tier universities. This is the kind of student who gets featured on brochures; the kind of student who "crushes" college after crushing high school and who is well on the way to crushing whatever comes next. But this also happens to be the kind of soon-to-be graduate who is already doing what William Fitzsimmons said the most successful graduates of fine colleges and universities often end up doing: "stepping back and wondering if it was all worth it."[23]

The antidote to the venom of the system is not to expect less of college students; in fact, the antidote is to expect more: they should be guided to be *more* fully human rather than little goal-gobbling achievement machines, especially since little goal-gobbling achievement machines eventually break down, whether during college or afterward. (*Full disclosure: I myself am a recovering goal-gobbling achievement machine, as I mentioned in the preface. I also suffer from relapses.*) After all, you can't enjoy a baseball game if you're obsessed with how much everything costs, who has the best seat, and how to consistently "upgrade your experience," just like you can't enjoy heaven if you keep thinking about how to get ahead, how to work the situation to your own advantage, or how to favorably compare your merits to those of others. None of those things are part of the condition of freedom—namely the freedom to enjoy, to discover yourself, to be at peace.

The college admissions game is a kind of bondage on young people, but that game does not exist in isolation. It is just one in a whole series of games where the assumption is that we are not yet enough and are always seeking after the next great thing, which basically restates the thesis of the "Your Verse" Apple advertisement I discussed in the last chapter. In this regard, when the exorbitant tuition fees change hands—even at Catholic colleges and universities—it is done with the consumer expectation that "I better get my money's worth." (*Another note in the interest of full disclosure: I don't think exorbitant tuition fees are okay, even though they help pay my salary.*) What you should get when you gain admission is an education for the sake of not what you think you like but what will help you to *enjoy* life on God's terms, unto life everlasting.

Behavioral Incentivizing

If testimonials like the ones I offered above cause concern—and there are indeed *many more* that I could have included, and I only teach a fraction of students at one "prestigious" institution among many others—then perhaps we need to advocate for change in what colleges and universities look for in their applicants. By and large, the top tier schools will remain the top tier schools and therefore continue to boast of the most coveted undergraduate spots, so what they do is bound to have a trickle-down effect on the whole system. And since there is no tier higher than the one on which Harvard sits, perhaps it is good news that Harvard is leading a reform in college admissions standards.

In a report emerging from the Harvard Graduate School of Education—with collaborators from a wide array of other institutions including all members of the Ivy League (and Stanford)—the power of college admissions processes for shaping our society is taken for granted. The title of the report speaks of the noble cause fueling this collaboration: "Turning the Tide: Inspiring Concern for Others and the Common Good through College Admissions." The problem at hand, in the view of the collaborators, is in the eye of high school students who "perceive colleges as simply valuing their achievements." As the authors of the report continue,

> This report advances a new, widely shared vision of college admissions that seeks to respond to this deeply concerning problem. It makes the case that college admissions can send compelling messages that both ethical engagement—especially concern for others and the common good—and intellectual engagement are highly important. Colleges can powerfully collaborate to send different messages to high school students about what colleges value.[24]

You'd be hard pressed to find anyone who would publicly declare that valuing individual achievement is more important than valuing contributions to the common good (however "common good" happens to be defined). All the same and at the risk of sounding chronically suspicious, we ought to pause before heaping uncritical praise on this effort. Each of those students whose testimonies I offered earlier—along with *most* of the students I teach—are already involved in great and worthy causes. The problem that they themselves are sensing is that those great and worthy causes are fitted into their individual profiles. Even with the best of intentions, they end up accumulating worthwhile experiences—even service experiences, and sometimes especially these—in order to build up their profiles, adding valuable lines to their résumés. If we recognize what the authors of this report recognize, which is that college admissions standards have the power to shape behaviors and values of teenagers and younger children, as well as their parents, then something else also becomes apparent. All of those noteworthy and noble pursuits that the report goes on to uplift, all the calls for balance and the reduction in competitiveness, all the recommendations for an increase in quality of investment in activities rather than simply the quantity of activities—all of *that* is going to factor into the college admissions selection process. In the end, a judgment will be rendered and, in the end, the verdict will still be "admit" or "non-admit." It is the admissions process that is still motivating people, still setting the agenda, still writing the script for children and teenagers. In some sense, "the game" has just expanded the boundaries for what's in play.

Notice how even what seems most basic, selfless, and non-prestigious gets accounted for in this "new vision":

> The admissions process should clearly send the message to students, parents and other caregivers that not only community engagement and service, but also students' family contributions, such as caring for younger siblings, taking on major household duties or working outside the home to provide needed income, are highly valued in the admissions process.[25]

"Highly valued in the admissions process." In other words, the rules of the process retain authority—that is the hidden assumption.[26]

The *Washington Post* asked college admissions officers from across the country what they are looking for in applicants. While the whole collection of responses is fascinating, I will focus on just one here. Martha Blevins Allman, the director of admissions at Wake Forest University, said this: "Concentrate not on being the best candidate, but on being the best person. Pay attention to what is going on in the world around you. If you do these things, not only will the world be a better place because you're in it, your greatest admissions worry will be choosing which college to pick from."[27] I wonder how much is hidden under those words "not only." As stated, it sounds as if the primary concern is making the world a better place, which will also, by the way, improve your chances of being accepted to the college of your choice. But if we allow ourselves to be just a bit suspicious a little longer, maybe we will recognize that in an article that is dedicated to providing useful information to students and especially their parents, what is really being stated is that becoming aware of and invested in your community and the world will "not only" get you the really desirable thing—a positive college admissions outcome—but also make the world a better place in the process. The primary driver for motivating behavior and establishing values is still college admissions. What we need is to reevaluate in whom or in what this powerful motivating authority is invested.[28]

The Authority of Hidden Assumptions

It is tempting and altogether too easy to start assigning blame for this bind of the "college preparatory" culture. The easiest targets of all are the colleges and the universities themselves, as we might imagine that motivations of self-interest from the institutions in broad terms and administrators personally are exerting undue control over the lives of others. Not only would such accusations be too blunt to be accurate, but also they would force us to miss the main point, which is this: it is our general, collective, even if typically silent agreement to the standards of evaluation implicit in this accomplishment-based narrative that actually makes it powerful. What college admissions committees "highly value" has so much authority because, in point of fact, advancement to college is treated as a prime goal. This may not be confessed, it may not be claimed, and it may not be discussed even among family members and friends, but written right into the institutions that shape our young people and beating in the hearts of us parents who are raising these children is the persistent concern about how we are preparing them to measure up to this one test. The young people feel it, and they adapt their desires and behaviors accordingly, or they shut down in one way or another in response to their perceived inability to measure up. This is not the only concern running through institutions and families and young people's lives, but it is the one that predominates when we seek to justify activities, evaluate commitments, or measure how much is enough. It seems that there is no other value, no matter how lofty or grand, that cannot be connected to "college" by a "but also," including "not only college *but also* sainthood." In that very formulation is a declaration of what's driving what.

What I have been at pains to portray is something very hard to see: the narrative assumption on which everything else in a life or even a culture builds. It is hard to see because it is hidden, and it is hidden precisely because it is just assumed. We do not question what we assume, unless and until we pause to ask what our assumptions are and take the time consider whether those are the basic assumptions we should have or even really want to have.

In his book *My Life with the Saints*, James Martin talks about the way he typically made judgments in the years leading up to college, through college, and immediately after college. After recounting his tale of entering the University of Pennsylvania's Wharton School of Business, having decided to study business because he and everyone around him could reason through how this course of study would lead to "a high-paying job after graduation," he offers this summative reflection:

> Wharton's reputation in the corporate world made finding a job ridiculously easy. At the beginning of senior year, hundreds of corporate recruiters flocked to the school to conduct interviews: in a few months I had received a number of excellent offers. After narrowing them down to three or four, I settled on a corporate training program at General Electric in New York City.
>
> Once again, almost no reflection was involved in my decision. To use some accounting terminology, I simply went with "generally accepted principles." For example, what should you do at the end of business school? Interview for jobs. Which job offer should you accept? The one with the highest salary. The more important questions were the ones that no one asked me, or rather, that I failed to ask myself: What do you desire in life? And what does God desire for you?[29]

"Generally accepted principles" speaks to ways of evaluating and judging that have become commonplace, and for precisely that reason they become incredibly powerful. In Martin's vignette, the "generally accepted principles" of the standard narrative of achievement and advancement drowned out other questions that, in retrospect, Martin recognizes as more important and indeed more desirable. Those "other questions"—the ones with which he ends—do not simply arise, though, in the absence of other narratives; rather, they arise out of another kind of definite narrative.

It might seem to some that freedom is about choosing without any preconditions, as if in a void. But that's a myth, because there are no presupposition-less positions and every one of us stands on some narrative, whether we admit to it or not. We cannot live without assumptions. We have to take certain things for granted and trust in particular base narratives. What we assume—what we trust fundamentally—is most important of all, because it sets the foundation, the standards, and the parameters for everything else we do, think, pursue, and desire. If we do not intentionally stand on a firm assumption upon which our narratives will build, then some generally assumed principles—some default assumptions—serve the purpose.

From a basic premise, all the possibilities for a narrative build. Put another way, the ways in which narratives may and eventually do expand are continuous with and depend on what came before and, most basically, what came first. The basis of a narrative wields absolute authority. Consider, if you will, the narrative of the Tooth Fairy. If a child takes as fundamentally true that the Tooth Fairy exists and fits a certain profile—namely, this creature desires your teeth and will take them from you in exchange for money—then it is possible that, when new information that might not seem to fit the narrative comes into play, the child will simply expand the narrative to account for it. This is precisely how an episode of the radio show *This American Life* began in 2001:

> (Host, Ira Glass): Rebecca remembers exactly when she learned the astonishing truth. She was in second grade and ran into her best friend Rachel at school one day.
>
> (Rebecca, now an adult): And she pulled me aside and said, "Last night I lost a tooth and I woke up while the Tooth Fairy was putting the money under my pillow. And guess who the Tooth Fairy was." And I said, "O my [goodness], who was it? I have to know!" And she said, "My dad. My dad is the Tooth Fairy."
>
> And I remember running home after school and telling my mom, "Mom, I know who the Tooth Fairy is." And declaring it as if I had grown up—that I knew who the Tooth

Fairy was. And she said, "Oh, well . . . who is the Tooth Fairy?" And I turned to her and I said, "Rachel's dad . . . is the Tooth Fairy. Ronnie Loberfeld is the Tooth Fairy."

And she said, "I can't believe you know. It's totally a secret; you can't let anyone else know. But you're right, Ronnie is the Tooth Fairy, and he works really hard. And, you know, it's a *secret*, so you can't let anyone else know. He is the Tooth Fairy but you can't let anyone else know."

And from that day on Ronnie Loberfeld was the Tooth Fairy. And all of my notes under my pillow were signed, "Love, Ronnie Loberfeld."[30]

In a low-stakes manner, this short excerpt testifies to just how formative a basic assumption can be when it comes to shaping a vision of reality. Because second-grade Rebecca was committed to the basic narrative of the Tooth Fairy, when the new information that her friend Rachel gives her comes along, she does not even consider what seems obvious to us and, at the same time, we do not consider what was absolutely certain to her. Rebecca's narrative therefore expands in an especially surprising way: she fits Ronnie Loberfeld into the narrative of the Tooth Fairy, even to the point of positing what must now, in hindsight, not only seem ridiculous but also a little terrifying: her friend's dad goes into the rooms of sleeping children to collect their teeth!

Of course, second-grade Rachel had no idea that what was really at issue in her experience was the hidden assumption that exercised authority over the narrative she would learn to tell. This is quite forgivable for a second grader—to say the least—especially because the stakes were so low (and, moreover, because it was the occasion for a brilliant piece of parenting on her mom's part). What is a bit more troubling, though, is that the narrative dynamics in play here are the same ones that James Martin recognized in retrospect when he saw that the important decisions of his late teens and early twenties were guided by "generally accepted principles" of which he was then unaware. Moreover, these are the same narrative dynamics in the testimonies of my students who are coming to see that the script running underneath their journeys to college was actually a script about habitually craving achievements and accomplishments.

The basic assumption or the core narrative is the answer to the question of "What's driving what?" If college admissions or comparable measures of "success" are treated as or secretly assumed to be the most important goal, then everything else will have to fit in to that narrative. This is not an issue of choosing success or holiness, but it is an issue of choosing which is more important and, therefore, what drives what, especially when difficult choices—choices of value, life's big decisions—must be made. And this is an issue that is at the heart of the *practical wisdom* of Christianity in large part because it was first part of the practical wisdom of Judaism.

What's First in the Judeo-Christian Imagination

That the most important thing in who you actually become and what you learn to love is what you actually treat as fundamental is itself an assumed truth of Christian transformation. When Christians profess their creed, they practice committing themselves to the firm foundation of belief in God the Father, Son, and Holy Spirit. This bedrock wisdom in Christianity's creedal profession of faith is itself continuous with the bedrock wisdom of Ancient Israel's daily profession of faith: the *Shema* prayer:[31]

> Hear, O Israel! The LORD is our God, the LORD alone! Therefore, you shall love the LORD, your God, with all your heart, and with all your soul, and with all your strength. Take to heart these words which I enjoin on you today. Drill them into your children. Speak of them at home and abroad, whether you are busy or at rest. Bind them at your wrist as a sign and let them be as a pendant on your forehead. Write them on the doorposts of your houses and on your gates. (Dt 6:4–9)

Here is Israel's fundamental assumption; here is the base narrative; here is the core commitment that critiques all "generally accepted principles." The foundation of Israel's life and imagination—the first and last standard for all its evaluations—is simply but absolutely that *the Lord is our God*. Whatever else is done in the course of a day or in the course of a lifetime, this one truth must be remembered. This is the most important thing to teach to children; this is the one great thing that, at all costs, must never be forgotten. Assume this and you shall live.

This prayer becomes elevated all the more when, in response to the question about what is the greatest commandment, Jesus himself answers with the *Shema*, before tying the twin commandment of love of neighbor to this first one, as we discussed in the first chapter (Mk 12:30–31; see also Lk 4:8). Everything else depends on making the most important thing first of all. By the wisdom of the psalmist: *Unless the* LORD *build the house, they labor in vain who build* (Ps 127:1), or again, *When foundations are being destroyed, what can the upright do?* (Ps 11:3). The foundation determines the quality of the house that may be built; if the foundation is faulty, no matter how wonderful and impressive the structure appears, it will not hold and all work will have been in vain. Committing to the right fundamental assumption is of utmost importance.

The Road Is Not Neutral

To return to considering those two disciples on the road from Jerusalem to Emmaus, discussed in the first chapter, we may now more fully consider how they were unaware of the authoritative power of their own hidden assumptions. It was not simply that they were ignorant of something or that they failed to remember something; their issue was with their base narrative. Even though they seemed to know what had taken place that fateful week in Jerusalem and that the tomb was now empty and that angels had announced to the women that Jesus was alive, they still could not see who was walking right beside them and conversing with them. Each of them had a memory set to the basic assumption that the messiah was to fit a certain profile, and so when new information and then this stranger comes to them, they do not do what we expect them to do, which is to see that this is Jesus and open themselves to belief in his Resurrection. Their expectations blind them—they are committed to another narrative.

They don't just need to remember something forgotten; they need a new way of remembering. They don't just need to see something new; they need a new way of seeing. They don't just need another element for their narrative; they need a new narrative.

How does Jesus give them a new way of remembering? He teaches them the scriptures, starting from the beginning (Lk 24:27). How does Jesus give them a new way of seeing? He shows them the gift of his body in the breaking of the bread (Lk 24:30–31). How does Jesus give them a new narrative? He gives them a story that they run to tell to the others, in haste (Lk 24:33–35). In response to a great need for transformation, Jesus acts directly and in specific ways for their own good. These movements establish the basic order of the Catholic Mass: the Liturgy of the Word, the Liturgy of the Eucharist, and sending forth.

This brings us back again—at long last—to the mother of all saints and the model of all disciples: Mary. We can recall that when the angel spoke to her, she recognized the sign of her cousin Elizabeth's pregnancy as continuous with the history of Israel's salvation. That history followed from Abraham and his wife Sarah, to whose likeness Mary's own kin was now configured. Her recognition of the signs in the angel's proclamation was not just about Mary remembering a few things, here and there; rather, Mary's own "base narrative" is revealed. She remembers according to a scriptural memory, she sees along the lines of the divine promise, and she allows herself to be located within the continuous narrative of God's mercy that is now, with her, narratively expanding.

At the beginning of Luke's gospel, Mary already lives according to the memory that the disciples at the end of the gospel will receive anew from Jesus in his Resurrection. Mary is unfailingly faithful to the *Shema*, remembering that the Lord is God even when she does not know what is happening. She stands on that trust, she places herself in that memory, she interprets from that basis, and, therefore, she claims the freedom to respond bravely.

If the first priority in becoming capable of the vocational discernment leading to missionary discipleship is to break from the tyranny of noise and reclaim the capacity for pondering through strategic patience, then the next priority is to practice a new memory. What we practice as fundamentally true—as the ground and ultimate horizon not only of our whole lives but also of our everyday comings and goings—will affect everything.[32] The problem, as I have been arguing, is that we have become well practiced in another kind of memory, one which, for American teenagers at least, is conformed to a "college preparatory culture." Breaking from one memory for the sake of another—moving from one base narrative to another—is no small thing. It would take something like "magic waters" to pull it off all at once but, with baptismal resonances momentarily suspended, no mere dipping would seem to complete the job. (Dante imagined a journey between two dippings, remember.) Moreover, if this were just something that could be done *for* us, that itself would be a violation of dignity and freedom—for the whole matter of Christian discipleship is to become something, not simply to arrive at some way of being all of a sudden. And so we are left with entrusting ourselves to the prayers of Mary as we seek after becoming what she already is by grace, and therefore we must journey as the disciples on the road to Emmaus journeyed under Jesus' own authoritative direction: through intentional practices of scriptural memory, of learning to see anew, and of telling a new story.

Renewing the Biblical Imagination

When Mary listened in openness to the announcement of the angel, her openness was not neutral; she was already inclined toward trusting, seeing, and believing in the narrative of the God of Israel. When the disciples on the road to Emmaus conversed with the stranger who drew near to them, their words were not neutral; they were already inclined toward a certain understanding of the messiah that blocked their ability to believe anew. When Jesus called them *foolish* to silence them and then teach them the scriptures, he was changing how their minds and hearts were inclined. The space of their imaginations took on new dimensions and prepared them to trust, see, and believe what was previously impossible for them according to their old ways.

The disciples on the road to Emmaus could not imagine the messiah that *had* come because they were fixated on the messiah they *thought* they wanted.[33] If Jesus drew near to these two disciples walking along today, what kind of messiah would he find them expecting? They would likely be expecting a messiah who would confirm commonplace moral maxims and who would help them become "the best versions of themselves." That does not sound so bad, but neither did the expectation for a messiah who would liberate the Jewish people from their Roman overlords through military revolution so as to reclaim the Promised Land as their own sovereign territory. Though the details of the expectation are distinct, the same problem exists now as then: we default to expecting God to conform to narrative assumptions that do not follow from God's own terms. The disciples on the road to Emmaus interpreted the scriptures according to their smallish desires for a religious revolution in political and militaristic terms, while the standard assumption today is for a god who will serve us by helping us to be nice, kind, and fair to each other while also making our problems go away.[34]

I mentioned something like this already in the first chapter in connection with the parable of the Good Samaritan. In the popular religious imagination, this parable is reduced to a message about doing good things for other people. While that is not completely wrong, it is also rather thin. That is a "message" that could get delivered in any number of ways, and it just so happens that Jesus tells this little tale to get the point across. What happens with an imbalanced moralistic reading of the parable is that once that message is grasped, the parable can be abandoned because it served its purpose. The parable becomes something like a grammar school lesson in morals, just like we might learn our ABCs by singing a song—once we grasp the alphabet and the order of the letters, the song is no longer necessary and we only come back to it when we have to remind ourselves that "u" comes after "t" but before "v." What really matters, it seems, is that we be civically tolerant above all, never too particular for fear of offending, and that we help each other out when we can.[35] That fits the profile of a "good person" in today's world, and a "good person" is one who is approved of, congratulated, and awarded the opportunity to advance. What is happening in the meantime is that ignorance of scripture is becoming commonplace, and as St. Jerome captures so poignantly, "ignorance of Scripture is ignorance of Christ." In this ignorance, we also become ignorant of ourselves.[36]

I have seen exactly this happening not only with the students I teach in college theology courses—*most especially* those who have come to college by way of Catholic education—but even in my own eldest son, Caleb, who attends Catholic school. My son is sharp, he's a good reader, and he thinks very quickly. He is rewarded for these traits in his schooling. He gets to the answer quickly and usually his answer is correct. He has learned how to infer meaning in what he reads. And he is predisposed to doing precisely this when he reads scripture in school—he looks for the message and, once he has it, he rests because he has the right answer. By the time he gets to college he would most likely be like most of the students who sit in introductory theology courses: he would already know what scripture is about, he would get that "it is about being a good person who is fair and kind to others," and he would be predisposed to disinterest in turning to scripture again. The more likely outcome for someone like him, though, is that he would just tacitly conclude that this is what religion is really all about and now that he's got the message, he doesn't need religion. He will just be a "good person" without the baggage of having to be "all religious." Maybe he'll just be "spiritual."[37]

I just happened to notice this about my son when he was still rather young, almost by accident. Though I was eager for him to grow in his Christian faith, as a young father I didn't really know what that would mean and, honestly, I didn't specifically plan for how I would take a leading role in forming him in faith. But since I had that general desire I figured—mostly by chance intuition—that while I was helping him practice reading on his own one day, I might as well include some faith formation with that. So we sat down to read the beginning of the Gospel of Mark together. I chose Mark because it is the shortest gospel, because everything happens "immediately" (this word appears no fewer than forty times in Mark), and because I quickly calculated that it was the least complicated of the four. What I failed to remember, however, is that by midway through only the first chapter of Mark, Jesus heals a man with an "unclean spirit" (Mk 1:21–28). When I considered this gospel, I wasn't expecting to have to address any difficult questions right away, but sure enough, there was my son slowly reading through this passage and immediately the question arose, "Daddy, what is an unclean spirit?"

So I did what any teacher caught off guard does—I responded with, "Well, what do you think it is?"

He said, "I don't know."

So I said, "How about if we look back at the story?" I was mostly stalling as we slowly went over the details of the passage again. After making a second pass and still unsure of how to explain this to my son in a way that would make sense to him, I said again, "So now what do you think an unclean spirit is?"

And he said, "I guess it means wanting to live in the world without God."

I was closing in on a PhD in theology at that point in my life. I had been studying theology for longer than I had studied anything else. I could tell you lots of things about God, but I could not express with such eloquence what this young child—who only had the story itself to teach him and not a whole lot of other things from which to infer—ended up seeing very plainly in this scriptural passage. He did not paraphrase, he just saw clearly what is presented clearly: Jesus heals a man who was trying to live in the world without God. Caleb was probably six at the time, and he taught me something absolutely crucial about how a disciple should read scripture: always begin with what is *actually* there, on the page, paying close attention to what is actually said and how it is said.[38]

It was this memory of my son's childlike openness to scripture that stirred my concern when, a few years later, he told me what he was learning about the parables in his school. Essentially, he said that the parables were moral lessons and Jesus' words were maxims to help us live better. Suddenly, what mattered most of all was not whether you wanted to live in the world with or without God but whether or not you were a "good person." That sounds like a slight difference, but a slight deflection in a train's trajectory at its origin means a radically different destination at journey's end. My son was being taught to look for the moral lesson that would help him live better as a good person, and since "good person" was subtly untethered from the definitiveness of God's terms, "good person" was now subject to being shaped and defined in whatever mold was most powerful otherwise. The density and concreteness of the text of scripture did not really matter—what mattered was what it was pointing to: its message. As I was becoming aware of this, I happened to ask a slightly older parent whose son was set to move on from eighth grade to high school what she thought about his Catholic education to date. She said that he and all his friends were, generally, "really nice kids" who "received a really good education" and were prepared to do well in high school. Then she concluded, "And I just don't think that's enough."

What that parent said clarified for me what had started to disturb me in my son's education and training in the Christian life. Her words also helped me to interpret what I began to see more and more with the "really nice kids" I taught in college theology courses and whom I supervised in college ministry programs. I started to see how the approach to scripture stood as a kind of litmus test for the approach to the Christian faith as a whole: when it is reduced to a repository of moral maxims designed to help you live better as "a good person," then once you get the message you can leave behind the medium.[39] Scripture and, therefore, the Church are seen as the grammar school of morals, and you outgrow grammar school. Oddly enough, the more successful kids become in their studies and other activities, the more common it will be for them to take for granted what they have already learned and move on to what seems more challenging, esteemed, and sophisticated. After all, you learn your ABCs so you can learn other stuff—the stuff that really matters.

Against this movement, we ought to again think of Mary. When she heard the sign of her cousin Elizabeth's pregnancy, she had not moved on from the old things she had learned. Rather, the old things formed her memory and she continued to marvel at them, sticking to their concreteness and density. Unlike Zechariah, she recognized that Elizabeth invoked Sarah because, for Mary, the scriptures were alive and active in her memory. She was a student of God's ways, so she interpreted herself and the signs of the times according to how God had revealed himself in the course of salvation history. In his fear, Zechariah missed the sign completely while, later, the disciples on the road to Emmaus who were committed to an alternative narrative were unready and unwilling to receive the definitive gift of God in the world that is the Risen Christ. I recognized that if I wanted my children (and even my students) to grow in holiness on God's terms first and foremost—with every other hope or desire falling in line behind that—then I would need to help them to become familiar with God's language, God's customs, God's narrative—that is, in short, to shape their imaginations to God's own terms. And, of course, in order to do that I would have to become more familiar with God's terms myself.

Developing a scriptural memory is essential to missionary discipleship because if we do not practice imagining within the dynamic of God's mission through history, then the sense of mission in our own lives will move toward other ends. We are always searching for a context and we will assume some context or other whether we mean to or not. Disciples receive their context in the love of God the Father incarnate in Jesus Christ and communicated in the Spirit. God's ways are not our ways, so we have to study God's ways (see Isaiah 55:8–9).

With my preteen eldest son, I have begun to make a habit of studying scripture together on Sundays. My primary and almost sole hope at this point is to allow him to discover how scripture "functions." For example, we spent seven separate Sundays reading the "seven last words" of Jesus from the various gospel accounts.[40] I did not concern myself with teaching him too much; rather, I allowed him (read: occasionally *I made him*) follow the annotations in the text itself.

In Luke 23:46, for instance, Jesus says, *Father, into your hands I commit my spirit* (RSV). In the notes in my son's Bible, Psalm 31:5 is referenced. So we moved from the Gospel of Luke to the psalms, where he read, *Into your hands I commit my spirit; you have redeemed me, O Lord.* That is the immediate connection, but we read around in this psalm a bit more to try to understand the reference in its context. Just before that verse, the psalm reads, *Be a rock of refuge for me, a strong fortress to save me! Yes, you are my rock and my fortress* (vv. 2b–3a).

At this point I asked my son, "Why a rock?"

And at this point he was permitted to "infer" from within scripture, so he said, "Jesus said to Peter, 'you are my rock on which I will build my Church.' So God is what we will build our Church on, and he will give us a foundation." From reading within scripture and not being told "what it is about," my son discovered that in committing his spirit to the Father, Jesus was also saying that his Father was his foundation and on that very same foundation he builds his Church.

When we looked at John 19:28 to read *I thirst*, we found Psalm 69:21 referenced in the notes: *They gave me gall for food, and for my thirst they gave me vinegar to drink*. That is the direct connection. But then when we read around the psalm, we found these lines: *I am weary with crying; my throat is parched* (v. 3); *I am the talk of those who sit in the gate, and the drunkards make songs about me* (v. 12); and *Insults have broken my heart, so that I am in despair. I looked for pity, but there was none; and for comforters, but I found none* (v. 20). After reading the whole psalm and writing down these different lines, I asked Caleb how he understood Jesus' thirst on the basis of this psalm. He wrote this note in the reading journal I asked him to keep: "the one who is suffering wants mercy not too much wine, or any really." Was Jesus' throat parched for water? Yes. But the psalm taught Caleb that Jesus' whole body and soul were thirsting for compassion.

We went through the other last words in similar fashion, and time and again we found ourselves sent back to the psalter. At some point I asked Caleb what he thought about all these lines from the psalms coming from Jesus' lips on the Cross. Honestly, I expected him to say something like "Jesus was using the psalms to explain what was happening to him on the Cross"; in fact, that is pretty close to what I would have said. But here is what Caleb actually said and wrote: "I think Jesus was probably praying the psalms the whole time he was on the Cross." I had never thought of it that way, just like I had never thought about the simple and direct description of what an unclean spirit is. Scripture was teaching my son how to know Jesus on God's terms, and I was learning from my son. While he—and even and especially I—was ignorant of scripture, he was in some significant respect ignorant of Christ. As he learned scripture, he was learning who Christ is. Knowing who Jesus is—on his terms—is the condition of the possibility of saying "yes" to him and following him. This is precisely what we see in those disciples on the road to Emmaus, who have to allow their imaginations to be conformed to the dimensions of scripture to see Christ. You cannot rely on a "personal relationship with Christ" to save you when the "Christ" you imagine is made in your own image and likeness. Studying scripture forms and re-forms our memory as configured to God's ways.[41]

The narrative of discipleship always builds on a biblical imagination because God's ways do not conform to our "generally accepted principles" but rather critique and renew those basic assumptions in every age.

The Light of Eucharistic Seeing

As the foundation of the imaginations of the disciples on the road to Emmaus was reset through Jesus' authoritative teaching of scripture, they were then made ready to see him in the mystery of the Eucharist—the breaking of the bread. In the Catholic Mass, the gift that those who receive from the table of the Lord may give to those who do not receive—or, moreover, the gift that those who receive may give to one another—is a vision of the world shot through with the light of Christ. We might be tempted to think that the world just is what the world is, but as I argued in my previous book, *Witness*, how we see the world and how we tell the story of life to one another is not set out for us in advance. We can give each other the gift of seeing the world within the Body of Christ. Perhaps more than anyone else, parents can give this gift to their children, as I first learned from my father and then had the opportunity to teach one of my younger sons.

My greatest education in parenting comes from what my dad chose to build his parenting on. After my mom left him when I was seven and my brother was three, my dad raised us on his own at a time when single parents were not as common as they are today, and a single dad was downright rare. With a broken marriage and shattered finances, followed by job insecurity and one health problem after another, my dad gave himself over to both the obvious and the millions of imperceptible daily duties of bringing up two young boys. But most important of all, he attended daily Mass every morning at 6:30 a.m.

In and of itself, this practice was neither a form of overt piety nor heroism; in fact, when I asked my dad more than two decades later why he went to Mass every day, he said, "I just enjoyed it. It was a good way to start my day."

Mass always ended a couple minutes before 7 a.m., and he would race home afterward to pack our lunches and get my brother and me ready for school.[42] Otherwise, his days were no different than the great many parents who tend to their kids, work their jobs, cook meals, pay bills, attend school meetings, drive to sports practices, and maybe find a half hour or so of downtime at the end of the day. In all those ways, what he did then is much like what my wife and I do now. And yet I can't help but think about the sheer volume of it all for one person, about the way he poured himself into it all, and about the simple routine that started all those days.

Once, when I was being particularly obnoxious during my early teenage years, my dad's friend sort of reprimanded me, saying, "Someday you'll realize all that your dad's done for you." Those words have stayed with me. Now that I am the age my dad was when he was undertaking his parenting tasks, I can't imagine trying to care for my children's needs without their mother (especially since she is the superior parent of the two of us). Indeed, I'm starting to realize the immensity of what my dad did for my brother and me.

The most important thing he did for us, though, was that he went to Mass every morning. It is not that all the things that happened the rest of the day were the effect of this one cause; rather, each of those days that I lived under his care were days spent with a man who practiced giving both his joys and his sorrows to the Lord, a man who stuck to

3. *Memory and the Authority of Hidden Assumptions*

that familiar ritual of receiving the Eucharist through all the ups and downs of life. As much as he had to improvise in those days, he made that one constant his firm foundation. And for two boys who had lost the stability of a familiar home, he became our stability.

Though the translation of the Roman Missal was different then, I like to think of my father sitting at those early morning Masses when I recite these words before approaching the altar: "Lord, I am not worthy that you should enter under my roof; but only say the word and my soul shall be healed." For my father, that "roof" covered our home, and our home was a perpetual reminder to him of the fracture that had occurred in his life—it was a reminder of what once was but was no longer. Under *that* roof, we all erred and we all failed. For all his virtues and heroic deeds, my father also had more than his fair share of poor decisions. Like all families, ours was, in many ways, unworthy of blessing.

But. I love that word right in the middle of that prayer. *But* I turn to you, O Lord. *But* I trust in you, O Lord. *But* your Word is not my word, Lord, because your Word heals even when my words wound. *But* my dad practiced opening himself to more than he was by himself, and at a few minutes before 7 a.m., he would race home to make our lunches.

Even with all (*I think*) I know about the Eucharist now, there is nothing I could ever think or say or write that would exceed the eloquence of what my dad did, day after day: he went out before we woke to receive the Eucharist, and he brought the Eucharist back to us within himself. My dad carried what he received into our home and shared him with us in the uncountable small acts of love he performed on a daily basis. We fed on his love; he became our bread.

My vision of the world was forged in my childhood home, and because my dad received the Eucharist daily, our home was shaped by that love, even though I didn't consciously recognize it at the time.

Nearly three decades later, my wife and I were sitting with our children at dinner one night. We were in the early months of 2017, and my kids started talking about things we might do when we drove out to the East Coast in the summer. In passing, one of my older kids said

that maybe we could go to the White House. Almost immediately, my
wife and I noticed that our five-year-old, Josiah, clammed up and looked
really distracted. After a few minutes, I went with him into another room
to see what was going on. He said nothing at first, but it was clear that
there was something wrong. I asked him if somebody said something
that bothered him—he nodded yes, reluctantly. I asked him if it had
something to do with the White House—again, he nodded yes. After
several minutes of my gently reassuring him that he could tell me, he
said that he didn't want to go to the White House because he'd heard
someone say that "Donald Trump is going to destroy the world." He
was five years old—this wasn't any kind of political opinion or bias that
he was expressing. In his childlike imagination, he'd heard something
like that in passing and he feared it. He didn't want to go to the White
House because someone said that the man who lives there is going to
destroy the world.

My first instinct was to tell him that Donald Trump is not going
to destroy the world, but I didn't say that. After all, if any single person
could actually destroy the world, it would be whoever holds the most
powerful office in the world (I definitely didn't say that to him!). I also
felt like the most important thing to do was not to try to diminish the
reason for his fear but rather to try to increase the reason for his hope. I
also knew that my wife—who runs a Catechesis of the Good Shepherd
atrium in which Josiah participates—has helped him and his older sib-
lings to develop an eye for and an imagination about the symbols of the
Catholic liturgy.

My response, therefore, was to ask him a question: "Josiah, who
holds the whole world in his hands?" I was pretty confident—thanks in
no small part to a VeggieTales jingle—that he would say what he said:

> "God."
> I told him that no matter what, God will always hold
> the whole world in his hands. "And you know what else?
> You know when we go to Mass and the priest holds up the
> bread—the Eucharist?"
> "Yeah," he said.

"Well, that is God's love coming into the world. When
we go to Mass, we can look up there at that moment and
see God's love coming into the world." He smiled, and even
giggled. Then we went back to the dinner table.

A few days later when we went to Mass, I nudged him just as the
priest was raising the host. I said, "Remember—that's God's love coming
into the world." He smiled and giggled again.

Even without making the case, my hope is that he can learn to see
every terrible thing that might happen in the world in light of that one
central action: God's love coming into the world.

Not two months later, I got home late from work one night, just after
Josiah and his younger brother, Isaac, had gone off to bed. I went into
their room to kiss them goodnight, but I found Josiah sitting upright
on his bed, staring out the window through parted curtains. He said he
was waiting to watch the sunset.

I told him that wasn't possible because (a) it was cloudy and (b) his
window faces east. I told him that if he wanted to, he could look out
there in the early morning and maybe he'd see the sunrise.

The next morning he woke before dawn and rushed down to remind
me of the sunrise. He rushed upstairs again, sat upright in front of the
window, and watched through parted curtains as the sky turn "yellow,
then orange, then pink, then blue." He watched the whole thing until
the day was illuminated. I sat there with him, while Isaac leaned against
his big brother's back. I told them that God's first command was *Let
there be light* (Gn 1:3).

As I went about my day, I found myself thinking back to what happened that morning and also back to a couple of months earlier when
he'd been stricken with fear at the thought of someone destroying the
world. That same child, whose imagination is so open to being filled and
shaped, sat there to watch what most of us either sleep through or forget
to marvel at. He marveled at the possibilities of a sunrise, he took in
its beauty, he watched the whole thing, and he found it to be the most
amazing occurrence imaginable. He was open to wonder rather than
closed up in fear. That's the condition of the possibility of the freedom

of discipleship, and it is the gift that Christ gives to his disciples who
gather around the altar and learn to see the world in his love.[43]

Embodying the Christian Narrative

Every Sunday at my parish—just after the communion lines end and we
observe several moments of silence—our pastor or associate pastor asks
for "those who are taking communion to the homebound to please come
forward." Every Sunday, two, three, or four parishioners come forward
to receive the Blessed Sacrament in their hands as well as a blessing that
they are instructed to bring to those members of our parish who are
absent, "assuring them of our prayers and of their communion with us
in the Eucharist." Every Sunday, those ministers then take Communion
and that blessing to those who were not there to hear what was said or
to receive what was given. Every Sunday, those ministers do what those
disciples first did on Easter morning, when *they rose that same hour and
returned to Jerusalem . . . [and] they told what had happened to them on the
road, and how he was made known to them in the breaking of the bread* (Lk
24:33–34). In other words, they do what all those who receive the gift of
the Eucharist are called to do: to build on that gift as our base narrative
and take up the mission of making Christ's love known in our charity for
and blessings of those who were not there to receive. Even if we came in
with venom, we are sent out with benedictions as missionary disciples.

As I wrote at the beginning of this chapter, Christian discipleship
is about who you become when the mission God gives you shapes your
identity, and the transformation by which disciples become saints always
begins with the gift of a new memory. The Eucharist is that new memory.
I want to draw this chapter to a close by offering two recollections from
within my own humble, quite ordinary parish in which the transformation from gift to mission was embodied in very unassuming ways in the
lives of fellow parishioners. In these two "snapshots," we might begin to
ask ourselves if and how we are forming young people to offer this kind
of witness with their lives as disciples practicing sanctity.

First there was Robert who, with his outsized personality, was diagnosed with ALS several years ago. In the months following his diagnosis,

I watched him receive Communion each week. At first, he received as he always had—upon his hands. After some time, I noticed how his shoulders had narrowed and how raising his arms became more difficult, until he couldn't raise them and so was only able to receive on the tongue. The last time I saw him receive was on the fourth Sunday of Advent several years ago: his wife wheeled him up with the oxygen tubes bringing air to his lungs, connected to the breathing machine she wore around her neck. In that one instant, I saw the mystery of the Eucharist and the mystery of marriage joined together in a single image of sorrow and of joy. The habitual journey up to the altar—whether with ease or with immense difficulty—became a setting for telling the story of the mission of marital love and of believing beyond the limits of words.

Then there was Joe, who was a parishioner at our parish for the last eighty of his ninety-four years of life. Every week for those eighty years, he dipped his fingers in the baptismal waters at the front of our church and made the Sign of the Cross. Every week since we had become parishioners there, he stood next to those waters as the self-appointed Head Greeter and Chief Usher. He welcomed people, he chatted with everyone (both before and during the liturgy), he laughed with children, and he found late-arriving people seats, even when they didn't want him to. He stood around those baptismal waters as hundreds and hundreds of children and adults were baptized; he was right up front when our youngest daughter, Gianna, was baptized—standing in the foreground of the best photo. When he died a couple of months later, those same baptismal waters were sprinkled over his casket. For those who pass through those waters, the parish is meant to become a stable community of the faithful—as the *Catechism of the Catholic Church* states (see no. 2179)—and for eighty years, Joe both found and gave stability to our parish. At his funeral, even those of us who knew him well learned something about him that we had not known previously, which is that every night since he was a child he had prayed the same prayer before he went to sleep. For just about anyone who knew him, we recognize how his daily journey of praying this prayer transformed who he was so much that, in retrospect, his whole life seemed to say nothing other than what he practiced saying daily:

> My Lord and my God,
> I adore thee my Jesus,
> I adore you.
> I love you my Jesus,
> I love you.
> Grant to me and all my family
> a holy life and a happy death.
> Amen.

He prayed that prayer in secret, but it wielded immense authority over his life. Those who met him received the fruits of that prayer in a man who had become a missionary disciple, one who became a living sign of the faith he professed, as if he had passed through magic waters.

4. Prophecy and the Cultures of Mercy

> Contrary to the laws of physics,
> we can stand straight, according to
> the Gospel, only when our center of
> gravity is outside ourselves.
>
> —Gustavo Gutiérrez, O.P.

Indifference is an acquired skill. Actually, that is not quite right: indifference has more to do with *deskilling*. We are created good—and even *very good*—with a natural sensitivity to the suffering of others and a natural desire to heal the wounded. Lack of practice means loss of skill. The desire to heal diminishes when we fail to heal, and the ability to perceive suffering diminishes as we neglect the condition of others. Compassion is natural; indifference is not, but when indifference becomes common, compassion has to be reacquired, like recovering a lost skill buried under mounds of neglect. That work can be laborious, even painful.

The good news buried under the bad news of the Rich Young Man who walks away from Jesus' invitation to *sell what you have and give to the poor* is that his steps were painful. *His countenance fell and he went away sorrowful* (Mk 10:21–22, RSV). This is a tragic moment, but it could be worse: the young man might not have cared at all—that would have been the absolute tragedy. He feels regret and he feels loss, and that is good news because those are the pangs of memory and desire of someone who was created for compassion.

You might imagine yourself walking past a homeless person begging: you notice him, you feel for him, you want to do something, but you are in a hurry or whatever, and so you walk on by. The next day, you see the same person and it still hurts to pass by—you feel a bit guilty—but you do it again. After ten times, it is considerably easier to keep walking and after a hundred times, you probably don't even notice the guy—he's just disappeared from your view. The Rich Young Man made the first painful step away from compassion, and each successive time he walks away, it will get easier for him. By this pattern, he will eventually become the rich man who ignored the poor man Lazarus lying at his gate day after day, which renders that rich man incapable of seeing Lazarus since his habitual indifference opened a yawning chasm between them (see Luke 16:19–31). We know the Rich Young Man is not yet lost because walking away bothers him, but we also know that every time he walks away, he gets closer to becoming the kind of person who loses the capacity to see and the desire to care for the needs of others.

By contrast, when *this poor man cried out, and the LORD heard him, and saved him out of all his troubles* (Ps 34:6, RSV).[1] In other words, *the LORD is merciful* (Ps 103:8).[2] God perceives suffering and acts—that is how God "sees" the world. To be created in the image and likeness of God entails receiving the gift of seeing the world in God's own vision: it is natural to perceive suffering and move to remedy it. In fact, standing before the Rich Young Man who is himself suffering from habits of neglect and indifference, *Jesus look[ed] upon him and loved him* (Mk 10:21). Jesus sees the young man as he is; Jesus sees him as he is created to be; Jesus sees him as he ought to be—then Jesus gives him what will heal him: the invitation to practice mercy. As the young man walks away sorrowful, he is walking into a different way of seeing the world, a way that is not conformed to how God sees the world.

The way the young man saw things, leaving behind his private treasure was too costly and so he assumed the cost of leaving Jesus' *heavenly treasures* behind (Mk 10:21). We could say that he made a value judgment, but what he really did was ratify a way of valuing, a way of judging, and a way of seeing. If we simply say that he made a moral choice, we risk missing the deeper significance because we might think that he just rationally weighed everything and then decided. But as Richard Gula argues when he writes about the relationship between conscience, character, and vision,

> most of what appears in our decisions and actions is the result of what we see going on, rather than the result of conscious rational choices. . . . What we see sets the directions and limits of what we do; it generates certain choices rather than others; and it disposes us to respond in one way rather than another. What is a choice for someone else may never occur to us as a choice at all, for we simply do not see the world that way.[3]

We are not told exactly what the young man saw when he looked at his possessions, or what he saw when he looked at the poor, or what he saw when he looked at Jesus. All we know is what he did and how he looked when he walked away. I imagine that Jesus *look[ed] on him and loved him* because he wanted to change the way the young man saw things. Jesus wanted to give him the gift of a new vision—a vision of mercy. In that sense, Jesus was concerned not only with a moral choice but also with how the young man sees the whole world. For those responsible for forming and empowering young people, this look of love and this desire for transformation often come through us.

We owe it to young people to tell them the truth: in the face of suffering and the needs of others, there is no neutral position: it is either God's way of mercy or the tragedy of indifference.

Marian Prophecy

Following our focus on memory and the power of hidden assumptions in the last chapter, our focus in this chapter is on prophecy and how particular cultures give rise to certain ways of seeing and, inversely, how intentional practices slowly build up cultures. In the most direct terms, the prescription of mercy has to do with the question of what is true and what is false, what is health and what is sickness. In the pages that follow, we will consider the culture of the family home, the necessity of the Works of Mercy, college parties, and the humble beginnings of larger-than-life saints. But first, as is our custom, we take our lead from Mary.

The power of Mary's prophecy is that she speaks a vision of the world that is conformed to God's vision. She sees the One who does great things, who shows mercy, who scatters the proud and knocks down the mighty while lifting up the lowly and filling the hungry. She sees the One who sends the rich away empty, for they have great possessions from which they refuse to part (see Luke 1:46–55; cf. Mark 10:22). Mary prophesies by seeing the world as it truly is, as God's creation. She accepts the truth and treasure of God's way rather than treasuring some illusive private way.

Mary's words strike as revolutionary not because they are unnatural, but because they are shockwaves of health in a world grown unnaturally indifferent. She who is immaculate is preserved from the tragedy of indifference that we each opt for seemingly by instinct. Moreover, grace immunizes her to the indifference we teach one another, with our pedagogies that give rise to whole cultures of indifference. The prophecy of Mary is the charter of a new culture, built within the reign of Divine Mercy, who is her beloved son.

There is violence to this prophetic vision only in the way that the removal of an addictive substance stirs the symptoms of withdrawal in the addict. The mighty are addicted to power, the rich are addicted to being filled, the proud are addicted to their own ways, but Mary proclaims that the cure has come and so the pain of withdrawal begins in a sin-sick world. Mary sings of her son, who looks upon sinners and loves them in order to heal them. But addictions are anesthetizing, and health can hurt at first.

What Mary clearly sees and sharply proclaims is the truth found in God that pierces the Rich Young Man's illusions—he is sick and he needs the medicine of mercy. Mary sees in God's mercy and proclaims God's reign. She is the model of human health and human wholeness, with pristine vision and true words. The movement from sickness to health is not about a single decision or even a series of decisions; rather, it has to do with *how* to live life. The young man is challenged to begin again in learning how to live and see things. That healthy education is offered in the school of discipleship, a school that for the rest of us begins where life begins: in the family home.

Reviving Cultural Catholicism (Because That's the Only Kind There Is)

In chapter 2 we joined Pope Francis in contemplating St. Paul's great hymn on love, and in the last chapter we considered the words of *New York Times* reader Colleen Smith, who voiced her concern that her "choice to let my girl play will eventually leave her wanting in the eyes of an admissions committee." We saw how each recognized—in quite different ways—the importance of what is regularly practiced and valued at home. It is also true, however, that neither example ultimately focuses on a single decision or even a set of decisions; rather, what is at issue is the kind of home that is fostered. Pope Francis and Colleen Smith are focusing on the whole project of the home and the whole orientation that parents set for their children's upbringing. They are talking about the *culture* of the family and how children are formed to see things.

In a recent study on religious transmission and the role of parents, Justin Bartkus and Christian Smith contend that "parents represent not simply *an* influence on the development of children's religious worldviews, but the *arch*-influence over it."[4] What parents value is the basis for what children learn to value. "Parental influence," they continue, "is the condition of the possibility for other influences to take effect. What's more, parental influence does not disappear as children mature."[5] Parental influence is *incomparably important*, and their influence is not limited to what they say or profess; deeper still, it is carried through in their habitual practices, the strength and quality of their commitments, and, most of all, in how they organize and incline the home. The home that parents take the lead in crafting embodies the fundamental assumptions and ways of seeing that wield the strongest formative influence on young people. The family home is the most intimate and persuasive culture.

After interviewing 245 parents in 145 households—with 73 of those parents being Catholics of "varying ethnicities, socioeconomic classes, religious commitment levels, and family types (single parent, two parent, etc.)"[6]—Bartkus and Smith came to this summary conclusion:

> We believe that any parent who wishes to pass on their Catholic faith must understand their home as a miniature *culture*, a project which initiates children into certain core values, practices, and modes of experience, all of whose validity is constantly tested by what parents do and say in interpretive reinforcement of those convictions. . . . The idea of parenting as the building of a *culture* is often underappreciated; more prominent is the notion of parenting as a series of decisions regarding which experiences and investments will maximize children's well-being. Yet, whether parents realize it or not, children are generally inclined to follow the grain of parents' own attitudes and commitments, especially when it comes to religion. That is, in addition to providing for their well-being, parents inevitably teach their children *how to live their lives.*[7]

When parenting is treated as "a series of decisions" aimed at the vague horizon of "maximizing the children's well-being," it does not follow that the home ceases to be "a miniature *culture*"—rather, it means that the home is a *culture of vagueness*, one given to the sway of whatever happens to be the most powerful influence or apparent value by default. In the previous chapter, I argued that in modern American life this often ends up being the "college preparatory culture," so that the goals and values embedded therein end up creating the standards by which the maximization of children's well-being is measured. In line with this recent study, then, I argue that the family home remains the most formative of all cultures for young people, *whether or not* the parents intend for it to be so.

What is valued and practiced in the home—what the space of the home "says" and how it is inclined—makes those raised in the home more likely to be formed in whatever mold is thereby given. At minimum, a maturing young person has to reckon with that mold, whether for the sake of rejecting it or else for accepting it, and especially for critically and conscientiously accepting it. The family home is where a vision of the world is practiced and, therefore, it possesses the incomparable opportunity to become a *prophetic culture.*

Saintly parents tend to understand the cultural influence and prophetic potential of the family home. The difference between saintly parents and other parents is that, by and large, saintly parents recognize the incomparable importance of their role and the formative power of the home, and they intentionally craft their home environment according to the ideals of what they value most. They are intentional in this regard, driving out vagueness with the clarity of their commitment. From the very start, I have drawn special attention to a particular saint who lived at the beginning of the modern period and who grew in an intentional family culture: Thérèse of Lisieux. I previously showed how her father's habitual practice of Sabbath rest—in keeping with the third commandment—redeemed the meaning of time in God, while allowing patience and contemplation to bloom. Now I want to turn to the witness of Thérèse's mother and Louis's wife, Zélie, who took the leading role in inclining that open space of their family's home to the desired end of holiness. Zélie Martin's clear commitment in crafting her family home was about following the designs of divine mercy. These designs can inform not only how parents order their homes but also how pastoral leaders order their ministries, especially for young people.

The Inclinations of the Martin Household

The Martin home was an intentional culture, through and through; the conditions for mercy were cultivated there. The conditions for mercy are human beings' natural environment, but this environment breaks down under the banality of neglect. Intentionality disperses neglect, and regular practices give rise to and reinforce intentionality. No less disciplined than her clock-making husband, Zélie Martin crafted her household with a vision of a definite end and with the kind of care that does not overlook the details. Zélie was a master of her craft.

Like Louis, Zélie initially desired to enter the cloistered religious life, but also like her husband, she was not permitted to pursue this desire. When the two of them married, the ideals of their earlier religious desire did not relent; in fact, they continued to pursue those ideals within the home they shared, not only in terms of the intentionality of their religious practice but even—odd as it may sound to us—in terms of living celibately. For ten months after their wedding they embraced sexual abstinence as if living together in a cloister until a spiritual director instructed them to carry out the pursuit of their pious ideals in another way: in and through childbearing.

Looking back in light of the family they created—and especially in view of their ninth and last child, Thérèse—that first period of marital celibacy does indeed strike an odd chord. Perhaps it is best considered as the waning days of impractical wishes or an exercise in nonsensical, even unnatural religious fervor. But if we remain stuck on how odd this seems to us then we risk missing the true genius of their unconventionality. Their primary desire was to live in obedience to and pursuit of the love of God.

You might think of receiving a precious piece of jewelry from a beloved family member and guarding it in a safe because the gift means so much to you. When the gift-giver learns of how you cherish it and lovingly tells you that you would honor her by wearing the jewelry, you promptly do so in accordance with her wishes. Above all, Louis and Zélie honored their gift-giving God. When they learned that the way to honor God in and through their marriage was through their conjugal union and childbearing, they retained their primary intention for holiness while changing their practice.

It was on the basis of their longstanding religious commitments that Louis and Zélie learned to see the gift of their own children as a call or even a command from God. Along with the power they shared to create life through their conjugal union, they were given the responsibility to raise children who would love heaven and be capable of it; this is the intentional end to which all their efforts of forming and educating their children were directed. To them, each child was a covenant between themselves and God. The consistent emphases in Zélie's personal correspondences show that to her each child was, in the words of the family's chief biographer, "a trust received from the Creator's hands; she must serve it by uplifting it, and she must not fear to aim too high. . . . She wished to fashion Christians and saints."[8] There is nothing vague about this—Zélie did not operate from a cloudy view of "maximizing well-being" but with a firm commitment to guide disciples toward sanctity.

The Collective Masterpiece

Zélie was especially well suited to guiding all the work and movement of her household toward a single, holistic end. Her "training" for the office of intentional and faithful motherhood began, as it were, well before her first child arrived. When she was denied admittance to the Sisters of Saint Vincent de Paul as a younger woman, she petitioned the Blessed Mother for guidance. On the Feast of the Immaculate Conception in 1851, she discerned these words spoken within her heart: "See to the making of Point d'Alençon."[9] Once she received this clarity, she did not delay in entering lace-making school. In her own childhood, she had developed the basic skills for lace making, and now she trained her hands and her nerves to create the exquisitely delicate and subtly varied designs of Alençon lace. She was a quick study, and so, before long, she was a master with her own shop in which she not only exercised her own finely honed skills but also orchestrated those of others.

Zélie was not the saintly mother of saints because she learned how to make lace; Zélie was the saintly mother of saints because she transferred all her skill for lace making and adapted all her capacities for intentionality from her workshop to her household. The fine lace that her workshop produced was both a metaphor of and preparation for the masterwork of her household. She began with the end in mind, always. She was definitive and committed in creating a culture for her home: it was a culture conformed to the religious ideals she had practiced pursuing for years, beginning with her own childhood all the way through what we would now call "young adulthood." In this school of artistry, Thérèse and her sisters "learned to sympathize with the sufferings of the lowly, to grieve over their humiliations, and appreciate the eminent dignity of the children of God."[10] Zélie's intentional care for her children was oriented toward and translated into her children's intentional care for those who suffered. They learned to see suffering, and they were guided to act on what they saw. They were formed for mercy.

Holy on Purpose

The Martin children were not accidentally holy. If ever there were a saint whom we might think was just born a saint, Thérèse would likely be it, but the witness of her parents reveals that she was raised in an intentional family culture shaped by parents who took as their basic assumption that their duty was to educate disciples for the joy of sanctity. When reflecting on her own childhood and the intimacy of the culture of her family, Thérèse later confessed that "God was instructing me in secret."[11] In all the discrete and routine movements of the Martin household, holiness was growing like a sapling that matures without pomp or spectacle.

The pattern of growth in which the Martins raised their children is visible in the charitable actions they were formed to do outside the home. These actions became routine in the best possible way: they were simply part of the life they shared. Notice what Thérèse mentions almost in passing before talking about a rather significant encounter with a poor, crippled man when she was six years old: "During the walks I took with Papa, he loved to have me bring alms to the poor we met on the way."[12] Thérèse was prepared to *see* and *respond to* the poor man she encountered well before she ever crossed paths with him, since it was just a family custom to carry alms to give to the poor.

Indeed, the Martin children learned to set out in haste to meet others, like Mary running to Elizabeth to accompany, serve, and proclaim (see Luke 1:39).[13] All the charitable activity that happened outside the home and became a regular part of the family's life was rooted in the practices exercised within the home. The family embraced the suffering that visited them, bearing suffering together as the cost of love. This did not mean that suffering was any less acute for them, but it did mean that suffering was not in vain and that they bore it together in God's company. Zélie held the dead bodies of four of the fruits of her own womb, and she gave the kind of testimony that only a mother of sorrows can speak: "I did not regret the pain and cares I had borne for them. Several people said to me, 'It would have been better if you had never had them,' but I could not endure this sort of language. I did not think that the sufferings and anxieties could be weighed in the same scale with the eternal happiness of my children."[14] This spiritual disposition to suffer pain for each other in love was the soil out of which the corporal and spiritual works for the poor outside their home grew.[15]

Zélie and Louis prepared to suffer for and delight in, to labor for and rejoice at, the children they would help create and raise in the ways of holiness before those children ever took flesh in their lives. They practiced saying "yes" to God so as to set the turning and weaving of their lives to the movement and the pattern of divine love, rather than to their own expectations or ideas of happiness. Indeed, as Joseph Piat points out, the dimensions of their life together expressed the Mysteries of the Rosary, whereby the memory of Mary's own heart was beating within the secret life of the Martin home:

> They were to experience the joyful stage, marked out by four cradles; the laborious stage: five more births, six deaths [including aunts], sorrows mingled with smiles; the sorrowful stage: their Calvary and the sublime sacrifice of parents;

to end at last with the glorious stage—the day Thérèse, the
last conquest of love, would carry their name to the altars.[16]

The joyful, sorrowful, and glorious stages are familiar enough as
Mysteries of the Rosary, but the truly ingenious one here is the laborious. Even though writing fifty years before St. John Paul II promulgated
the Luminous Mysteries, Piat recognized that this family of saints were
aglow with the illumination of Jesus through Mary. In the oscillations
of sorrows and smiles, the labors of love—in season and out of season—
slowly lit up the true meaning of the life that Louis and Zélie were called
to craft and which took flesh in their home. The Rosary meditates on
Mary's contemplation of her blessed child, while the Martins contemplated their children in the likeness of Mary's. There is a definite Marian
character to the Martin home, where the whole mystery of salvation
turned within household subtleties.

The world first knew Thérèse, and only because of her did we ever
look toward Zélie and Louis. But without Zélie and Louis, there would
have been no St. Thérèse. Of course, together they conceived her but,
even more, together they created the kind of culture where it was easier
to be holy, to learn the movements of mercy, to suffer with those who
suffer and to rejoice with those who rejoice. Zélie's craftsmanship was so
masterful, in fact, that Thérèse most of all—as the youngest of the nine
children—benefitted from the culture her mother fostered even when
her mother was not personally present. Zélie died when Thérèse was four
years old, and even during those first four years, Zélie was in declining
health. Zélie's formative influence was thus enfleshed in Thérèse's older
sisters, who became as mothers to her, and most of all in the rhythms
and designs of the household. Zélie set the pattern and prepared everything so well that the masterwork could continue without her direct
involvement. Nothing redounds to the credit of this master lacemaker
more than this.[17]

Forming Parents to Form Young People

The household Zélie crafted alongside Louis testifies to the claim I cited earlier, which is "that any parent who wishes to pass on their Catholic faith must understand their home as a miniature *culture*, a project which initiates children into certain core values, practices, and modes of experience, all of whose validity is constantly tested by what parents do and say in interpretive reinforcement of those convictions."[18] By allowing our gaze to pass from Thérèse herself to the parents who formed her, we see more clearly what a comprehensive approach to forming young people in faith entails and even demands: an unbridled commitment to investing in the formation of parents. As we have contemplated the witness of Thérèse's parents—and especially here her mother—we see how that work of formation begins well before parents ever become parents.

It is really hard to be a good parent, one who both wants to and is capable of creating the kind of culture that embodies the best values, ideals, and practices of the Christian faith. Taking the long view, we must see that if we want to form young people well, then we have to form their parents well, and if we want to form their parents well as parents, then we cannot wait until they are already parents to form, support, and guide them. As with Zélie and Louis, parents begin their formation for the kind of parents they become when they themselves are teenagers and young adults. This means, of course, that we must shift our focus from wanting to form those who are teenagers and young adults right now simply as teenagers and young adults. Instead, we have to think about forming them as the mature adults and indeed *parents* we hope they become.

The greater part of forming and educating young people today is actually investing in the young people they themselves will form and educate ten and twenty years from now. Parents not only provide and make decisions for their children but also and especially create *cultures* in which their children mature. Future parents must therefore be formed to become initiators of miniature cultures conducive to holiness, with the habits of mercy as integral to the overall pattern.

Mercy is the keynote of Mary's prophecy; mercy is how God's will is done on earth as it is in heaven. An intentional home—even if it isn't quite brimming with canonized saints like that of the Martins—is the kind of culture in which the practices of pondering and of memory are steadily translated into word and action through regular works, and these regular works allow those growing in that culture the opportunity to strengthen a "way of seeing things" that corresponds to the divine way of seeing. God's will is *not* regularly done on earth as it is in heaven, but missionary disciples set out to make it so, and the saints give their lives as witness to the validity of holiness. Saints help cure our blindness to God's way. And as with physical therapy for those whose capacity or ability has been somehow diminished and must be reacquired through specific exercises, in this prophetic culture the spiritual incapacitation and disability that goes by the name "indifference" is cured by the specific exercises of the "Works of Mercy."

The Works of Mercy

The Martin household is something of a Catholic ideal. Both parents were not just saintly but later canonized saints, while their youngest child has been called "the greatest saint of modern times,"[19] and even the "difficult sister"—Léonie—is now on the road to canonization herself.[20] What I have been suggesting in this chapter, though, is that the exceptionality of the Martin household is in the intentionality of its cultural formation. The Martins patiently and—but for their posthumous recognition—secretly grew in holiness, like the Holy Family tucked away in Nazareth. What this family witnesses to is both the validity of cultural formation and the prophetic dimensions of the Christian life. The normal conditions of their family home that appear uncommon against the backdrop of what seems normal by the world's standards are in fact the proclamation of the right, just, true, and even properly *natural* conditions for human beings created in the image and likeness of God. Especially in their habitual perception of and response to suffering, whereby they allowed the good of others to become their own desired good, the vision of the world according to God's mercy that

Mary proclaimed in her Magnificat became the very vision by which the Martin family learned to see the whole world, starting from inside the walls of their home.

Just as Mary's prophetic words disrupt the sickness of indifference in a world obsessed with power and grandeur on its own terms, so does the Martin household disrupt and even critique what passes for "normal" both within and outside of family life. As I suggested earlier, this is something like what happens when the shock of health—like a strong medicine—touches a sickened system. This painful sting is what the Rich Young Man felt when Jesus instructed him in the way of mercy, and that young man went away sad rather than embracing the pain of becoming truly healthy.

What would the Rich Young Man have looked like had he embraced the pain of mercy? He would have looked like St. Francis of Assisi, who is the Rich Young Man gone right. When Francis first handed over his cloak to a beggar, and when he first kissed a leper begging for alms, he passed through the pain of his aversions and began the practice of seeing in mercy.[21] When he stripped himself of his old garments before his unrelenting father, he began to put on new garments of charity that his heavenly Father bestowed on him.[22] With each step into mercy he gave more and more, but the steps became more natural to him, and he grew ever more capable of greater acts of penance and charity. He didn't simply make a series of moral choices but rather grew into a new way of valuing, judging, and seeing himself, the poor, and the whole world in God's light. He saw Jesus and loved him. Practicing mercy and knowing Jesus were inseparable for Francis because those two things are simply inseparable. Francis is a revolution in perspective, as he became "rich in poverty, exalted in humility, full of life in the midst of mortification, wise in simplicity."[23]

Born Giovanni di Pietro di Bernardone, Francis did not arise from the Catholic ideal like Thérèse of Lisieux, but his education in humanity and holiness progressed along a common path: he batted away indifference by practicing the Works of Mercy. *Saint* Francis was a man well practiced in mercy, so much so that it became natural to him, restoring him to what he was created to be. The Works of Mercy are practices that, paradoxically, heal the one who performs them because they are all about healing the ones who receive them. Practicing the Works of Mercy is how indifference is driven out because these works teach you how to say to someone else "What are you going through?" and mean it.

Even if St. Francis did not arise from the ideal Catholic home like St. Thérèse, it still seems he became an ideal unto himself, and so he stands at a distance from us, like a star we could never reach. Part of the reason for that is we are probably more comfortable looking at the finished product of Francis and thinking it too unattainable than taking seriously the practices that built toward that end. That is similar to looking at Thérèse and just assuming that she was born a saint, rather than taking seriously the intentionality of her familial culture. Perhaps what we need is the help of someone who grasps and is captivated by the final vision of these saints but does not overlook the painful and liberating practices that led to their strangely joyful end in gospel holiness. That intermediary guide may well be the co-founder of the Catholic Worker movement: Dorothy Day.

Stepping into Holiness

Dorothy Day grew to love the image of Thérèse of Lisieux and she cherished the brilliance of Francis of Assisi. But Day did not become so obsessed with where those saints ended up that she missed the lesson about how to love *what* they loved, *whom* they loved, and *how* they loved. She recognized how essential are the Works of Mercy, and she learned from the saints which ones are necessary to practice: namely, "all of them."[24] She knew that the malaise of indifference—that sluggishness of heart, that dullness of vision—seeps in whenever we become content with our own happiness alone and relax our concern for others. Indifference is unnatural, but it's addictive. So Day not only advocated but also set about practicing the Works of Mercy—regularly, daily, building up communities and cultures and Houses of Hospitality that depended on these works—because, as she wrote, "It is with these means that we can live *as though* we believed indeed that we are all members one of another, knowing that when 'the health of one member suffers, the health of the whole body is lowered.'"[25]

The incredible wisdom of Dorothy Day is captured in just two words in that last sentence: "as though." She recognizes that only rarely does purity of intention or the power of fervor motivate our actions, especially on a day-to-day basis where habits are formed. Rather, it is much more common that intentions develop, values form, and understandings emerge after we spend a long time—day after day, by little and by little—practicing as true what we *hope* to always believe as true but quite often don't feel like doing. We practice acting "as though" we were already fully convinced of what we are trying to believe. The decision to move toward suffering and away from comfort is *never, ever* automatic, so the Works of Mercy are prescribed as medicine to lead us toward the health we do not yet feel and cannot yet grasp but will eventually learn to enjoy if we faithfully take our medicine.

It is just as easy to assume that Francis of Assisi got it right all at once as it is to assume that the Rich Young Man got it all wrong in one fell swoop. Sometimes it seems it is all about one step, one choice, or maybe even having or not having something like a gene for compassion or a gift for holiness. This is false. What is true is that the first step matters but only in the sense that it is the next step to be taken. A step toward indifference means that opting for indifference next time is more likely; a step toward mercy gives you practice in mercy and makes mercy a little more likely even if no less demanding next time. In Day's own words,

> The older I get, the more I see that life is made up of many steps, and they are very small affairs, not giant strides. I have "kissed a leper," not once but twice—consciously—and I cannot say that I am much the better for it.
>
> The first time. . . . A woman with cancer of the face was begging (beggars are allowed only in the slums) and when I gave her money (no sacrifice on my part but merely passing on alms which someone had given me) she tried to kiss my hand. The only thing I could do was kiss her dirty old face with the gaping hole in it where an eye and a nose had been.

It sounds like a heroic deed but it was not. One gets used to ugliness so quickly. What we avert our eyes from one day is easily borne the next when we have learned a little more about love.[26]

The Hinge of Heaven

To Dorothy Day there is a question that should haunt all Christians— the question that the poet Charles Péguy imagines God asking each of us in the end: "Where are the others?" As Day writes, "We cannot live alone. We cannot go to heaven alone."[27] Learning "a little more about love" means learning that truth more fully. If we come to Jesus like the Rich Young Man and ask what we must do to inherit eternal life, he will tell us what he told the Rich Young Man: "give to the poor." In other words, treat the sufferings of others as your own suffering, make their happiness your happiness, practicing relocating your center of gravity in their direction.[28] We might respond with something like, "But Jesus, I only want to love you." And Jesus would only say, "I know. That's why I command you to love those I love." Or in Day's words, "He made heaven hinge on the way we act toward Him in His disguise of commonplace, frail, ordinary humanity."[29] If we are opposed to learning how to love those whom Jesus loves then we will never be able to love heaven, where his way, his truth, and his life are everything (see John 14:16; cf. Revelation 21). To Dorothy Day, that means constantly looking around ourselves and looking within ourselves to ask "Where are the others?" Where is their good, where is their joy, where is the space for their wishes?

Right at the beginning of chapter 1, I shared the story of my daughter on one Sunday when she saw and remembered and cared about what I rather quickly forgot: the young boy in the wheelchair who passed by our home. She had something like an instinct that had become dulled in me for taking notice of that boy, remembering him, and wanting to do something for him. Frankly, she cured me of a little bit of my blindness that day. I have seen much more suffering than she has, mostly because I have lived decades longer. I can "deal with suffering" and I know how to "live with it"—provided, of course, that it is other people's suffering and not my own. To Felicity, someone else's suffering was not strictly separate from her—it impacted her so that within her, there was room for another.[30]

Just like Thérèse, though, Felicity was not born a saint. If she does not continue to practice mercy as first seeing the suffering of others and acting on it in some way, her capacity for mercy will diminish, as will her ability to act mercifully. She will become comfortable by guarding herself and retreating into some form of staid security. That move is addictive because it is immediately rewarding—it doesn't seem to cost as much. She'll become a little bit more like me, which is to say that she'll be a little more comfortable with *not* being moved, with finding different ways to look away, with letting the stirrings of compassion or even guilt settle down and soften. And as Day shrewdly observes, "people insulated by their own comfort lose sight of it."[31]

Vocational Discernment and the Works of Mercy

Vocational discernment is not possible without the Works of Mercy. The Works of Mercy train us to habitually take the needs, sufferings, and joys of others as a primary concern. If not for this regular training through these specific exercises, then the comfort of our own preferences, our own self-interest, and our own way of seeing things warps our vision and weakens our hearts. It will likely happen to young people unless we create intentional cultures built on the regular practice of mercy in homes, schools, and parishes. Like all of us, young people are created for compassion. As we saw all the way back in the first chapter, God initiates *neighborly love* by asking us in the Incarnation, "What are you going through?" It is both in response to and along with this way of loving that we are called to exercise neighborly love in union with our love of God. The Works of Mercy teach us how to see things as God sees them, and vocational discernment relies greatly on the way we see things. Again, "most of what appears in our decisions and actions is the result of what we see going on,"[32] and the Works of Mercy teach us to see what's going on with others instead of what we would become consumed with otherwise, which, for each of us, is the comfort of maximizing my own well-being (or at least seeming to).

The Works of Mercy change our location, sometimes physically. When we change locations, we see different things, which means that the sort of options for decisions that are presented to us also change. When Dorothy Day set out to live the Gospel in midst of the poor of New York, the first decisive step she took was where she placed herself, physically. That is, her place of residence and therefore where the Houses of Hospitality were situated was key. If she was going to learn how to love others, she had to place herself in the midst of others. "One must live with them," she wrote, "share with them their suffering too. Give up one's privacy, and mental and spiritual comforts as well as physical."[33]

In this sense, the Rich Young Man would not change locations. What continued to appear in his decisions and actions was the result of what he saw going on, which was confined to the space of his own possessions. What might these possessions be for those of us who are challenged by the invitation that Jesus gives to the Rich Young Man? They might be my own goals and ambitions, or "generally accepted principles" as James Martin called them, or the constant onrush of things that fill my daily schedule.

The concrete reality of others is inconvenient because it slows us down. We can make ourselves more aerodynamic by painting on layers of indifference. These habits of neglect seem harmless at every stage: *just don't go there, just don't talk to that person, just walk by, just plug in, just close the door, just don't ask, just forget that look in her eye.* These things can all become insulations against the loneliness of others, the poverty of others, the love of others.

But because Thérèse's parents taught her to carry alms, she went *toward* the poor during her regular walks with her father—that is, she saw them. And because Dorothy Day took up residence where the neglected members of her city lived, her decisions and actions were in response to what she saw. True vocational discernment requires the Works of Mercy because God's call is never for private happiness; God's call is always about the freedom and bravery to act on behalf of the good of others with the love of Christ. Practicing mercy empowers young people for making big decisions about how to live one's life.

A Tale of Two Dorms

I want to turn once again to the writing of one of my students, who for an assignment analyzed the residential cultures in which he lived in college. For this cultural analysis, he juxtaposed events in two residence halls on two separate but related occasions. What is common about both occasions is that he was spending time with other men with whom he lived immediately after the death of a fellow student. What is different about each occasion is the conditions in which they were sharing time together (or not) and therefore the ways in which they related to each other (or not).

> It was a cold February evening and I was going to a party in [another dorm] with a few friends from [my dorm]. Being a non-drinker, I was the only sober member of this group of seven guys, and I was focused on a single trouble. Earlier that morning, the news broke that a former member of our dorm who now lived off campus had died, and there were rumors circulating that it had been a suicide. I brought up to the other guys how very sad this was to hear. Only one of the guys said anything back: "Yeah, I heard that too. That was really sad." That was the entirety of our conversation—no one else said anything.
>
> We then arrived at the party, and what a rally it was. The hallway in [the dorm] was packed wall to wall with college students. The resident assistants manned the entrance, filtering people in and out. The rest of the guys I came with quickly squeezed their way into one of the dorm rooms on a frantic search for beer, leaving me alone.
>
> I started to look around . . . absolutely everyone had a red Solo cup in his or her hand. But what was most striking of all was that no one was actually talking to each other. If it weren't for the blaring rap music, the screaming between

people on opposite corners of the hallway, or the sound of trapped bodies bumping against each other, you could probably hear a pin drop. Flustered, I left the hallway and walked into one of the rooms. There I saw one of the guys I came with, so I walked over and yelled, "Hey!" over the background noise. He looked at me, and with a monotonous demeanor said, "Hey," then returned to his drink. That was the entirety of our conversation. So I decided to turn around and leave the party alone.

Looking back, I can see that the entire party was not a body of college students meeting each other, but a collection of individuals that just happened to be partying next to one another. It was the subtlest yet the most sinister form of hedonism: the inability to talk to each other, and the fixation on the music and drinking. All of it was centered around one key question: "Am I personally having a good time?"[34]

On this first occasion, a lot of people packed together was not community but instead the convergence of private agendas. The alcohol, the music, and the preset expectations for the gathering serve as insulation against what might disturb the comfort of the partygoers: conversation with one another, paying attention to one another, and especially the thought of the tragic death of someone just like them. Louis is describing a miniature culture of indifference in which the question "What are you going through?" is neither spoken nor heard.

As his reflection continues, Louis then recalls a second occasion in which the setting is his own residence hall community following the sudden death of another one of their members:

That evening, our entire [dorm] community, along with many others, went to the Grotto. Our rector led us in prayer as we stood arm-in-arm with one another. The situation was horrifically tragic and oddly beautiful. We refused to construct our own realities around our private lives. We refused to be indifferent to the truth. We saw [his] death as it was, rather than how we wanted to see it. This quiet evening firmly contrasted with the script [from that previous party]. On this night, students left and right poured out their emotions to friends and strangers alike, and friends and strangers responded with sympathy.

The second evening was different for a few important reasons. There was silence rather than noise. The leader of the community—the rector, not unlike a father on this night—led them in prayer. The focus was not on each person's own private agendas but rather on their neighbor who had died, and on the shock and grief that they shared together. They were not insulated from suffering but bore it together as the cost of love. They exercised mercy, most especially in praying for the dead and consoling the afflicted.

In Louis's sharp eye, these two nights show two different kinds of cultures, which happen to exist side-by-side in his own college environment. One culture isolates persons from one another even when they are packed tightly together, while the other culture helps them to find one another and share life together, even in death. One culture induces deafness and a form of blindness, while the other facilitates hearing and seeing and feeling. The sort of choices and decisions that might arise from one culture are starkly contrasted with the choices and decisions likely to become apparent in the other. If and how someone *hears the word of God and acts on it* depends a great deal on how we recognize and pay attention to one another, and these two nights show how important the environments we create and cultivate are to the way we see the world.

Of course, there is a distinctively collegiate quality to these examples, where strangers live in close proximity to one another in some kind of residential living system where alcohol-soaked parties are rather common. But the insights that this kind of cultural analysis bears are not limited to just this particular setting. What Louis observes is how the expectations for private happiness anesthetize us to the presence, needs, and well-being of others, while intentional practices for sharing pain and joy with one another reawaken us to the compassion that ought to be natural to us. On that second night, Louis and his companions did not hide from tragedy and so experienced the beauty of a culture shaped with the intentionality that had also been common to the home of Louis and Zélie Martin, where the labors of love slowly lit up the meaning of the Christian life.

Back Home from College

Except for our children's penchant for leaving their things lying on the floor, there is not much about our home that resembles a college dorm. Yet, separating thoughts of my home from thoughts about the college setting too much would be a mistake. For what we see in the college setting that Louis describes in the din of the dorm party is rather consistent with a culture where the emphasis is routinely placed on maximizing one's own well-being, chasing after goals and accomplishments, and building up résumés and profiles. That is the kind of culture where people are formed to focus on individualized ends: work hard, play hard. In such an environment, the outbreak of community on the second night might strike us as wonderful but rare, like a miracle. This is precisely why considerations of my own home should be connected to those collegiate examples—because what we practice in our home is what becomes the base narrative, the standard for normalcy, and the recommended worldview in which our children are raised. What we do now inclines them to eventually see one or the other of those two nights as "normal."

A couple of years ago my wife, Lisa, thought of a simple yet brilliant way to shape our home according to the Works of Mercy. She purchased a very small chalkboard that sits on a table in our living room (it's about the size of a nameplate on someone's desk) on which she wrote one of the Works of Mercy every two weeks. She then guided our kids in practicing that one Work of Mercy in some way.

Even though practicing especially the corporal works required us to go out of our house to specific places where those with material needs were to be found, it was not terribly difficult to figure out how to perform many of those works. What was difficult was figuring out how to visit the imprisoned, since our children are young and walking into a prison is not all that easy. This is where a little innovation came in to play:

Lisa got in touch with a priest who regularly ministers to the inmates at a federal prison about forty miles from our home to ask him for advice. He said that the guys like to receive letters and cards, so he recommended that we send things like that as a way for our kids to "visit" them. This is exactly what we did. Because that Work of Mercy was prescribed, we had to figure out how to do it, which stimulated a little bit of creativity and allowed a small bond of communion to be established across the prison walls that separate "them" and "us."

We did not need to go so far or get so creative when we were tasked with feeding the hungry. On our way home from church one Sunday, we noticed a somewhat older man with a cardboard sign sitting on a corner near our house. We were sort of predisposed to recognize an opportunity for mercy when we saw one because of Lisa's chalkboard routine. My daughter Felicity and I drove back to where we saw him, parked the car, and walked over to meet him and ask what he needed. We learned his name is Chuck and that he'd like a sandwich and a drink. So we took his order, drove down the block to Subway, got him a turkey sandwich without lettuce or tomatoes, a bag a chips, and a Sprite. When we saw him there again the next week, we drove to Subway first and then went back to talk with him, even though he was always short with his words. This became a little Sunday routine with our kids, until Chuck just suddenly stopped showing up on that corner. We didn't know why.

During our family's night prayer, though, our kids—beginning with Felicity—would remember to pray for Chuck throughout the week. We would pray for him somewhat regularly even after he stopped showing up on "his corner." We talked a little about where he might be, hoping that maybe he ended up in a better situation, especially since we knew that he frequented our local Catholic Worker drop-in center and our city's Center for the Homeless. Then just as suddenly as he "disappeared," we saw Chuck again on the other side of town one day, begging on a different corner. One of our children recognized him first.

There was another woman we came to know because we saw her asking for alms one day at the corner near our local farmers' market, again on a Sunday. We stopped to talk to her and see what she might need. We learned her name is Sheila and she was hoping for some groceries to help her daughter and grandchild, who were in danger of being evicted from their home. We met Sheila on that corner a few times, offering her different kinds of support each time and trying to figure out what was going on with her family and how we might be able to offer them some assistance. As with Chuck, our kids started praying for Sheila during night prayer and again, as with Chuck, they spotted her on another corner on a different side of town some time later.

Here is what I learned from these encounters with Chuck and Sheila. First, our kids remembered the people whom they met and for whom they did something, and they wanted to pray for them when we took time to offer intentions during night prayer. Second, it mattered to our kids that they knew their names. Third, they noticed when Chuck and Sheila were gone and they were able to recognize them after not seeing them for quite some time—they became anything but "anonymous poor people." Fourth and finally, our kids actually started to "map" our hometown according to the places where they had interacted with or seen Chuck and Sheila (or others). "That's Chuck's corner" or "That's Sheila's bench."

Summarily, practicing the Works of Mercy changed what our children saw, whom they noticed and remembered, and even how they interpreted the spaces of our town. In other words, we have seen first-hand the formative power of the Works of Mercy, which is why it is so concerning that we have let the intentionality of these practices slip. We didn't make a decision to stop; we just became less focused over time.

One of the hazards of writing a book like this one, and especially focusing on the Works of Mercy, is that I am directly confronted with Jesus' words to the Rich Young Man: if you want treasures in heaven, if you want to follow me, then give to the poor. Sometimes what is most comforting of all is the space between where I am and where the poor are—that is, the space between what I am just doing otherwise and what others might need, materially as well as spiritually. The imprisoned do not happen to show up on my front door, and the hungry are not typically in my kitchen. When we were more intentional about practicing whatever Work of Mercy appeared on the chalkboard in our living room, we had to change our center of gravity.

The gift of the Works of Mercy is that we do not have to invent ways to follow the pattern of divine love—the pattern is given to us. The challenge of the Works of Mercy, though, is actually performing them, regularly and consistently. Not doing the Works of Mercy is a form of indifference and perhaps the most dangerous kind: it is the indifference of staying within routines where our hearts get directed to other priorities. When we do the Works of Mercy, though, even how we see the streets and the places we pass every day starts to change, especially for young people.

The Geography of Compassion

Seeing the same old places in the light of mercy presents new possibilities for choices and decisions. If we do not see the suffering or needs of others, then the choices for how to respond simply do not occur to us at all. We remain bound in our ignorance and unseeing. That is not the realm of freedom, and without freedom there can be no bravery. The contentment, comfort, and even what seems like the happiness of staying away from the suffering or needs of others are difficult to pierce through—the longer we stay in that cozy state, the harder it is to step out of it. The true cost of staying there is that it just sets the terms of how we see the world. What the Works of Mercy provide is a means for reconfiguring our vision of the world, both near and far. No one understood that better than St. Teresa of Calcutta.

Teresa of Calcutta's life is the story of leaving happiness for the sake of joy. The temptation of happiness was in the avoidance of suffering while the promise of joy was in enduring suffering in hope. When she left her family for India at the age of eighteen, she left behind a happy family and even a beloved mother whom she would never see again. When she left the Loreto Order for the slums of Calcutta, she left the deep happiness she experienced in her first religious community. When she left Calcutta time and again to go all over the globe, she left the happiness of *not traveling* and the happiness of being at home in her mother house. With each journey from happiness to joy, she was remapping the world she and others saw.

From the middle of the 1960s until the middle of the 1990s, when her mission as the Apostle to the Unwanted was reaching the dimensions of the entire world, Mother Teresa crisscrossed the globe in the fierce obedience to and joyful passion for the call she started to hear in 1946 to serve the "Poorest of the Poor." She who had formerly been a history teacher as a religious sister in the Loreto Order became the poor jet-setting explorer who found, in lands long ago discovered and populated, the *undiscovered* loneliness of those abandoned to the neglected regions of modern life. She who had formerly been a geography teacher became the Lord's city planner who redrew maps on six continents—not according to commerce and convenience, but according to the care and concern for the poor, situating her Missionaries of Charity in the midst of the unclaimed to bring companionship and comfort where it was lacking in her reimagined "geography of compassion."[35] She did not settle for seeing the world according to the designs of power and pomp, but practiced instead seeing it prophetically as Mary had, in light of divine mercy.

Once again, though, by evoking Teresa of Calcutta we come up against one of those seemingly inimitable figures like Francis of Assisi or her namesake Thérèse of Lisieux, whose remarkable holiness seems so distant even if so admirable. Yet again, though, this fixation on the "final product" might cause us to miss the practices that built toward that glorious end. The mature genius of the saint who redrew the maps of the world was rooted in the humble soil of her family home, where Nikola and Drana Bojaxhiu created a miniature culture in which their children practiced leaving their own comfort to find joy in giving comfort to others.[36]

Teresa's father, Nikola, was a politically astute man who was deeply involved in the civic life of Skopje and later in the Albanian independence movement. He conducted his home with discipline but also, and more importantly, with charity. The Bojaxhiu home was an open home, where guests were always welcome as one might expect from a man active in political and civic life; what is unexpected is that the most special welcome was given to the poor, whose company had nothing at all to do with political connections or social status. In regard to one particular elderly woman who would come to their home regularly for meals, Nikola instructed his children to "welcome her warmly, with love . . . never eat a single mouthful unless you are sharing it with others."[37]

For her part, Drana raised her children in regular prayer at home and in "errands of mercy" outside the home. On a weekly basis, Drana went to feed and clean the home of a widow whose family had abandoned her. She regularly bathed and tended to an alcoholic woman covered in sores. She took over the maternal care for six children who were orphaned when their parents died in close succession. *Out of* a happy home, Drana led her own children toward those who were suffering, neglected, hungry, dirty, sick, and lonely. The Bojaxhiu family gave the comfort of their home to those who needed it, and they left the comfort of their home to serve those in need.

St. Teresa, who became the master cartographer for a world redrafted in mercy, learned how to sketch the designs of mercy in her childhood home when she was a little girl named Agnes Bojaxhiu.[38]

The Truth behind the Lie

The Bojaxhiu home, the Martin home, the Franciscan Order, a college dorm community that prays and weeps together—all of these might seem like wonderful, rare examples of humanity touching noble heights. In point of fact, these are nothing other than glimpses of what is true. The truth is that we are created for compassion and that the conditions for mercy are our natural environment. Indifference is a lie: it hides the truth of who we are and who we are created to be. Vocational discernment is possible only as we move out of indifference through practices of mercy.

There is no neutral position between mercy and indifference—it is either one or the other. Even hatred is a form of indifference made possible once compassion has been severely injured or even killed.[39] Jesus calls the Rich Young Man out of the illusion of being separate from the suffering of others—Jesus tells him that he will not find the joy he most deeply desires in that illusion. Jesus calls him into a more human way, which happens to find its pattern in the divine way. The human being can become what the human being is meant to become when he is surrounded by compassion. When he himself is filled with compassion, he is who he is meant to be. For young Catholics, life's big decisions should be matters of compassion, matters of love.

In her dialogue with the Lord from the depth of her contemplative prayer, St. Catherine of Siena encounters the truth of our humanity that hides under the malaise of indifference and all those various subtle assumptions about some kind of neutral position when it comes to the needs of others in this world. Catherine hears the Lord say to her:

> Here you owe each other help in word and teaching and good example, indeed in every need of which you are aware, giving counsel as sincerely as you would to yourself, without selfishness. If you do not do this because you have no love for your neighbors, you do them special harm, and this as persistently as you refuse them the good you could do. . . . I have told you how every sin is done by means of your neighbors, because it deprives them of your loving charity, and it is charity that gives life to all virtue. So that selfish love which deprives your neighbors of your charity and affection is the principle and foundation of all evil.[40]

We are created in and for a world that is itself charity—creation springs from God's charity. The charity that is not done for our neighbors is an act of withholding from them what we owe them, like we are undoing the truth of the world. What Catherine grasps in her prayer is that our humanity is not neutral: we are created to bestow charity upon one another—this is where the joy of others and our own joy become one, in the divine pattern. In the end, there is only the life of charity or no life at all. Indifference is the illusion of some other way, which does not exist. The prophetic vision in light of mercy is nothing but the clarity of this truth. This is how Mary sees the world in her son, it is how saintly parents intentionally form their children to see all things, and it is how the faceless masses on nameless streets are revealed to us as brothers and sisters among whom we may begin to discern choices and decisions as missionary disciples on the way to saintliness.

5. Sacrifice and the Joy of Trust

> Man should take joy as seriously
> as he takes himself. And he should
> believe that he is created for joy.
>
> —Alfred Delp, S.J.

God eternally says *I AM*. God creates by saying *let there be*. God waits to hear what his beloved creatures will say, hoping they say exactly what he has already said but with their own voices. God had the end in mind at the beginning.

The mystery of vocation is the interplay between God speaking then listening and our listening then speaking. In response to the divine *I AM*, God opens a space to receive our own "I am." This mystery is complete first in Mary. The angel stopped speaking, heaven rested its case, and a space opened. In this space, Mary responds *Fiat: I am the handmaid of the Lord; let it be to me according to your word* (Lk 1:38). Divine freedom meets the fullness of human freedom, and *the Word became flesh*. God dwells in his creature who dwells in God.[1]

Mary's "yes" is given in a moment and yet unfolds over time. She says "I am . . ." and yet those words also mean "I will be." Her *fiat* is not only "I do" but also "I will." She pledges herself in trust to the Lord, and she takes responsibility for what her "yes" will entail. Her response is anything but automatic; it is a gift, and this gift is a sacrifice.

Sacrifice is always loss and gain. What does Mary lose? She loses indeterminacy: the question of who she shall be begins to narrow as this call and commitment take flesh. She loses arbitrariness: the latitude to maneuver this way or that within the broad confines of God's will constrict as *this* reality takes hold. She loses possibilities: an uncountable number of "somedays" and "maybe ifs" are sealed off as she consents to this mission and identity. She is the mother of *this* child, the Son of God. She loses the future of her own private choosing.

Yet at the same time Mary gains the future of God's choosing. She chooses it. This is the paradox of freedom at its fullest. She gains a definite mission at the cost of other imagined missions. She gains a particular identity at the cost of any number of other alternate personas. She gains a reality at the cost of other possible destinies. She shows us that vocation is not simply about doing something but rather *being* someone: concretely, definitely, everlastingly.

The Mysteries of the Rosary track the full range of Mary's "yes." In the twenty mysteries beginning with the annunciation and concluding with her coronation as Queen of Heaven and Earth, Mary's "yes" deepens in depth and stretches in breadth, assuming sufferings and illuminations and renunciations and restorations. She could not see all the details from the start—that wasn't the point. The point was to say "yes" to *Someone*: to her God, whose Word was spoken to her and who asked her for trust. Trust is the altar on which she sacrificed her own expectations. She said "yes" to him in that quiet moment with the angel, and in the end, the volume of that "yes" amplified to fill both heaven and earth.

By exploring the meaning of Mary's sacrifice, this final chapter is about the hardest thing of all because it is about what all of vocational discernment, discipleship, and the Christian life leads to: taking responsibility for being someone in response to God's call. This is about the culmination of *hearing the Word of God* and then—upon hearing well, which is always harder than it sounds—*acting on it.* This response is anything but automatic, even and especially for the one who has heard well. At the end of any process of discernment—no matter how good, how thorough, how well-informed, and how faithful the "process" may be—the discerner comes to a gap that only he or she can cross: the gap of trust and responsibility. The heart of vocational discernment is in saying "yes" to *Someone*, and that "yes" makes you *someone*.

Timothy Radcliffe expresses this quite nicely: "A vocation, whether to be a priest or a religious, married or to practice a profession, goes against [the] grain. It is a witness to our hope that my life as a whole may have some sense. I do not just do things; I am called to be someone, and a vocation is part of saying who I am."[2] Part of what makes "vocation" so difficult is that there is no such thing as a private vocation, which means, in other words, that there is no Christian calling that is about me alone. Perhaps the greatest danger for true Christian vocation is when we instrumentalize "discernment," subtly believing that God's call is all about *my* fulfillment and therefore God happens to be participating in guiding me on my course. This is really the dominance of my plans and preferences masquerading under the cover of what I might call "God's will." In the end, though, my vocation as *God's* call is the liberation from the overwhelming, futile burden of having to create myself. Discerning and responding to my vocation is my way of saying that I have been created by God, with and for others. This is the point of being a Christian: giving *my* yes in harmony with God's yes in Christ.

Harmonization requires hearing and acting; it permits extraordinary creativity but only based on extraordinary discipline.[3] In the pages that follow, then, we will consider how the true freedom of a Christian is tied to taking responsibility for being someone, what it means to remain tuned to the Word of God whom the true Christian discerner never stops heeding, and, as we move toward the completion of this work, that the fullness of Christian living is in suffering out of love for others, to grant them the space of freedom and support them in becoming brave. In the first section, we will consider the importance of trusting yourself to others and to God. In the second section, I will emphasize the importance of remaining committed to the disciplines upon which vocational discernment builds—namely: solitude and community. In the third and final section, we will heed the witness of three saints (or two saints and one beatified, as it were) that show us how the practices of discipline undergirded their creativity to give their lives as a resounding "yes."

What matters most is that we become Christians whose lives say "yes" to God the Father—"yes" to our Creator, who says "yes" to us in Christ with the Holy Spirit. For those of us called to form and educate others in the Christian faith, what matters most is that we empower them to speak this "yes" while helping them to know the One to whom they are saying "yes" and to love him. The "yes" we utter in life's big decisions and, ultimately, with our whole lives is the "yes" of trust, of responsibility, of sacrifice, where we humble ourselves to serve the good of others in response to the God who humbles himself to serve our good. In this is our joy made complete.

Developing Nature in Openness to Grace

Something like "muscle memory" is necessary for making, claiming, and living into vocational commitments. On a minute-to-minute basis, those of us living today seem to have more choices and options presented to us than ever before. Looking at digital culture, as we did in chapters 2 and 3, allows us to glimpse how this proliferation of possibilities emerges: we are bombarded with information, we are typically always reachable, and we have the means for increasingly rapid communication. We can and often do change things on the fly, and other people change things on us with equal ease. More and more seems transitory, less and less seems permanent, except for the ability to change everything around.

Committing to something means possibly missing out on the new thing that comes along later, which might be even more appealing because novelty is always more appealing. This is but one reason why every commitment demands sacrifice. Staying focused on one person or group means not checking in on whatever is going on with others, and that means possibly missing out on something. The same is true of remaining situated in one place and not scanning other scenes through, say, social media. The tendencies to want to keep things open, keep commitments flexible, keep plans changeable, and keep ourselves adjustable build up certain habits and proclivities that are not, in the end, conducive to acting with the singular trust necessary for responding to a vocational call and the mission of discipleship. Small habits and practices shape character, therefore making each of us more or less capable of acting with the freedom and bravery of a Christian disciple, as someone committed to Christ.

For instance, I have asked my students on numerous occasions over the years when they make plans for an ordinary Friday night. What they eventually admit—by and large—is that they do not really finalize their plans until right before something happens. Where they are going, with whom, when, and for how long are all kept open as long as possible. They want to wait and see how things develop, what other people might be doing, or if something else will pop up. They have become quite skilled at managing multiple forms of soft potential commitments, any of which could be abandoned or morphed at a moment's notice. In fact, on more than one occasion my students have jokingly—but also not so jokingly—told me that plans are not really finalized until the thing has *already* happened. Only afterward can they consider plans firm!

It seems that it is becoming increasingly rare for someone to say, "I will go there, with you, on this day, at this time, for this long. Count on me." What happens when you make firm plans and commit yourself to those plans with actual people is that you may very well have to make some small sacrifices along the way to keep to your commitment. Something else may come along that you will have to turn down. Your feelings may change or your excitement may wane, and you have to motivate yourself to stick to your word. Occasionally, you may actually have to break a commitment for a legitimate reason and then you have to communicate this to those with whom you made plans, even if you have to take responsibility for some error like not managing your time well or double-booking, or even because you actually changed your mind about what you are going to do. (On "values inventories" that I have administered, very few people say that they will give a full and honest reason to someone else when they have to break a commitment.)

What is going on all the time is that we are becoming practiced in and comfortable with letting go of commitments, keeping our pledges malleable, and allowing ourselves to sway and dawdle with less and less compunction, resistance, or predictability, save the predictability of not wanting to tie ourselves down. There might appear to be some distance between how plans are formulated for Friday night and how we live into and through vocational commitments, but the habits necessary for supporting the latter are developed—or not—in these lesser venues.[4]

With this in mind, perhaps it is not so surprising that when "discernment season" rolls around on college campuses, the well-rehearsed practice of holding on to or even increasing the number of soft potential commitments becomes apparent again. "Discernment season" tends to start halfway through the fall term, typically for seniors but also increasingly for underclassmen whose summer plans have steadily become issues of great concern. On the one hand, everyone just wants to get beyond the "discernment" and arrive at whatever the future destination will be, or at least know that destination with clarity. On the other hand, many people seem to revel in the drama of "discernment." It is as if being undecided, especially with as many potential futures as possible, makes people feel more alive. It is more enthralling than living into one definite future because many potential futures are filled with novelty. It seems that shopping is more enjoyable than purchasing and owning.[5]

As anecdotal evidence to this, I have observed a strange occurrence that tends to happen when someone approaches the culminating moment of a discernment process, when a choice is to be made: they sometimes undo the work of discernment they have already done. For example, a college student may have decided early on and for good, informed reasons that he did not want to practice law and so ruled out law school as a post-graduate option. After more than several months of researching graduate programs in other fields, taking the GRE, and earning the support of professors to write recommendations, he gets anxious. All of a sudden, he starts cramming for the LSAT, hurriedly completes a dozen law school applications, and begs his recommenders to craft another set of letters to suit his new "backup plan." (Some ideas are legitimate backup plans, but law school is not one of them.) Moreover, if a recommender were to question where this new interest was coming from, the student is unlikely to produce any compelling reason besides, "I just want to keep my options open." What is lost in the frantic shuffle is that previous decision he made in regard to not wanting to practice law, a decision that was precisely about narrowing his possible options as part of the process of discernment.

Something not dissimilar to this is occurring with modern-day dating practices, especially as facilitated through apps that collect and present a wide array of possible partners to each user. The "thrill of the chase" gives way to the monotony of swiping left and right to disapprove or approve of persons' images as presented on your screen. Tinder is perhaps the most widely used of these apps—at least at the time I write this—and it happens to cater to the mentality that, as one user puts it, "You can't be stuck in one lane. . . . There's always something better. If you had a reservation somewhere and then a table at Per Se opened up, you'd want to go there."[6] There is perhaps no softer commitment than one in which the moment you swipe one way or another, another image is already entering your screen to present you with a different, potentially better option. And if that option is not better, surely one of the ones down the line will be.

If we consider these scenarios further, we might come to recognize that the possibility of choosing from among a greater set of options becomes more important than what is actually to be chosen. The proliferation of options seems to expand the range of freedom, but in reality, this sudden expansion functionally does three things: first, it numbs us to the reason we started searching for a future job or a partner in the first place—that is, to actually commit to one. Second, it causes us to lose perspective, since now the solid building blocks of the decision we will eventually make have been scattered as new, under-considered factors come into play, ones that seem to make "law school" or whatever the new option is seem more enticing precisely because of its novelty. Third, it sets us up to be less satisfied with the choice we make—the more options we consider for a longer period of time, the greater the "buyer's remorse" and the feeling of loss for other possibilities.[7] This probably also increases the likelihood of going back on a commitment afterward.

We cannot underestimate the allure of what seems new and exciting, or overestimate our aversion to having to follow through on making a vocational decision at the end of a process of discernment, especially when the choice is difficult.

Trusting in the work you have already done in discernment is part of claiming yourself as a whole person, one who is much more than the product of the present moment. It means believing in who you were and what you were able to decide in an earlier stage of the discernment process, which allowed you to make progress in an informed and conscientious manner. It protects you from falling prey to the feeling of the moment, when the loudest influencers, the most available advisers, the most popular options, the most exciting feelings, or the paths of least resistance exert undue influence over the decision you make. It means accepting the unavoidable fact that you are ultimately responsible for gathering up the entire process of discernment into one decision to which you will commit *yourself*, which *you* claim as your own. If the "process" of discernment is actually going to lead somewhere and not be undone, then trusting what you have already done is imperative. Otherwise, you end up training yourself how to never be at peace with any decision you actually make because of the sense of loss regarding all the options you did not pursue. You also allow yourself to become more sensitive to and desirous of whatever the novel or unexpected thing may be in the future, which corresponds quite nicely with the non-continuous logic of "Now . . . this" that we discussed in chapter 2, but is not proper to true vocational discernment. "Being open to the Spirit" does not mean perpetually revising everything—it more precisely means trusting in your practice of being open to the Spirit as you have gone along. In the future, it means seeking the guidance of the Spirit to help you follow through on how you have pledged and committed yourself.

When all is said and done, it is a greater act of faith to commit yourself to a particular path, assume responsibility for that choice, and perhaps be forced to repent of and revise your plans later than it is to obsess over getting things exactly right (whatever that means) or perpetually keep things open. If grace truly does build on nature, then becoming a mature, responsible human agent is foundational to living a life of grace. This is about trust in God. In responding to God's call after taking the time and putting in the work to listen to his voice, you do not say "yes" to something but indeed to *Someone.* And this *Someone* is worthy of trust.

To become the sort of person who accepts this light burden of freedom and the yoke of responsibility is the whole point of discernment, in the end. We do well to recall that before the "yes" came forth in Mary's voice and she began the journey of claiming responsibility for her mission, she had already relied on her practices of pondering and memory to hear well the Word of God that came to her. In the course of responding to what she heard, she heeded God's way of doing things—the way of mercy—and spoke about the truth of the world as corresponding to this way. These very human practices provided the foundation for her own discernment, and as she lived into her unique calling, these practices not only continued but even developed: she pondered more and more the mystery of her son, her memory was more and more conformed to the narrative of salvation, and her vision was more and more illumined with the light of God's merciful deeds in creation.

As we consider what it means to both form others for vocational discernment and take up the challenge to become ever more capable of hearing and acting on God's Word ourselves, among the very best things we can do is to promote and practice the stable disciplines that lead to ongoing attentiveness to God's call and the poised readiness to respond. This is about learning to entrust ourselves to God, who asks us to trust his Word. There are two key disciplines that form us to become ever more capable of trust: the discipline of solitude and the discipline of community.[8]

The Discipline of Solitude

I have become increasingly aware of the lack of silence in my life. I go for evening walks in our relatively unbusy neighborhood, and though no one is speaking, I can hear the hum of traffic in the distance, the rattle of a train more than a mile away, or even the buzz of electrical lines here and there. Sometimes at night when everyone else is sleeping, I will sit alone on the floor of our living room, in the dark, settling into the silence of a relatively still house (which isn't absolutely silent, but it's close). It is the silence that I have been craving, and yet a strange thing happens: as I sit in silence, my mind fills with noise. Worries from the day ping around my head and jostle my heart. Even when there isn't anything in particular that draws my attention, there is still some unspecified anxiety lingering. Though the air around me is silent, my interior life remains unquiet.

I recently had the opportunity to spend time in a small cottage bordering some woods. As soon as I got there, I went running in the woods, eager to seek out the quiet away from roads and digital screens. The wooded trails were indeed quiet, and no one else was in sight. I could not hear cars or trains in the distance; there weren't any buzzing electrical lines, or creaks of a house. It was really quiet. But as I ran, some bird or critter would stir in the brush alongside the path and I would jump. Each time this happened, I would startle and even, for a moment, feel fear. I was not familiar with the terrain, I did not know what was in the brush, and my instinctual reaction was to jump away.

Both in the dark of my living room and the sun-speckled opening of that wooded path, I came to realize something: I am not comfortable in silence. Silence is not the terrain that I can control. In the first instance, what I have been harboring or ignoring starts to swirl inside me even as everything around me is still. In the second instance, when I am not filling the quiet with my own noise, I am easily unsettled by what stirs in the silence. It is not hard for me to understand how Zechariah would be overcome with fear when the angel stirred the stillness of the sanctuary.

The discipline that makes us comfortable in silence is also the discipline that can only be practiced in silence: the discipline of solitude. Solitude is not simply being alone, not simply refraining from speaking, not simply being *in* silence. Solitude is, rather, composure in silence. Silence is the occasion for practicing solitude and solitude only develops for someone who routinely enters into silence, getting more comfortable with it, more used to it, more welcoming of it. Those who only enter into silence periodically find themselves at dis-ease in silence, and altogether rather jumpy.

Henri Nouwen writes that "without solitude it is nearly impossible to live a spiritual life. Solitude begins with a time and place for God, and him alone. If we really believe not only that God exists but also that he is actively present in our lives—healing, teaching, and guiding—we need to set aside a time and space to give him our undivided attention."[9] Silence is God's terrain and God's native language. God is fluent in our language, but God prefers silence. Silence is where we learn to listen to God's voice.[10]

The aptitude for listening well is built up over time and must be continually practiced. The paradox of the discipline of solitude is that it is not about waiting on *something* but rather simply the willingness to wait, without expectation. Solitude is the discipline of just waiting, in silence. This goes against the predominant tendencies of our modern lives: to calculate our efforts, to seek out one new thing after another, to look for what we want to find and to listen for what we want to hear. More to the point, solitude is waiting without demands on *Someone* who waits and speaks and dwells in silence, as in the Eucharist.[11]

When discussing "pondering" in chapter 2, we focused on 1 Corinthians 13 and St. Paul's declaration that *love is patient.* I wrote then, following Pope Francis, that patience is about giving time and giving space for another to be, for another to change, and even for us to grow. The first place in which love as patience is to be practiced is in the home, where the basic rhythms of life are rehearsed. Solitude is itself the practice of patience in which a time and space are given within the interior home of our minds and hearts.[12] By returning regularly to silence and developing the discipline of solitude, our habit says to God what St. Augustine prayed: "The house of my soul is too small for you to enter: make it more spacious by your coming."[13] Silence makes us more welcoming of God.

Just as St. Paul then followed up "patience" with "kindness" in describing "love" in order to show that while we wait on others, giving them time and space, we ought to color that time and incline that space to their own benefit, so too with solitude. While the discipline of solitude is founded in the habitual, even daily practice of returning to silence and becoming more comfortable there, we ought to color that time and incline that space to God's liking by becoming more naturally mindful of him. The authority of hidden assumptions that I spoke of in chapter 3 furtively rule even when we are unaware, which means that we must become more attuned to what God's presence is like, who God is, and what God does so that our solitude may be welcoming of him as he is, and not as we otherwise imagine him to be. Indeed, "the important thing is that the place of solitude remains a simple, uncluttered place,"[14] where the Lord may come to rest with us and we may rest in him. But preparing that open space for this guest means preparing ourselves to focus our attention on God's presence. For this, the simple recitation of "a psalm, a parable, a bible story, a saying of Jesus, or a word of Paul, Peter, James, Jude, or John"[15] can color the time and incline the space of our waiting to be more conducive to welcoming the Lord's dwelling.[16]

The discipline of solitude is not about reaching a certain end; it is about becoming a certain kind of person. Solitude forms us to become persons who are ready to ponder and primed to remember who God is through what God does. In her discernment, Mary shows the marks of one who practiced solitude and was therefore capable of not only hearing, but also trusting.

The Discipline of Community

Just as being in silence is not the same as solitude and yet necessary for cultivating the discipline of solitude, so too being with others is not the same as community and yet necessary for cultivating the discipline of community. More than just coming together, the discipline of community encompasses the alternations between activity and passivity, giving and receiving, boldness and humbleness. The discipline of community is the free and open space to practice obedience together—obedience to God through our obedience to one another's needs and wellbeing, sufferings as well as joys. This discipline is necessary for the Christian disciple, who is called both to love of God and love of neighbor (see again Mark 12:30–31).

In his short and remarkable book *The Stature of Waiting*, W. H. Vanstone tells of new British housing developments that were being established in which the feeling of "neighbourliness" was lacking and greatly coveted. In these new developments, all manner of activities and programs were initiated to "create a community." All the while, in one small district within these new developments, the signs of neighborliness were abundantly evident: people talking in their yards, entering one another's homes, sharing tools, and caring for one another's children. What made this one district of some fifteen or twenty houses different was simply this:

> At the centre of the small area lived a woman, the mother of five children, who was confined strictly to bed for several months with ulcerated legs; and the common decency of those who lived nearby would not allow them to ignore the helpless predicament of the mother. They attended to her and her family. In so doing they came to know one another and, in an informal way, to work together in sharing out the necessary tasks; and so the much desired "neighbourliness"... was soon created.[17]

Vanstone goes on to point out that it was not due to any particular virtue or generosities of this infirm woman that this community developed—quite to the contrary, she was apparently rather dour and difficult to get along with during this period. The singular thing that she contributed to the neighborhood was the most important thing of all: she could not hide her wounds or her particular forms of incapacitation. The community formed around her infirmity. This seems an odd thing to those of us who are more concerned with what we can do, achieve, and actively contribute. What Vanstone is pointing out is that what is sorely lacking in the modern world is precisely what would allow us to really get to know one another: the sharing of our burdens, the bearing of our wounds, the appeals to our natural compassion that the clear observance of need allows to arise.

In his speech upon receiving the Laetare Medal at the University of Notre Dame's 2017 Commencement, Fr. Gregory Boyle, S.J., told the story of José, who had told his own story to a group of six hundred social workers in Richmond, Virginia, some years earlier. José's upbringing was horrendous, filled with violence and abuse, both emotional and physical. His back is covered with scars from the arbitrary punishments his mother exacted on him, beginning in his early childhood. He loathed his scars for years, hiding them from everyone. But, as he tells his story—and Fr. Boyle tells it on his behalf—José learned to cherish these scars. Again, that sounds rather odd, but as José asks, "How can I help heal the wounded if I don't welcome my own wounds?"[18] The discipline of community depends on at least someone allowing himself or herself to be known and potentially loved for who that person is, wounds and all. It is no wonder that when Jesus appeared to his disciples in the glory of his Resurrection, he showed them his wounds (see Luke 24:39–40; John 20:20, 27).

Like the discipline of solitude, the discipline of community is about a kind of composure. This is not the composure of pretending to have it all together, but rather the composure of being real just as we are. This is the discipline of continually coming together with others, to share ourselves honestly, to be willing to see others for who they are, to be humble enough and brave enough to show ourselves for who we are, right now.

In the previous chapter, I attempted to draw attention to the necessity of practicing mercy for learning to see as God sees. I related this to participating in Mary's prophecy. It is a basic truism that mercy is impossible so long as we remain distant from one another. In order for me to perceive the need for mercy, I must draw near to you to recognize precisely how you suffer; to ask what you are going through. In order for me to receive mercy, I must allow you to draw near to me to recognize how I suffer. It is worth remembering that as those disciples who walked with their backs to Jerusalem—where their hope died—made their steps toward that village called Emmaus, *Jesus himself drew near and went with them* (Lk 24:15). This approach is what made community possible. Of course, drawing near to "dwell with" is utterly consistent with the character of the Only Begotten Son of the Father, so much so that it is the normative principle for all those who wish to share in his life. The discipline of community, then, is foundational for those who would *hear the word of God and act on it.*

Ways and Means

The goal of those who mentor, raise, and educate Catholic young people cannot be to get them to make one specific vocational commitment or another. The goal for those who care for Catholic young people must be to form them in certain dispositions. In reading the witness of Mary, mother of the saints and model of discipleship, I have named pondering, memory, and prophecy as leading to and powering her sacrifice. So far in this chapter, I have re-presented this kind of formation in two disciplines: solitude and community. In the full measure of Christian formation, the hope—*the hope*—is to prepare those maturing in discipleship to offer God the trust that cannot be coerced, to assume the freedom that cannot be forced, and to claim the responsibility that can only be willed. The whole point is, as I wrote in the first chapter, to free young people from what binds them, to direct them toward what it means to be free, and to prepare them to take responsibility for their freedom, with bravery. There is no such thing as individualistic Christianity, but likewise there is no such thing as automatic discipleship or accidental vocation. In some way and at some point, by some means and with some volume, those whom the Lord has looked upon, loved, and claimed as his own must say "I am," "I will be," "I do," "I will," or, in brief, *fiat*, and step into the wild, disciplined creativity of living into that "yes" so as to become *someone* to the *Someone* who gives meaning to all things.

The smaller, routine sacrifices of adhering to certain practices conducive to missionary discipleship—practices like pondering, memory, and prophecy, with disciplines such as solitude and community—build up the "muscle memory" for the lifelong sacrifice of accepting a particular mission from the Lord. That mission is always to say "yes" to God in the concrete circumstances of your life, amid the actual persons with whom you live, using the limited resources that you have at your disposal. Even for those who seem to do incredible things for and with God, there are always small sacrifices, small practices, small commitments that provide a foundation for their missionary "yes." In fact, it seems that the greater the acts of trust, the more concrete the forms of devotion for those who perform them.

It turns out that we learn to say "yes" to God in the same way in which we learn to do anything well: by practicing, by developing routines and habits, by slow and sometimes repetitive steps. Grace does indeed build on nature, and nature is always strengthened when touched by God's grace. For those of us who take on the sweet and serious responsibility of forming others in faith, we do well to help those we form to develop the right kind of disciplines for listening and responding to God's call in their lives. As we will now see in turning to three outstanding Christian witnesses—even and especially those who gave the most they had to give: their very lives—the practices they developed over years of formation and devotion provided both the foundation and the power for the "yes" they spoke to God.

St. Thomas More, according to Robert Bolt

Since the 1960s, the most popular account of St. Thomas More has been Robert Bolt's *A Man for All Seasons*, first written as a play and then adapted into a film that swept the top prizes at the 1967 Academy Awards, including Best Picture. It is often considered a splendid portrayal of Thomas More as a "man of conscience," and just as often critiqued by certain Catholic critics for misrepresenting Catholic conscience. What is undeniable is that the play—and then the film—offers a stirring account of a man who remains consistent in a certain outlook and set of convictions, even and especially when his historical situation makes it more and more difficult to do so. This kind of consistency is rare. In fact, that is precisely what caught Robert Bolt's eye in the first place.

Bolt, who confessed that he was "not a Catholic nor even in the meaningful sense of the word a Christian" found something striking in this figure who was quite serious about the connection between taking an oath and committing himself to what he had pledged.[19] By his observation, Bolt sees this connection held less and less tautly, with large and small perjuries more and more common in everyday life. What he sees in More "is a sense of selfhood" that is consistent, in which he means what he says and refuses to say what he does not mean.[20] What matters to Bolt is that "the self" is consistent for More—that he can stay the course and not equivocate on his word or view. To Bolt, what More believes is far less important than the consistency of his belief. For those who critique this portrayal, especially from a Catholic perspective, it is with this focus on "the self" that Bolt gets More wrong since what really matters, in their eyes, is that More held to God's truth rather than his own—that is, *what* he believes is the more important part.

This grievance with Bolt's play usually revolves around one scene and, in fact, one statement from More, and on the basis of that statement alone, the critique seems well founded. But if we look to this one statement in connection with how Bolt's More further develops his thought later in the play, we come to see that perhaps even in spite of his own intentions, Bolt ends up presenting More not only as a shining example of Catholic conscience but also as a man whose sacrifice is undeniably one of trust in God. And the reason why Bolt cannot avoid this presentation is because he had to reckon with More's actual words.

The scene at the center of this dispute occurs about halfway through the play in a passionate though somewhat playful debate between two friends: Thomas More and the Duke of Norfolk. The matter at hand is, of course, More's unwillingness to support King Henry VIII's divorce of Catherine of Aragon without a dispensation from the pope. Norfolk is trying to reason with and persuade More to offer his support, and their conversation touches on the "theory" of the pope's authority as the successor of St. Peter. This is where Bolt's More speaks the famous words that are central to the debate about the play's Catholic credibility:

> The Apostolic Succession of the Pope is—Why, it's a theory, yes; you can't see it, can't touch it; it's a theory. But what matters to me is not whether it's true or not but that I believe it to be true, or rather, not that I *believe* it but that *I* believe it.[21]

It is the emphasis on the "I" over "believe" that is the point of contention. Here we see Bolt's interest in More on full display. It is More's unflinching commitment to *his own principle* that draws Bolt's admiration.

What often happens is that this scene and this specific line are offered as the key evidence against Bolt's presentation of More. This means, of course, that this line is lifted from the play and presented as if everything that needs to be said is said right here. But this is not everything that needs to be said, as it is not nearly everything that is said on the point within the play itself. More's debate with Norfolk is intended to continue in further scenes with Norfolk, which includes the one in which More intentionally breaks off his friendship with Norfolk, not for lack of affection but because they are at an utter impasse in regards to the question of More giving his support to the king. The climax of this later conversation comes in this exchange:

> MORE (*Gently*): I can't give in, Howard— (*A smile*) You might as well advise a man to change the color of his eyes. I can't. Our friendship's more mutable than *that*.
>
> NORFOLK: Oh, that's immutable, is it? The one fixed point in a world of changing friendships is that Thomas More will not give in!
>
> MORE (*Urgent to explain*): To me it *has* to be, for that's my self! Affection goes as deep in me as you think, but only God is love right through, Howard; and *that's* my *self*.[22]

In this exchange, Norfolk is holding to what More said earlier: that this whole issue is a matter of More's "I"—that is, the consistency, quality, or substance of his "self." Here we ought to notice, though, that More is giving a further account of his "self." What his "self" consists of is what God sees, right down to the bottom. We might think of Norfolk here as presenting Bolt's own view of More, which has to do with the stunning quality of a man who can "stand for" something so staunchly, so consistently, and at such an eventual cost. And yet, right up against this is the figure of More himself, who, in appealing to God's vision going right to the bottom of who he is, shifts the perspective from what he "stands *for*" to what he "stands *on*." His consistency in holding to his view is only half the matter—and the lesser half at that. What really matters is the matter he is "standing on," the place where he takes his stand. Where this is revealed in full is in More's trial, when, after being condemned, he finally speaks freely and divulges his full opinion.

The reason why I say that Bolt—like Norfolk—had to contend with the actual Thomas More in constructing this play (despite whatever intentions Bolt had for presenting More according to his own fancy) is that when Bolt began to construct More's final testimony, there were actual, documented words he could not ignore. Bolt could not shape More in his own manner because he ran right into how More presented *himself*. Norfolk is again in the room, and he is the one who pronounces More's verdict and then asks More if he has anything to say. More takes this opportunity to discharge his mind. What I offer here is his actual court testimony, which Bolt had obviously read and included in the play itself, although he condensed it somewhat and smoothed out the language for modern ears:

> Seeing that I see ye are determined to condemn me (God knoweth how) I will now in discharge of my conscience speak my mind plainly and freely touching my indictment and your statute withal. And forasmuch as this indictment is grounded upon an act of Parliament directly repugnant to the laws of God and his holy Church, the supreme government of which, or of any part whereof, may no temporal prince presume by any law to take upon him, as rightfully belonging to the See of Rome, a spiritual pre-eminence by the mouth of our Saviour Himself, personally present upon earth, only to St. Peter and his successors, bishops of the same see by special prerogative granted; it is therefore in law, amongst Christian men insufficient to charge any Christian man.[23]

After all the maneuvering and conflict, all the pressure and attempts at persuasion, Thomas More discloses in his own words what is at the bottom of this whole affair. It seems folly: he stakes himself in fidelity to what the Church professes to be true, which is that while "personally present upon earth" Christ gave to St. Peter alone, and therefore to those who follow him, the prerogative to decide on spiritual matters such as those in question. In brief, More "stands on" Christ's own words, as they have been handed down to him. This is the foundation of his "self," at the very bottom.

Bolt was drawn to More because of the evident consistency of his character. He was the same man in one season as in another: "a man for all seasons." What More himself ends up showing, however, is that who he is had much less to do with the strength of his will or the force of his character—though he was indeed remarkable in both those respects—than with the solidity of the ground that he takes as his own foundation. He stands on Christ, on Christ's very own words. He trusts these words most of all and gives whatever he must over time for the consistency of this trust.[24]

Perhaps the most famous of all of Thomas More's own words are these: "I die the king's good servant, but God's first." This, in the end, is the irreducible truth of Thomas More—the stable truth of his "self." This is what Robert Bolt—the playwright—could not ignore, even though, by his own admission, he was not interested in finding this. Yet, in one of the subtler but ultimately most important moments of Bolt's play, the priority of More's allegiances—the very ground on which he stands—is made plain. When the king is bound for More's estate, to meet with him and insist on his support for his divorce and remarriage, More is nowhere to be found. His wife, his daughter, his steward, and Norfolk are all looking for him, rather frantically, as the king approaches. Where is he? At vespers: the evening prayer of the Church.

"Does the king visit you every day?" Norfolk asks, snidely.

"No, but I go to vespers most days," More responds, coolly. Between vespers and Tower Bridge, the volume of More's "yes" amplified.

Bl. Franz Jägerstätter, Conscientious Martyr

In his life and as a saint, Thomas More is as well known as Franz Jäger-stätter is relatively unknown. One held the highest office in his land while the other tilled the land as a farmer in an obscure Austrian town. One gave a very public witness, and the other gave a "solitary witness," known to us now only because of the accidental discovery of one researcher or, if you prefer, because of providence.[25] Yet, with all that separates Jägerstätter from More, he is like the far more famous "man of conscience" in terms of the stability of his foundation and the sacrifice of his commitment, even unto death.

Franz Jägerstätter refused conscription into military service on behalf of the Third Reich. He would not bear arms, nor would he pledge his allegiance to the Nazi party, which he learned to see, with great clarity, as directly repugnant to laws of God. He was imprisoned for his conscientious objection and eventually executed for his non-complicity. As with More, Franz's death is the seemingly spectacular thing and yet what he took as the foundation of his life is the basis of his witness.

What remains from Franz Jägerstätter are letters sent between him and his wife, Franziska, while he was imprisoned, along with his journal entries from both the years before and then during his imprisonment. The letters are mostly unremarkable in their ordinariness: they reveal often-mundane correspondence of a husband who cannot be with his family, who talks about the maintenance of the farm and the education of his children in a consistently warm and compassionate tone. If anything is remarkable, it is the very tone that he maintains, which emerges from a prison in which compassion was intentionally rooted out and in which increasing harshness surrounded him. But perhaps it is equally remarkable that he is so concerned with the education of his children and the daily duties of domestic life, especially considering that he was well aware that execution was his inevitable end at the hands of what he knew was an evil regime. This simplicity in the midst of increasing complexities of life is not accidental, for in the year before his arrest, Franz wrote in his journal where he routinely reflected on scripture, the Christian faith, and the issues of his day that "all of us must strive therefore to become like children [before God] while also being adults."[26]

Reading the record of his words and correspondences, which divulge—over and over again—what mattered most to Franz, we can get a sense of what he means by the paradoxical pairing of childlikeness and adult-likeness. What is childlike is a lavish commitment. Like a child who throws himself into his play with abandon, or who is willing to thrust his whole body into the arms of a parent without a second thought, Franz testifies to the directness and even the recklessness of a primary and unflinching sort of trust. What is adult-like, though, is learning how to recognize the "signs of the times," to see what is going on in the world and in one's own life with patience and clarity, to assess and judge these things prudently, and then to figure out how to negotiate these particular complexities in such a way that the childlike trust might remain primary.

It just so happened that Franz lived in a time and place where a particular order—the Third Reich—demanded absolute fidelity from its subjects and absolute dominion over the whole of each person. For Franz, he saw patiently and clearly that in the complexities of his time, the prevailing political power was directly opposed to the Christian faith, which also asks for primary fidelity and claims the whole person. As an adult, with the maturity of a conscience formed over years of practice, study, and prayer, he makes the choice to accept the consequences of not serving one order for the sake of remaining faithful to the other. For Franz, this is not a choice between his family or his own life, on the one hand, and his faith and principles on the other; rather, he commits to being a Christian father, Christian husband, and even a Christian citizen of Austria by assuming the cost of what it means to be a Christian in these circumstances.

The childlike trust that became strong enough to negotiate adult-like circumstances had matured over time and through practice in Franz's life. After a somewhat rebellious youth, he married Franziska who was, by the accounts of those who knew them, more devout and observant in her Catholic faith than Franz. Franz settled into this life, and the changes that were already taking place in him as he was growing out of his mercurial state took more definite shape. The two of them spent their honeymoon on pilgrimage in Rome and vowed to make another pilgrimage for their tenth wedding anniversary, an anniversary they never reached because of Franz's death. Franz moved toward Franziska's practice of the regular reception of the sacraments, even becoming a daily communicant. He offered himself as a sacristan at his parish, tending to the duties of maintaining the grounds and setting the altar alike. He took vows as a Third Order (secular) Franciscan, which committed him to not bearing arms or bringing harm to others in the model of St. Francis. Even as a child, he participated in Passion Plays in which his role was as one of the soldiers who crucified Jesus, and the significance of this perspective made a subtle mark on him. All the while, as he matured into adulthood as a father and husband, he spent a considerable portion of his leisure time reading and reflecting on scripture, working out the intricacies of his conscience in regard to contemporary moral issues, and writing out his thoughts and convictions, combing over them again and again, in order to seek further understanding for what he believed by faith. The time of crisis that came when the Third Reich pressed down on his simple, unspectacular life hit upon someone whose character was structured according to these practices and basic commitments, which had been worked on for years and which gave him a stable place to stand when everything else suddenly became unstable.

This is why his letters and reflections from prison are filled with concern for the education of his children. He recognized that the Third Reich's most brilliant and sinister approach to their totalizing ideology was the Hitler Youth, in which young people were formed in seeing the world in a certain way, apart from whatever other beliefs their parents may have harbored. "Children who are poorly educated in the faith," he wrote, "often continue to practice their faith as long as they fear the punishment of their parents. Years later, as adults, they may live as lukewarm Christians and interiorly may be more similar to nonbelievers."[27] In other words, when the costs of adult-like fidelity are felt with all their weight of responsibility, those who have not learned to love firmly, warmly, and passionately like a child who entrusts himself wholeheartedly to the arms of a parent will seek an easier path rather than accept what it means to be *someone* of substance.

Franz Jägerstätter assumed the cost of being all but erased from history in order to give to his children "a solitary witness" of what was true, what was stable, what was worthy of allegiance and capable of bearing the weight of meaning in our lives. In what he believed to be his final letter to his wife, Franz offers what is most precious to both her and his children:

Now my dear children, when your mother reads you this letter, your father will already be dead. . . . Out of my experience I can say that life is painful when one lives as a lukewarm Christian. To exist this way is to have more the existence of a vegetable than to truly live. If a person were to possess all of the world's wisdom and be able to claim half the earth as his own, he could and would still be less fortunate than a poor person who can claim nothing in this world as his own other than a deep Catholic faith. I would not exchange my small, dirty cell for a king's palace if I was required to give up even a small part of my faith. All that is earthly—no matter how much, nor how beautiful—comes to an end. But God's Word is eternal.[28]

He tells his children that this Word will bear you up, you can trust in it. It is worth studying and learning by heart (see again Deuteronomy 6:4–9; Mark 12:30–31). To this Word, he himself has entrusted all his weight—the weight of his very life, the weight even of his love for his children, whom he loves with tender affection and devotion. He has practiced giving his trust to this Word—like a child, even as an adult—and he offers to his children, as his last wild act of love, the commandment to go and do likewise.

St. Gianna Beretta Molla, in the Arms of Love

Like Franz Jägerstätter, Maria and Alberta Beretta were Franciscan tertiaries who practiced intentional devotions of penance, prayer, and charity in their everyday life. When their tenth child was born on the Feast of St. Francis, they named her Giovanna Francesca in observance of the liturgical feast. "Gianna" was raised in this Franciscan spirituality in the sort of formation that inclined her toward committed, active Catholicism.[29]

In the full bloom of her life—a life that ended when she was thirty-nine—Gianna offered the following teaching to the Young Women of Catholic Action whom she addressed in a conference talk:

Love and sacrifice are as intimately connected as sun and light. We cannot love without suffering or suffer without loving.

Look how many sacrifices are made by mothers who truly
love their children. They are ready for everything, even to give
their own blood. Did not Jesus die on the Cross for us, out
of love for us? Love is affirmed and confirmed in the blood
of sacrifice.[30]

Gianna learned this Gospel truth both from the home her parents
created and from her own regular participation in Catholic Action.
Within the regular and ordered way of life that this fraternity promoted,
Gianna took as her own motto what the fraternity itself routinely practiced: "prayer, action, sacrifice."[31]

In reflecting on his own participation in Catholic Action, her husband Pietro recalls that the most important thing that he learned was
"respect for my neighbor." As unspectacular as this sounds, the importance of this kind of formation cannot be underestimated in Pietro's life.
Because he regularly spent time with others in such a way that he got
to know them, wait with them, serve them, and allow himself, when
necessary, to be served by them, he learned that difficult and necessary
Christian task of asking others, "What are you going through?" and listening attentively to how they respond, in the way they respond, which
is often inaudibly. Catholic Action trained him so well in the *discipline
of community* that he credits it with saving him from the appeal and
influence of Fascism in the years of its favor in his homeland.[32]

Gianna received this same regular formation, from her early years
through her adult years when she became a leader in Catholic Action,
teaching and forming others. After her parents' own example as committed members of a lay society, Gianna gave herself over to the formation of this particular society and allowed herself to be formed through
its practices. This was a key way in which she observed the *discipline of
community*.

Alongside this discipline, she also observed the *discipline of solitude*.
By her husband's testimony as to the devotions that his late wife regularly
observed, Pietro offered this:

> Besides daily Mass, which she hardly ever missed, was the visit
> to the Blessed Sacrament with some minutes of silence talking
> intimately with Jesus. There was the daily recitation of the
> Rosary. . . . Silence was very important to her. . . . Certainly,
> it is easier for wisdom to emerge in silence.[33]

Her reverence for the Blessed Sacrament in silence informed and
inspired her action, both through her charitable activity with Catholic
Action and through her professional practice as a doctor. "Whoever
touches the body of a patient," she often repeated, "touches the body of
Christ."[34] In solitude she became more comfortable welcoming the one
who hastens to those who suffer, who suffers in his own body for love of
them, and therefore she came to see in the suffering ones that she treated
the very wounds that Christ was asking her to heal in love, with skill and
compassion. When she reflected on her calling as a physician, she offered
this brief recitation on her own and others' duties as Catholic doctors:

1. Do our part well. Study your sciences well. There is a race
    for money today.

2. Let us be honest. Be trustworthy physicians.

3. Take affectionate care, thinking that they are our broth-
    ers. Act with delicacy.

4. Do not forget the sick person's soul. Given that we have
    the right to certain confidences, be careful not to profane
    the soul. . . .

    Our mission is not ended when the medicines are of no
    more use. There is the soul to take to God, and your word
    will have authority. . . . As the priest can touch Jesus, so we
    touch Jesus in the bodies of our patients—poor, young, old,
    children. May Jesus be able to make himself seen though us.[35]

In her times of solitude, she made room in silence for the Lord to
dwell with her. In her practice as a physician, she gave her own skill and
compassion as a space for Jesus to be made known to those who suffered.
In the complete witness of her Christian life, one in which she practiced

hearing the Word of God and acting on it, she practiced giving time and space to God and others, and she colored that time and inclined that space with warm welcome and charitable concern.

Gianna Beretta Molla's most famous act was her final one, when she chose to give her own life in the delivery of her and Pietro's fourth child—Gianna Emanuela. "Gianna envisaged a Christian family as a cenacle gathered around Jesus,"[36] and so it is more than fitting that she gave the time and space of her own life to the child who bore not only her own name, but also the name of "God with us." With the simplicity of a child, Gianna the mother entrusted herself to the *Someone* she had practiced trusting from childhood in this last wild act of love, which was the act that summed up her whole life. At the same time, with the keenness and prudent discernment of an adult, she recognized the cost and assumed the responsibility of saying "yes" to the end.

From where does such freedom and bravery come? From whom? More than anyone, Gianna knew she could not supply it on her own, nor could she give that gift to others on her own. And so after each of their children were baptized, Gianna would insist that she and Pietro consecrate each child to Our Lady, who had a chapel dedicated to her near their home. "Gianna was very devoted to her," Pietro remembers, "and I think that her final choices were brought to maturity in the shadow of the Madonna."[37]

Gianna entrusted her children to the care of the Blessed Mother because she herself practiced giving herself to Mary's care. Mary is the one in whom the Word of God was pleased to dwell and who bore the cost of love for him, well beyond the limits of any possible expectations. In Mary, Gianna encountered the paradigm for Christian vocation—a call that is discerned through patient pondering and a faithful memory, that is enacted in the prophetic terms of mercy, and that comes back again and again to small sacrifices that make disciples capable of even greater sacrifices in the name of love. "Each of us must prepare ourselves for our own vocation and prepare ourselves to be givers of life," Gianna confessed, and so beginning well before she gave her children to Mary's care, she was in the regular habit of entrusting herself to the arms of the

Mother of Jesus. In Mary, Gianna found the one who nurtures the disciples her son calls his beloved, whom he calls into his own mission of uniting the love of God to the love of neighbor. And so Gianna would pray:

> O Mary, in your maternal hands I commend and abandon myself entirely, sure of obtaining what I request. I rely upon you because you are my sweet mother; I confide in you because you are Mother of Jesus; I entrust myself to you.
>
> In this trust I rest sure of being heard in everything, with this trust in my heart I greet you *Mater mea, fiducia mea* [my mother, my confidence]; I consecrate myself entirely to you, begging you to remember that I am your own, guard me and defend me, sweet Mary, and in every instant of my life present me yourself to your Son, Jesus.[38]

Mary taught this disciple how to harmonize with God's voice and become a giver of life. "I am," now "let there be."

Epilogue
The Ones Who Give Life

The saints who appear in this book not only gave their lives to Christ; they also built their lives on Christ. In silence and gathering with others, they practiced listening to him and trusting themselves to him. They became capable of saying "yes" to him in greater ways through the "muscle memory" of saying "yes" in smaller ways. They learned commitment, they learned sacrifice, and they learned joy. They would not be parted from that joy even for title or security or comfort. They harmonized with the Word of God, and in the end, they testified to the truth and offered to others the space and the confidence for what matters most. In response to the One who gives life, they became ones who give life to others.

The saints whom the Church raises up are both a gift and a challenge to those of us who feel rather ordinary, even unexceptional. Again, this is probably an indication of our tendency to look at the saints as finished products and miss the long, slow path of formation that led to that end. Even more, though, there is something about the circumstances of the saints that seems enviable. It may seem to us that, at some point or other, the opportunity to make choices in response to God's call was just clearer for them: they seem to have "yes" or "no" moments that are better defined than ours. Mary would stand at the head of that line, for we are told that an angel spoke directly to her. Here, though, we should consider again what is clarity and what is uncertainty. If we heed the witness of the saints patiently and fully, we see that their times and their personal circumstances were every bit as uncertain as we feel ours to be. They were first-timers at this discipleship-thing, just like us.

The uncertainty surrounding them was no less than ours, and yet their clarity came from the practices in which they worked out and built up their capacities for trust. Their practices and disciplines provided them with stability in uncertainty, giving them somewhere to stand so as to give themselves in commitment to Christ.

In his book *The Power of Silence*, Cardinal Robert Sarah includes a lengthy excerpt from a letter written by the mother of a family. The mother's name does not appear—she is anonymous, like the rest of us. And yet if we incline our ear to her voice, we will discover in her testimony the echo of the saints, who harmonize with the voice of God:

> When my children were little and I thought for them and made decisions for them, everything was easy: my freedom alone was in question. But the time came when I realized my role was gradually to get them used to making choices, and as soon as I agreed to do that, I felt worried. While allowing my children to make decisions, and therefore to take risks, I at the same time took the risk of seeing freedoms other than mine arise. If, too often, I continued to make choices in place of my children, it was, I must admit, to spare them from suffering the consequences of a choice that they might have to regret. Yet there was another reason at least as important, if not more so: in order not to risk a disagreement between their choice and the one I would have liked to see them make. I essentially tried to shield myself from possible suffering, the pain I felt each time my children committed themselves to a way different from the one that to me seemed best for them. This way I manage to glimpse the fact that the "Father" can suffer. We are his children. He wants us to be free to build our own lives, and the infinity of his love makes any constraint on his part impossible. Perfect love, without a trace of self-interest but that implies the acceptance from the outset of some suffering inherent in this total freedom that he wants for us.[1]

She is speaking about matters of love, and perfect love drives out fear (1 Jn 4:18). In the faces of those given to her care, those whom she cares about and for whom she wants what is best, she glimpses the immensity of the Father's love for us. It is tempting to want to control the freedom of others so as to secure for them what we think is best for them. We fear they will choose otherwise. In the depths of her honesty, though, she also confesses that she feared encountering freedoms that were not the same as hers, that were not univocal to hers and therefore would necessitate her harmonization if discord was to be avoided. That discord, though, may very well be between her own expectations and the realities of the lives of others. In short, she discerned that the fulfillment of her vocation—her calling—was to give to others what she herself had been given: the space of freedom in which to speak. This is at once radical risk and radical trust. But that is precisely where she glimpses the immensity of God's love.

God speaks and then God listens. Listening means waiting, and waiting is painful. Waiting requires restraint. Actually, it requires power. For the God who waits on us to speak in response to his Word, divine waiting is the form of divine power: God is not compelled by urges, comforts, fleeting novelties. Instead, God gives time and space for his creatures to be, and unceasingly colors that time and inclines that space to our own good, all to give us, his beloved, the freedom to become brave. God gives us the privilege of bearing the costs of love so as to accept ourselves as *someone*, both to him and to one another.

This anonymous mother is recognizing that she is called to give in a manner that is like God the Father's way of giving. The fulfillment of her vocation tends toward that end. She stands as a model for all of us who have been called, whether explicitly or seemingly by happenstance, to form others for Christian discipleship, helping them to become capable of vocational discernment. Whether parent or mentor, minister or teacher, the fulfillment of our own call is to form them to be free and brave, so they can say with their own voice: *fiat*.

In order to say what Mary said, what are those whom we are asked to raise, teach, and form looking for?

Young people are *not* looking for someone to say "yes" for them, as tempting as it is to trade away that responsibility. What they are looking for is what they really need: preparation for and support in learning to say "yes" to God, and to take responsibility for that choice in and through their vocational commitments.

They are looking for what Zechariah and the two travelers on the road to Emmaus were looking for, even though they didn't realize it: someone to teach them how to be silent, to learn how to listen, to take time for new ways of thinking. They are looking for the challenge and the support to become capable of Mary's pondering, who drew into her heart the mystery of God in the midst of the mystery of her life.

Young people are looking for liberation from the hidden assumptions—those "generally accepted principles"—that hold too much power and fill the space of their own freedom with expectations and demands that exceed their due proportion. They need the gift of a memory that sees what God has done, giving them a vision of the world and themselves as created out of love. They are looking for the memory that Mary revealed, where the new, uncertain things of God were connected to the former things of God, making it possible to find sure footing in a constantly changing world.

They long to be re-centered. The choices and options for true, meaningful living are much rarer in some places than in others. Going to the places where mercy is needed, being among the people, is how they will take on a new vision of the world, remapping it even. Practicing mercy is practicing the presence of God. Young people need someone to present the more challenging path that promises the true treasure. They are looking for the kind of vision Mary exercised in seeing the world in God's light, which unveiled the sham of pride and uplifted the priority of those who suffer, those who present us with the opportunity to become fully human together.

They are looking for the privilege of sacrifice: to become someone of substance and to become capable of assuming that cost. They desire to be the same person of quality in one season and the next, which means they need firm ground on which to stand. They want help in becoming capable of saying what they mean and meaning what they say when those quiet moments of personal decision arrive, when they must claim the responsibility for who they will be and how. They are looking to become capable of the serene confidence of Mary, who could recognize her moment and commit herself wholeheartedly to the glorious uncertainty of saying "yes" to God.

They are looking for us to be their guides, their mentors, their pastors, their catechists, their teachers, and especially their parents who will provide credible testimony to what matters most. They need us to practice what we preach, but also to preach something of substance, something true and bold and beautiful. They deserve people of confidence and compassion, who both model for them what it means to live in Christ and who help them to do it.

They are looking for us to be witnesses who show them what Christ looks like, and who show them how Christ looks upon them. They are waiting for someone who asks, over and over again, "What are you going through?" and who cares about what they say and lets it impact them. They want someone to teach them to say and mean these words to others. They expect someone who cares so much that they might even call them "foolish" and take up the difficult task of redirecting, reeducating, and accompanying them for the whole journey. They are looking for honesty, they are looking for humility, they are looking for consistency, and so that is what we must be.

It is part of our vocation to help them become capable of theirs. Ones who give life beget ones who give life.

> Pray for us, O holy Mother of God,
> That we may be made worthy of the promises of Christ.

Notes

1. From My Daughter to the Blessed Mother

1. The inspiration for selecting this particular question comes from Simone Weil, who ties together love of God and love of neighbor with insight and clarity in the brief essay "Reflections on the Right Use of School Studies with a View to the Love of God," in *Awaiting God: A New Translation of "Attente de Dieu and Lettre a Un Religieux,"* trans. Bradley Jersak (Maywood, CT: Fresh Wind Press, 2013), see especially 64.

2. Joseph Ratzinger, *The God of Jesus Christ: Meditations on the Triune God*, trans. Brian McNeil (San Francisco: Ignatius Press, 2008), 28; see also 52.

3. For more on the revelation of God's name and the action of mercy in the Book of Exodus, see my *Work of Love*, 195–202.

4. Ratzinger, *The God of Jesus Christ*, 28.

5. As St. Paul preached, *If God is for us, who can be against us?* (Rom 8:31).

6. Francis, *Evangelii Gaudium: The Joy of the Gospel* (Washington, DC: United States Conference of Catholic Bishops, 2013), §282.

7. Benedict XVI, *Jesus of Nazareth, Part II: Holy Week: From the Entrance into Jerusalem to the Resurrection* (San Francisco: Ignatius Press, 2011), 276.

8. For more on enriching our reading of the Parable of the Good Samaritan, see Henri de Lubac, *Catholicism: Christ and the Common Destiny of Man*, trans. Lancelot Sheppard and Elizabeth Englund (San Francisco: Ignatius Press, 1988), 205–6.

9. See Gary Anderson, *Charity: The Place of the Poor in the Biblical Tradition* (New Haven, CT: Yale University Press, 2013), 32, 69, 104–10.

10. St. Catherine of Siena, *The Dialogue* (New York: Paulist Press, 1980), 121; cf. Karl Rahner, "Why and How Can We Venerate the Saints?" in *Theological Investigations*, trans. Cornelius Ernst et al., vol. 8 (Limerick, Ireland: Mary Immaculate College, 2000), 20. Compare this to what Mother Teresa says about the love of God and love of neighbor: "Because we cannot see Christ we cannot express our love to him; but our neighbors we can always see, and we can do to them what if we saw him we would

like to do to Christ," in Malcolm Muggeridge, *Something Beautiful for God: The Classic Account of Mother Teresa's Journey into Compassion* (New York: HarperOne, 1971), 113.

11. For more on how love of God and love of neighbor are united and, in particular, how God takes on neighborly love in regard to us, his creatures, see Rahner, "Why and How Can We Venerate the Saints?" 16–21. St. Augustine contemplates the persuasiveness—indeed, the sweetness, the eloquence—of God's neighborly love for us in *Teaching Christianity: De Doctrina Christiana*, trans. Edmund Hill (Hyde Park, NY: New City Press, 1996), 1.30.33.52–56; see also John Cavadini, "The Sweetness of the Word: Salvation and Rhetoric in Augustine's 'De Doctrina Christiana,'" in *Augustine's De Doctrina Christiana: A Classic of Western Culture*, ed. Duane Arnold and Pamela Bright (Notre Dame, IN: University of Notre Dame Press, 1995), 170.

12. For an extensive study of the theology of vocation with special attention to the historical development of this theology, see Edward P. Hahnenberg, *Awakening Vocation: A Theology of Christian Call* (Collegeville, MN: Liturgical Press, 2010). The "fullest sense of the term ['vocation']" redounds to the "universal call to holiness" that the Church explicitly reclaimed at the Second Vatican Council (see especially *Lumen Gentium*, chapter 5). Henri de Lubac ties the vocation to the mystery of salvation in particularly striking ways, such as when he writes that "for each one salvation consists in a personal ratification of his original 'belonging' to Christ" (*Catholicism*, 39).

13. In his characteristic style, Karl Rahner suggests as much with a great quantity of words in his "Being Open to God as Ever Greater," in *Theological Investigations*, trans. Cornelius Ernst et al., vol. 7 (Limerick, Ireland: Mary Immaculate College, 2000), 35.

14. For the dogmatic statement on the mystery of the Church, see Austin Flannery, ed., "Dogmatic Constitution on the Church: Lumen Gentium," in *Vatican Council II: Constitutions, Decrees, Declarations*, Revised edition (Northport, NY: Costello Publishing Company, 1996), §1.

15. In the preface to Hans Urs von Balthasar's short and illuminating work dedicated to "the world's salvation in Mary's prayer," Erasmo Leiva-Merikakis writes that "the uncreated Lord cannot have a mother; the redeeming Lord must. And, because there are not two lords but one Lord, Mary unexplainably becomes both the Mother of God and the Mother of all those redeemed by the incarnate God, who wills that man should receive from Mary the life he has deposited in her corporeally. But because this life is actually himself, no one can be found in Christ who is not also found in Mary" (*The Threefold Garland: The World's Salvation in Mary's Prayer* [San Francisco: Ignatius Press, 1982], 11–12).

16. Compare to Psalm 55:5, *Fear and trembling come upon me, and horror overwhelms me* (RSV).

17. In fact, the words that are translated as "troubled" in both narratives in the RSV are not precisely the same word in the Greek; rather, the word translated as "troubled" for Mary is a stronger word than the one used for Zechariah: *tarassō* (ἐταράχθη)

for Zechariah and *diatarassō* (διεταράχθη) for Mary. Luke Timothy Johnson elects to translate these terms as "agitated" for Zechariah and "utterly confused" for Mary. The point is that Mary is comparatively *more* astounded, *more* caught off guard, *more* destabilized by the appearance and greeting of the angel than is Zechariah. See Luke Timothy Johnson, *The Gospel of Luke*, Sacra Pagina Series 3 (Collegeville, MN: Liturgical Press, 1991), 31, 37.

18. See Mark Coleridge, *The Birth of the Lukan Narrative: A Commentary on the Infancy Narratives in the Gospels of Matthew and Luke* (Sheffield, England: Sheffield Academic Press, 1993), 43. Cf. Johnson, *The Gospel of Luke*, 39.

19. See Coleridge, *The Birth of the Lukan Narrative*, 63; cf. Raymond Brown, *The Birth of the Messiah: A Commentary on the Infancy Narratives of Matthew and Luke* (New York: Doubleday, 1993), 280. By responding in faith and seeking to understand, Mary is hereby acting as a true theologian, for whom "faith seeking understanding" is the single and constant exercise.

20. See Coleridge, *The Birth of the Lukan Narrative*, 43–44, 62–64; cf. Francois Bovon, *A Commentary on the Gospel of Luke 1:1–9:50*, ed. Helmut Koester, trans. Christine Thomas (Minneapolis: Augsburg Fortress, 2002), 38.

21. See Joseph A. Fitzmyer, "The Virginal Conception of Jesus in the New Testament," *Theological Studies* 34, no. 4 (1973): 569.

22. See Ben F. Meyer, "'But Mary Kept All These Things . . .' (Lk 2, 19.51)," *Catholic Biblical Quarterly* 26, no. 1 (January 1964): 44–45; cf. Johnson, *The Gospel of Luke,* 51.

23. See Coleridge, *The Birth of the Lukan Narrative*, 28.

24. Darrell Bock, *Proclamation from Prophecy and Pattern: Lucan Old Testament Christology* (Sheffield, England: Sheffield Academic Press, 1987), 55.

25. See Brown, *The Birth of the Messiah*, 268–71.

26. Coleridge, *The Birth of the Lukan Narrative*, 61.

27. See Jean Daniélou, *The Infancy Narratives*, trans. Rosemary Sheed (New York: Herder and Herder, 1968), 8; Coleridge, *The Birth of the Lukan Narrative*, 30.

28. Ratzinger, *The God of Jesus Christ*, 28.

29. See Johnson, *The Gospel of Luke*, 37; Brown, *The Birth of the Messiah*, 229.

30. For one of the best, most probing, and most meditative readings of these figures at the beginning of the third chapter of Luke's gospel, see Alfred Delp, *Advent of the Heart: Seasonal Sermons and Prison Writings, 1941–1944* (San Francisco: Ignatius, 2006), 128–30.

31. On the prophetic dimension of the early part of Luke's gospel, see Bock, *Proclamation from Prophecy and Pattern*, 55–58; and Johnson, *The Gospel of Luke*, 63–82.

32. Timothy Verdon captures the mystery of Mary's prayer in union with her son's prayer when he writes, "in his supreme hour in Gethsemane Jesus will reproduce Mary's original 'Fiat'" and yet, in another respect, "the infinite value of [Jesus'] 'Fiat' at Gethsemane and later on the cross anticipated and made possible his mother's own freedom" (*Art & Prayer: The Beauty of Turning to God* [Brewster, MA: Mount Tabor, 2016], 15–16).

33. Ibid., 62.

2. Pondering and the Meaning of Time

1. The most accurate clock in the world is not really a clock, though it is the thing on which the accuracy of all clocks in the digital age is keyed. This "clock" is the NIST-F2 Cesium Fountain Atomic Clock and, though there is a lot to read about this, the best way to basically learn what it does is to watch this video about its predecessor (the "F1"): https://youtu.be/IXPmM2TPHms and then watch this video about the "F2": https://youtu.be/z-jE7DXy1x0. For a brief article about this clock, see Gayle Swenson, "NIST Launches a New U.S. Time Standard: NIST-F2 Atomic Clock," Text, *NIST* (April 3, 2014), https://www.nist.gov/news-events/news/2014/04/nist-launches-new-us-time-standard-nist-f2-atomic-clock.

2. Mumford, *Technics and Civilization*, (Chicago: University of Chicago Press, 2010) 13; cf. Marshall McLuhan, *Understanding Media: The Extensions of Man*, ed. W. Terrence Gordon, Critical edition (Corte Madera, CA: Gingko Press, 2003), 197–211.

3. Mumford, *Technics and Civilization*, 14.

4. For more on bells being used to order the day, see David S. Landes, *Revolution in Time: Clocks and the Making of the Modern World* (Cambridge, MA: Harvard University Press, 2000), 72–78.

5. For more on the innovation of the clock and its unseen, ubiquitous impact on the modern world, see Nicholas Carr, *The Shallows: What the Internet Is Doing to Our Brains* (New York: W. W. Norton and Company, 2011), 41–44; and Neil Postman, *Amusing Ourselves to Death: Public Discourse in the Age of Show Business*, 20th Anniversary Edition (New York: Penguin, 2005), 11–12.

6. One of the founding engineers of Instagram recognized that he was constructing an addictive mechanism that was "bottomless," just as "Facebook has an endless feed" and "Tinder encourages users to keep swiping in search of a better option" (Greg Hochmuth quoted in Adam Alter, *Irresistible: The Rise of Addictive Technology and the Business of Keeping Us Hooked* [New York: Penguin, 2017], 3).

7. Building on the work of Pierre Bourdieu and Zygmunt Bauman, Vincent Miller diagnoses this same veiled dynamic in consumer advertisements, calling it "seduction." Advertisers utilize this tactic, according to Miller, in order to "strengthen the joys of seeking, of reaching out." Consumers are trained to desire not simply what is available

on the consumer market but more insidiously to desire the delivery mechanism of the consumer market. For example, there is something intoxicating about Amazon.com that goes beyond the products that it makes available; that it makes products so readily and efficiently available is the real draw, and already embedded in that fact is the assumption that there is always more to search, more to find, more potential for consumption even if not everything can or will be consumed. It is the potential that is alluring. See Vincent Miller, *Consuming Religion: Christian Faith and Practice in a Consumer Culture* (New York: Continuum International Publishing Group, 2003), 116–19.

8. Consider this letter from the founder of Facebook: Mark Zuckerberg, "Building Global Community," Digital Letter, February 16, 2017, https://www.facebook.com/notes/mark-zuckerberg/building-global-community/10103508221158471.

9. NYU associate professor of marketing Adam Alter comments on the familiarity of swiping as with tablets—like an iPad—for infants and toddlers in contrast to the unfamiliarity of a print media in the following way: "The swiping gesture that Apple introduced with its first iPhone in 2007 is as natural to [a one-year-old featured in a viral YouTube video] as breathing or eating. But when she sits in front of a magazine, she continues to swipe, becoming frustrated when the inert photos before her refuses to resolve into new ones. She is among the first humans to understand the world in this way—to believe that she has limitless command over the visual environment, and the ability to overcome the staleness of any experience by welcoming its replacement with a dismissive swipe" (Alter, *Irresistible*, 244).

10. If this sounds a little bit like a drug addiction, that may be more than coincidental. There is at least a curious coincidence between the decline in teenage drug use and the increase in teenage use of smartphones (see Matt Richtel, "Are Teenagers Replacing Drugs with Smartphones?" *New York Times*, March 13, 2017, https://www.nytimes.com/2017/03/13/health/teenagers-drugs-smartphones.html). Furthermore, according to a 2015 Pew study, 76% of adults in America report going online daily, while "fully 36% of 18- to 29-year-olds go online almost constantly and 50% go online multiple times per day" (Andrew Perrin, "One-Fifth of Americans Report Going Online ' Almost Constantly,'" *Pew Research Center*, December 8, 2015, http://www.pewresearch.org/fact-tank/2015/12/08/one-fifth-of-americans-report-going-online-almost-constantly/). Cf. Brett T. Robinson, "Recreational Dubs: Constituting Apple's iPod Cult," in *Drugs & Media: New Perspectives on Communication, Consumption, and Consciousness*, ed. Robert C. MacDougall (New York: Continuum, 2011), 121–42.

11. Even though this is a fictitious news report from Waterford Whispers News, the reason it's funny is because it's basically true: "Miracle Teenager Survives on His Own for Almost 6 Hours with No Wi-Fi," *Waterford Whispers News*, September 23, 2016, http://waterfordwhispersnews.com/2016/09/23/miracle-teenager-survives-on-his-own-for-almost-6-hours-with-no-wi-fi.

12. Cory Doctorow, "Writing in the Age of Distraction," *Locus Online Features*, January 2009, http://www.locusmag.com/Features/2009/01/cory-doctorow-writing-in-age-of.html; cf. Carr, *The Shallows*, 91, 108, 115–43.

13. In fact, this is the famous claim that Marshall McLuhan made with his argument that "the medium is the message" in *Understanding Media*.

14. Postman, *Amusing Ourselves to Death*, 99–100.

15. Ibid., 65–75.

16. Ibid., 80.

17. Maggie Jackson, *Distracted: The Erosion of Attention and the Coming Dark Age* (Amherst, NY: Prometheus, 2009), 99. When virtual reality matures, it will allow us to instantaneously transport our perception and consciousness to any location to do anything with anyone for as long as we like (see Alter, *Irresistible*, 142).

18. See Andrew Sullivan, "I Used to Be a Human Being: My Distraction Sickness—and Yours," *New York Magazine*, September 2016, http://nymag.com/selectall/2016/09/andrew-sullivan-technology-almost-killed-me.html.

19. Though there is much more to say on this topic and to launch into that discussion here would draw us well off topic, it is worth noting that anyone who, in the name of Christian formation and discipleship, promotes the notion of "becoming the best version of yourself" is actually contributing to the problem more than helping. This is a therapeutic approach that has more in common with the waywardness of "the prosperity gospel" than it does with the healing of the actual Gospel. Both the "best version of yourself gospel" and the "prosperity gospel" are really about making your own gospel, to suit your purposes.

20. Apple, *Your Verse* (Apple, 2013), https://vimeo.com/85377877.

21. Consider the *Oxford English Dictionary*'s entries on "Anxiety, N.," *OED Online* (Oxford University Press), accessed March 16, 2017, http://www.oed.com.proxy.library.nd.edu/view/Entry/8968: "(1a) Worry over the future or about something with an uncertain outcome; uneasy concern about a person, situation, etc.; a troubled state of mind arising from such worry or concern. . . . (4) A pathological state characterized by inappropriate or excessive apprehension or fear, which may be generalized or attached to particular situations." Cf. Soren Kierkegaard, *The Concept of Anxiety: A Simple Psychologically Orienting Deliberation on the Dogmatic Issue of Hereditary Sin (Kierkegaard's Writings, VIII)*, ed. Reidar Thomte (Princeton, NJ: Princeton University Press, 1981), especially xv–xvi, 42–43.

22. For a penetrating inquiry into the religious dimensions of Apple and Steve Jobs's vision, see Brett T. Robinson, *Appletopia: Media Technology and the Religious Imagination of Steve Jobs* (Waco, TX: Baylor University Press, 2013).

23. For more on the disorientation of the modern world, see Romano Guardini, *The End of the Modern World*, trans. Elinor Briefs (Wilmington, DE: ISI Books, 1998);

and Cardinal Robert Sarah, *The Power of Silence: Against the Dictatorship of Noise,* trans. Michael J. Miller (San Francisco: Ignatius, 2017), especially chapter 1 (21–86).

24. Jennifer L. Roberts, "The Power of Patience: Teaching Students the Value of Deceleration and Immersive Attention," *Harvard Magazine,* 2013, http://harvardmagazine.com/2013/11/the-power-of-patience.

25. Ibid.; cf. Sarah Coakley, "Deepening Practices: Perspectives from Ascetical and Mystical Theology," in *Practicing Theology: Belief and Practices in Christian Life,* ed. Miroslav Volf and Dorothy Bass (Grand Rapids, MI: William B. Eerdmans, 2011), 78–93.

26. In a story about her own process of discernment and periods of waiting, the young poet Madeline Lewis writes about traveling to San Francisco to study how bread is made. One of the things she learned about was the importance of fog in aiding the chemical reactions that contribute to the quality of bread in the city. As she came to understand, this slow, uncertain time changes what comes to be: "I learned that in foggy places, bread flourishes. Fog allows lactic acid to ferment in the dough, lactic acid that in turn helps bread rise and grow thick in density. Lactic acid can change not only the composition of the dough, but also ourselves: the chemical composition of lactic acid is such that, when we knead dough with lactic acid, our hands soften. *In short, when we take bread that has been nurtured by fog, it softens us.*" See Madeline Lewis, "In a Fog," *Church Life Journal,* Stories of Grace, January 18, 2017, https://churchlife.nd.edu/2017/01/18/stories-of-grace-episode-9.

27. Jackson, *Distracted,* 260.

28. Ibid., 256.

29. Simone Weil, *Awaiting God: A New Translation of "Attente de Dieu and Lettre a Un Religieux,"* trans. Bradley Jersak (Maywood, CT: Fresh Wind Press, 2013), 57.

30. Ibid.

31. Ibid., 61–62.

32. Teresa of Avila, *The Way of Perfection,* ed. E. Allison Peers (Mineola, NY: Dover Publications, 2012), 135 [19.2]; cf. Sarah, *The Power of Silence,* 51, 83–84.

33. So as not to give off the impression that prayer is some kind of specialty reserved only for the well rehearsed, which would be the furthest thing from especially St. Teresa's spiritual vision, it is worth quoting this simple and true line: "To pray is not difficult, nor does it require special learning" (Timothy Verdon, *Art & Prayer: The Beauty of Turning to God* [Brewster, MA: Mount Tabor, 2016], v). What Msgr. Verdon goes on to teach, however, is that the formation of the imagination as the fertile space in which the fruit and intimacy of prayer ripens does require a certain kind of training, one which is first learned in families and in the Church, among other disciples and mentors, as well as in and through art and scripture. We will turn to the formation of the imagination in the next chapter when we attend to memory.

34. For more on this kind of assignment and the "painful" but rewarding experience of waiting on interpretation through attentiveness and patience, see Rika Burnham, "Intense Looks: Solitude, Scholarship, and a Teacher's Transformative Experience," in *Teaching in the Art Museum: Interpretation as Experience* (Los Angeles: J. Paul Getty Museum, 2011), 67–78; cf. Richard Wollheim, *Painting as an Art: The A. W. Mellon Lectures in the Fine Arts* (Princeton, NJ: Princeton University Press, 1987), especially 8, 45–75.

35. See Sullivan, "I Used to Be a Human Being."

36. This presentation on chapter 4 of *Amoris Laetitia* substantially mirrors that which I am concurrently offering in an essay titled "The Movement of Intercessory Prayer and the Openness to Encounter" for an edited volume entitled *Pope Francis and the Event of Encounter*, which is scheduled to be released around the same time as this book but from the Cascade imprint of Wipf and Stock Publishers.

37. Pope Francis, Apostolic Exhortation on Love in the Family *Amoris Laetitia* (March 19, 2016), § 91, https://w2.vatican.va/content/dam/francesco/pdf/apost_exhortations/documents/papa-francesco_esortazione-ap_20160319_amoris-laetitia_en.pdf. On the paradox of God's "hoping" for us, see Charles Péguy, *The Portal of the Mystery of Hope*, trans. David Louis Schindler Jr. (Grand Rapids, MI: William B. Eerdmans, 1996); cf. Hans Urs von Balthasar, *Theo-Drama: Theological Dramatic Theory, Volume V: The Last Act*, trans. Graham Harrison (San Francisco: Ignatius Press, 1998), 186; and Verdon, *Art & Prayer*, 15–19.

38. Francis, *Amoris Laetitia*, § 92.

39. Ibid., § 93.

40. See ibid., § 94–104.

41. Ibid., § 109.

42. See ibid., § 111–18. In the book that Francis said "did me such good," Walter Kasper writes that "love creates and grants space to the beloved, in which he or she can become themselves" (Walter Kasper, *Mercy: The Essence of the Gospel and the Key to Christian Life*, trans. William Madges [New York: Paulist Press, 2014], 92).

43. Roberts, "The Power of Patience."

44. See Timothy P. O'Malley, *Bored Again Catholic: How the Mass Could Save Your Life* (Huntington, IN: Our Sunday Visitor, 2017), which offers a delightful yet substantive reintroduction to the movements of the Catholic Mass as formative of our affections and character.

45. In 1911, Taylor published the hugely influential work that more or less solidified his vision of time ordered to industrial efficiency as *The Principles of Scientific Management* (Eastford, CT: Martino Fine Books, 2014). For more on Taylor and "Taylorism," see Carr, *The Shallows*, 149–50, 152, 173, 218; Nicholas Carr, *The Glass Cage: How Our Computers Are Changing Us* (New York: W. W. Norton and Company,

2014), 107, 108, 114, 158, 207; Jackson, *Distracted*, 81–93; and Robert Kanigel, *The One Best Way: Frederick Winslow Taylor and the Enigma of Efficiency* (New York: Viking Adult, 1997).

46. For more on Louis and Zélie Martin, see my "Blessed Is the Fruit: Canonizing the Parents of the St. Thérèse,"*Aleteia.org*, October 16, 2015, http://aleteia. org/2015/10/16/blessed-is-the-fruit-canonizing-the-parents-of-the-st-therese from which I draw some of the lines in this section.

47. To read Thérèse's childhood reflections about how her leisurely walks with her father taught her how to practice charity, see chapter 2 of Thérèse of Lisieux, *Story of a Soul*, trans. John Clarke (Washington, DC: ICS Publications, 1996); cf. my *Work of Love: A Theological Reconstruction of the Communion of Saints* (Notre Dame, IN: University of Notre Dame Press, 2017), 205–6.

48. Stephane-Joseph Piat, *The Story of a Family: The Home of St. Thérèse of Lisieux*, trans. A Benedictine of Stanbrook Abbey (Rockford, IL: Tan Books and Publishers, 1994), 14.

49. See ibid., 87.

50. The final chapter of Timothy Radcliffe's *What Is the Point of Being a Christian?* (London: Bloomsbury, 2005) is a timely and enjoyable reflection on the unparalleled importance of observing the Sabbath, especially in the modern world (see 194–208).

51. Thérèse of Lisieux, *Story of a Soul*, 98–99 (all italics are Thérèse's own). For her recollections of Sunday evenings with her father, who would sing and recite poetry to his daughters, teach them how to pray and then tuck them in to bed, see chapter 2, especially page 43. Significantly, it was on the Pentecost Sunday in 1883 that Thérèse "turned toward the Mother of heaven, and prayed with all her heart that she take pity on her. All of a sudden the Blessed Virgin appeared *beautiful* to me, so *beautiful* that never had I seen anything so attractive." What penetrated the depths of her soul, Thérèse says, was the "ravishing smile of the Blessed Virgin" (65–66, in chapter 3). This event was pivotal in her young life. She knew Sunday as the great feast day, where she tasted in advance the "everlasting repose of heaven" (42), which, in the fullness of her time on earth, became her ultimate desire (see *Thérèse of Lisieux: Her Last Conversations*, 102).

3. Memory and the Authority of Hidden Assumptions

1. Phil Alden Robinson, *Field of Dreams* (Universal Pictures, 1989).

2. W. P. Kinsella, *Shoeless Joe* (New York: Mariner Books, 1999), 252.

3. Eduardo Chávez, *Our Lady of Guadalupe and Saint Juan Diego: The Historical Evidence* (Lanham, MD: Rowman and Littlefield, 2006), 61.

4. A brief list of only some of the more recent and well-researched books that offer insightful diagnostic commentary on the effects of technological saturation in the

modern age include Jackson, *Distracted*; Sherry Turkle, *Alone Together: Why We Expect More from Technology and Less from Each Other* (New York: Basic Books, 2012); Postman, *Amusing Ourselves to Death*; Alter, *Irresistible*; David Brooks, *The Road to Character* (New York: Random House, 2015); Carr, *The Shallows*; and Carr, *The Glass Cage*.

5. See, for example, Guardini, *The End of the Modern World*, which definitively proposes more than any of the previously cited books because Guardini is committed to a thoroughly Christian vision of the world and of the human person.

6. Once again, I refer the reader to my previous book, *Work of Love*, in which I defend this view in what I call "a theological reconstruction of the communion of saints."

7. John Henry Newman, "Holiness Necessary for Future Blessedness," in *Selected Sermons, Prayers, and Devotions* (New York: Vintage, 1999), 5 (italics in original text).

8. Again, Timothy O'Malley's meditations on the Catholic Mass follow this central insight; see O'Malley, *Bored Again Catholic*.

9. Bl. John Henry Newman, "Remembrance of Past Mercies," in *Selected Sermons, Prayers, and Devotions* (New York: Vintage, 1999), 205. Newman's image is reminiscent of how St. Augustine contemplates the life of the saints in eternal beatitude in Book XXII of St. Augustine, *City of God*, trans. Henry Bettenson (New York: Penguin, 2003). I am obviously quite taken with this section of Newman's sermon since I also quoted it in full in *Witness: Learning to Tell the Stories of Grace That Illumine Our Lives* (Notre Dame, IN: Ave Maria, 2016), 67. Consider also Jonathan Edwards's remarkable sermon *Heaven: A World of Love* (CreateSpace Independent Publishing Platform, 2013).

10. Robinson, *Field of Dreams*.

11. Dante Alighieri, *Purgatorio*, ed. and trans. Robin Kirkpatrick (New York: Penguin, 2007), 28.125.

12. Ibid., 28.128; cf. Dante Alighieri, *Inferno*, ed. and trans. Robin Kirkpatrick (New York: Penguin, 2006), 14.136–38.

13. Dante Alighieri, *Purgatorio*, 28.129; cf. Dante Alighieri, *Inferno*, 33.124–32, 142–45.

14. See Dante Alighieri, *Purgatorio*, 30.73–75.

15. "Even supposing a man of unholy life were suffered to enter heaven, 'he would not be happy there'; so that it would be no mercy to permit him" (Newman, "Holiness Necessary for Future Blessedness," 6). The fitness or unfitness of disciples for heavenly bliss is likewise the premise not only of Newman's sermon on blessedness but also of C. S. Lewis's *The Great Divorce*. In this short novel that is, at once, something like an extended meditation on Newman's sermon and a *Reader's Digest* version of Dante's *Commedia*, Lewis features one character after another who is inordinately attached to some pleasure or preference or "love" that they just will not let go of even for the sake of gaining all of heaven and then ultimately receiving back what they let go of in

the first place. It sounds crazy, but if there is one thing that is true about hell and the "choice" of the damned, it is this: it just doesn't make sense.

16. For a little help separating truth from myth relative to what happens in the college admissions process, it is wise to listen to actual college admissions officers now and again (see, for example, Stephanie Klein Wassink, "What Really Goes on in a College Admissions Office?" *Time*, February 18, 2016, http://time.com/money/collection-post/4227671/what-really-goes-on-in-a-college-admissions-office).

17. William R. Fitzsimmons, "Guidance Office: Answers from Harvard's Dean, Part 5," *The Choice Blog*, September 16, 2009, https://thechoice.blogs.nytimes.com/2009/09/16/harvarddean-part5.

18. According to the University of Notre Dame's website, 80% of the class admitted in 2016 is Catholic, although for years the reported percentage of Catholic undergraduates was closer to 85 percent (see "Admission Statistics," University of Notre Dame Enrollment Division, *Undergraduate Admissions*, accessed April 8, 2017, http://admissions.nd.edu/apply/admission-statistics).

19. From Marissa Browne, University of Notre Dame Class of 2019. Used with permission.

20. From Abigail Dommert, University of Notre Dame Class of 2020. Used with permission.

21. From Yoo Jin Jung, University of Notre Dame Class of 2018. Used with permission.

22. University of Notre Dame Office of Undergraduate Admissions, "Evaluation Criteria," University of Notre Dame Enrollment Division, *Undergraduate Admissions*, accessed April 8, 2017, http://admissions.nd.edu/apply/evaluation-criteria. To glimpse these criteria in a single seventy-five-second video, see Neighborhood Film Company, *Any Given Day*, 2012, https://vimeo.com/48618719.

23. Fitzsimmons, "Guidance Office, Part 5."

24. "Turning the Tide: Inspiring Concern for Others and the Common Good through College Admissions," Making Caring Common Project (Harvard Graduate School of Education, 2016), http://mcc.gse.harvard.edu/files/gse-mcc/files/20160120_mcc_ttt_execsummary_interactive.pdf?m=1453303460.

25. Ibid.

26. For more on this shift in college admissions values, see Lisa Heffernan and Jennifer Wallace, "To Get into College, Harvard Report Advocates for Kindness instead of Overachieving," *Washington Post*, January 20, 2016, https://www.washingtonpost.com/news/parenting/wp/2016/01/20/to-get-into-college-harvard-report-advocates-for-kindness-instead-of-overachieving/?tid=a_inl&utm_term=.210bde2c4dd1.

27. Judy Mandell, "What College Admissions Officers Say They Want in a Candidate," *Washington Post*, August 30, 2016, https://www.washingtonpost.com/news/parenting/wp/2016/08/30/what-21-college-admissions-officers-say-they-want-in-a-candidate/?utm_term=.0c37314a25dc. In an odd twist, these new college admissions standards end up sounding quite a bit like Mark Zuckerberg's idea of what Facebook is and will become. Facebook may not be as cool as it was even a few years ago, but the vision that Facebook fosters as the "largest online community in the world"—one which, if it were an actual country, would be the most populous one on the planet—is too powerful to ignore. In a letter addressed "to our community" that Zuckerberg wrote in early 2017, he said that "research suggests the best solution for improving discourse may come from getting to know each other as whole people instead of just opinions." This sounds exactly right, but then he goes on to state that "Facebook may be uniquely suited" to help us know each other as whole persons because "connecting everyone to the Internet is also necessary for building an informed community." But the vision of whole persons that Zuckerberg fosters—the vision that Facebook pursues and shares in common with other social media giants—is one that runs through their algorithms (see Joe Miller, "How Facebook's Tentacles Reach Further Than You Think," *BBC News*, May 26, 2017, http://www.bbc.com/news/business-39947942, and DeLorenzo, "Facebook and Christian Time"). "You have one identity," Zuckerberg claimed elsewhere. "The days of having a different image for your work friends or co-workers and for the other people you know are probably coming to an end pretty quickly . . . having two identities for your self is an example of a lack of integrity," (quoted in Kirkpatrick, *The Facebook Effect*, 199). As Nicholas Carr dryly comments after citing these very words, "That view, not surprisingly, dovetails with Facebook's desire to package its members as neat and coherent sets of data for advertisers" (Carr, *The Glass Cage*, 206). What a social media profile presents to others is a composite image of your "whole self," or at least the carefully crafted self that sometimes includes sloppy moments that you forgot to delete or to which someone else tagged you. That hidden moment when you are "presented" around the table for the college admissions committee happens over and over again in plain sight in what Zuckerberg believes is happening more and more in and through social media. And so, naturally, college admissions officers will even look to applicants' social media profiles, because today that is part of a thorough examination. See Timothy Stenovec, "Facebook Is Now Bigger Than the Largest Country on Earth," *Huffington Post*, January 28, 2015, sec. Tech, http://www.huffingtonpost.com/2015/01/28/facebook-biggest-country_n_6565428.html; and Kaitlin Mulhere, "Lots More College Admissions Officers Are Checking Your Instagram and Facebook," *Time*, January 13, 2016, http://time.com/money/collection-post/4179392/college-applications-social-media.

28. One additional level of complexity here is that students are not the only ones under pressure in the admissions process; the institutions themselves are under pressure, with directors of admissions feeling the brunt of the burden. Every institution of higher education—like all institutions—has its own set of priorities and aspirations. More

often than not, these priorities and aspirations are synched with their peers (or their wannabe peers). While the applicants and someday-applicants are busy conforming themselves to what they consider to be the ideal image for admissibility, the institutions are busy trying to establish, affirm, or reinforce their own desired images. The institutions are therefore always—whether explicitly or by default—crafting their admissions classes according to the kinds of students whose profiles—no matter how homogenous or diversified those profiles end up being, by whatever measures—accentuate and advance the priorities and aspirations of the institutions themselves. The Harvards and Stanfords of the world seem less concerned with such self-curation, but that's because they embody the standards that the other institutions follow—even, often times, religious institutions of higher education. Harvard and Stanford can basically do whatever they want, and everyone else will follow. In the end, college and university admissions directors are therefore under pressure to meet their targets in terms of number of enrollees, selectivity, the profiles of admitted students, and graduation yield, among other things. For more on the pressures facing admissions directors, see Scott Jaschik, "More Pressure Than Ever: The 2014 Survey of College and University Admissions Directors," *Inside Higher Ed*, September 18, 2014, https://www.insidehighered.com/news/survey/ more-pressure-ever-2014-survey-college-and-university-admissions-directors.

I also want to admit that I recognize the irony in the fact that I am critiquing the rules of the college admissions process since, after all, I occupy the position and state of life that I do in large part because I succeeded according to the rules of the game. Even more, I now work and teach in one of these prestigious universities—the very one I attended, in fact. Then again, though, what I offered in the "preface" is intended to show that for me—but not only for me—the overwhelming desire for achievement left me a record of significant character deficits on the ledger that needed to be (and still need to be) addressed, corrected, and redeemed. It isn't just that paying attention to certain ways of valuing left me ignoring others, but rather that the very ways of valuing in which I have long been engaged are precisely the cause of the deficits. The habitual focus on individual achievement and self-advancement is *ipso facto* blindness to the needs of others and, ultimately, a form of deafness to the call to discipleship.

29. James Martin, *My Life with the Saints* (Chicago: Loyola, 2007), 47.

30. Ira Glass, "Kid Logic," *This American Life* (Chicago, June 22, 2001), https:// www.thisamericanlife.org/radio-archives/episode/188/kid-logic.

31. For more on the continuity and development between Israel's great prayer and the creed of Christian faith, see my *Work of Love*, 11–15; cf. John Henry Newman, "The Orthodoxy of the Body of the Faithful during the Supremacy of Arianism," in *The Arians of the Fourth Century* (Eugene, OR: Wipf and Stock Publishers, 1996), 445–68; Jaroslav Pelikan, *Credo: Historical and Theological Guide to Creeds and Confessions of Faith in the Christian Tradition* (New Haven, CT: Yale University Press, 2005), 341, 376; and Jaroslav Pelikan and Valerie Hotchkiss, eds., *Creeds and Confessions of Faith in the Christian Tradition*, vol. I (New Haven, CT: Yale University Press, 2003), 7–9.

32. The poetic prayer typically attributed to Pedro Arrupe comes to mind here: "Nothing is more practical than falling in love."

33. See the chapter "Talking to a Stranger" in Rowan Williams, *Resurrection: Interpreting the Easter Gospel* (New York: The Pilgrim Press, 1984).

34. See Christian Smith, "Is Moralistic Therapeutic Deism the New Religion of American Youth? Implications for the Challenge of Religious Socialization and Reproduction," in *Passing on the Faith: Transforming Traditions for the Next Generation of Jews, Christians, and Muslims*, ed. James L. Heft (New York: Fordham University Press, 2006), 55–74; cf. DeLorenzo, *Witness*, 6–13.

35. Regarding the commonplace moral platitudes in contemporary American religious life, see Smith, "Is Moralistic Therapeutic Deism the New Religion of American Youth?" especially 72–73.

36. A good indication that the living wisdom of the Gospel is being reduced and that, therefore, the imagination of the disciple is being impoverished is that a message is paraphrased. "The Good Samaritan means that you should do good things for other people, like holding the door for them." Or we might hear, for example, that "the Prodigal Son means that no matter how bad you've been, you can always go back home." This reduction in the Parable of the Lost Son (and that of the Lost Sheep and the Lost Coin could be added) closes off the imagination to the radical paradox of the Son of God making the journey from his home in *equality with God* (Phil 2:6) to *the far country* (Lk 15:13) to assume the condition of the one who is lost. Of course, the parable is as much about the older son as it is the younger son, for whom it seems that learning to live with his wayward, sinful younger sibling is an undue burden (see Lk 15:25–32). Jesus, who never leaves the obedience of his Father's house, assumes the older brother's condition, too. Then again, it is the parable of the father of both sons—*A man had two sons* (Lk 15:11)—and it is also the parable of the household as the place of abiding together in the father's love. As you continue to dwell with this inexhaustible parable, you come to see that "what it is about" is the whole history of salvation where younger sons always curry favor and older sons have to learn to yield to that order of blessing and the Father of the righteous and unrighteous alike gives a home for them to learn how to live together in his love. In short, our bumper-sticker-become-tweet-obsessed-imaginations dilute the magnificently rich narrative of salvation into a pithy message whose meaning we may quickly infer. In literary criticism, this kind of reduction has been called the "heresy of the paraphrase"; for more see especially chapter 11 of Cleanth Brooks, *The Well Wrought Urn: Studies in the Structure of Poetry* (Orlando: Mariner, 1956). Cf. Flannery O'Connor, *Mystery and Manners: Occasional Prose,* ed. Sally Fitzgerald and Robert Fitzgerald (New York: Farrar, Straus, and Giroux, 1969), especially 90, 96, 107–9.

37. Of course, the "spiritual but not religious" category may not be as large as assumed, but what recent research does suggest is that there is a strong correlation between seeing the moral value of religion and remaining religiously affiliated. This

suggests that religion is perhaps seen mostly as a moral creed, which corresponds to Smith's research as cited above (see Betsy Cooper et al., "Exodus: Why Americans Are Leaving Religion—and Why They're Unlikely to Come Back," *PRRI*, accessed April 17, 2017, https://www.prri.org/research/prri-rns-poll-nones-atheist-leaving-religion).

38. Though he was of course wholly unaware of the four senses of scripture by which the Church reads the sacred text within the body of the Church, Caleb was emphasizing the priority of the "literal sense" (reading at the letter of the text) upon which the other three senses all build (i.e., the "allegorical sense" or reading across the text from/to the person of Christ, the "moral sense" or reading the text as formative of the individual soul, and "the anagogical sense" or reading toward our final destiny in communion with God and full union with one another). For more on the sensus of scripture, see the *Catechism of the Catholic Church*, 115–19.

39. And again, once the moral relevance of scripture or religion becomes unconvincing, religion itself is typically abandoned in the modern world, especially in the United State (see again Cooper et al., "Exodus: Why Americans Are Leaving Religion—and Why They're Unlikely to Come Back").

40. These "seven last words" are found in Matthew 27:46 (and Mark 15:3); Luke 23:34, 23:43, 23:46; John 19:26–27, 19:28, 19:30.

41. This is one of the points on which I think that Sherry Weddell misses the mark when she deemphasizes catechesis in developing her "five thresholds of conversion." (See Sherry A. Weddell, *Forming Intentional Disciples: The Path to Knowing and Following Jesus* [Huntington, IN: Our Sunday Visitor, 2012], especially chapter 5). Without good catechesis, we cannot be sure that the person we are trusting is actually Jesus. The Church preaches and teaches and communicates Jesus by the power of the Holy Spirit. By reading scripture within the body of the Church and being empowered to read it well, patiently, and with the help of a guide and mentor (like a parent), you are actually coming to know Jesus for who he is, on God's own terms. Without good catechesis to discipline the grammar of this encounter, you are just as likely to end up trusting the "prosperity gospel Jesus," the "therapeutic happiness Jesus," or whatever other "Jesus" is actually easier to imagine than the one who is really the Word-made-flesh, the Father's only begotten Son, who often calls us *foolish* out of love.

42. Since I have since learned in telling this story that some people are horrified to think that my father left two young children home alone for a half hour every morning, I am happy to report that we were not left unattended. For those who are curious, one of my dad's friends lived with us for some time until that friend got married and moved out, and otherwise, our neighbor would just come drink her coffee in our living room while we were sleeping and our dad was at Mass.

43. This connection between the elevated host and the rising (or setting) of the sun appears in the short story "A Temple of the Holy Ghost," in *The Complete Stories* by Flannery O'Connor (New York: Farrar, Straus, and Giroux, 1971), 236–48. I always

loved that story but I didn't fully "get it" until I saw it through my five-year-old's hope-filled eyes, eyes that were previously clouded over in fear. I also find resonance with the second chapter of Gregory Boyle's *Tattoos on the Heart*, which is filled with stories of learning to see ourselves again as children held within the gaze of a God overcome with love for us (New York: Free Press, 2010), 41–60.

4. Prophecy and the Cultures of Mercy

1. Cf. Ex 2:24–25; 3:7–10, 16–17.

2. See also Ex 34:6; Nm 14:8; Neh 9:17; Ps 8:15; 103:8; 111:4; 145:8; Jn 4:2; and Jas 5:11.

3. Richard M. Gula, *Reason Informed by Faith: Foundations of Catholic Morality* (New York: Paulist, 1989), 113–14.

4. Justin Bartkus and Christian Smith, "A Report on American Catholic Religious Parenting," National Survey of Youth and Religion (Notre Dame, IN: University of Notre Dame: Institute for Church Life and Center for Study of Religion and Society, 2017), 8 (italics in original text).

5. Ibid.

6. Ibid., 9.

7. Ibid., 12 (italics in original text).

8. Piat, *The Story of a Family*, 182; cf. 48–49. See also Part 1 of Louis Martin and Zelie Martin, *Call to a Deeper Love: The Family Correspondence of the Parents of Saint Therese of the Child Jesus*, ed. Frances Renda, trans. Ann Connors Hess (New York: Alba House, 2011). In her letters, Zélie's trust in God, her confidence in the Blessed Mother, and her love of the saints all become vibrantly apparent.

9. Piat, *The Story of a Family,* 33.

10. Ibid.

11. Thérèse of Lisieux, *Story of a Soul*, 75; cf. Hans Urs von Balthasar, "The Timeliness of Lisieux," in *Carmelite Studies: Spiritual Direction* (Washington, DC: ICS Publications, 1980), 114.

12. Thérèse of Lisieux, *Story of a Soul*, 38; cf. DeLorenzo, *Work of Love*, 205–6.

13. See Raymond Brown, *The Birth of the Messiah: A Commentary on the Infancy Narratives of Matthew and Luke* (New York: Doubleday, 1993), 232.

14. Piat, *The Story of a Family*, 98.

15. Recent research has shown how teenagers are developing the skills for "perspective-taking" most significantly through the age of twenty-one, so that exercises in "empathy" during the formative years and especially as encouraged by parents bear fruit later on. For a quick summary of this research and some of the

takeaways, see Sue Shellenbarger, "Teens Are Still Developing Empathy Skills," *Wall Street Journal*, October 15, 2013, sec. Careers, https://www.wsj.com/articles/teens-are-still-developing-empathy-skills-1381876015.

16. Piat, *The Story of a Family*, 49.

17. As with the section on Louis in chapter 2, this section on Zélie draws on my article, "Blessed Is the Fruit."

18. Bartkus and Smith, "A Report on American Catholic Religious Parenting," 12 (italics in original text).

19. These are the words of Pope Pius X.

20. Philip Kosloski, "Leonie Martin: St. Therese's 'Difficult Sister' Continues on the Road to Canonization," *Aleteia.org*, January 26, 2017, http://aleteia.org/2017/01/26/leonie-martin-st-thereses-difficult-sister-continues-on-the-road-to-canonization.

21. Bonaventure, "The Life of Saint Francis (Legenda Maior)," in *Bonaventure*, trans. Ewert Cousins, Classics of Western Spirituality (Mahwah, NJ: Paulist, 1978), 187, 189; cf. Timothy Verdon, *The Story of St. Francis of Assisi: In Twenty-Eight Scenes* (Brewster, MA: Mount Tabor, 2015), 4–9.

22. Bonaventure, "The Life of Saint Francis," 193–94; Verdon, *The Story of St. Francis of Assisi*, 13–15.

23. Bonaventure, "The Life of Saint Francis," 320. G. K. Chesterton captures the paradox (or "problem") of St. Francis brilliantly in one swift and rather exhilarating paragraph in "Saint Francis of Assisi," in *Saint Thomas Aquinas and Saint Francis of Assisi* (San Francisco: Ignatius, 2002), 253–54.

24. Dorothy Day, *By Little and By Little: The Selected Writings of Dorothy Day*, ed. Robert Ellsberg (New York: Alfred A. Knopf, 1984), 98.

25. Ibid., 91 (emphasis added).

26. Ibid., 110.

27. Ibid., 91.

28. See the epigraph for this chapter, taken from Gustavo Gutiérrez, *A Theology of Liberation: History, Politics, and Salvation*, trans. Caridad Inda and John Eagleson, revised edition (Maryknoll, NY: Orbis Books, 1988), 118.

29. Day, *By Little and By Little*, 97.

30. For more on making space for others, discipleship, and evangelization, see Pope Francis, *Evangelii Gaudium: The Joy of the Gospel* (Washington, DC: United States Conference of Catholic Bishops, 2013), 133 (§ 274).

31. Day, *By Little and By Little*, 106.

32. Gula, *Reason Informed by Faith*, 113.

33. Dorothy Day, *The Long Loneliness* (San Francisco: HarperCollins, 1952), 219.

34. From Louis Filipiak, University of Notre Dame Class of 2018. Used with permission.

35. I first came upon this wonderful term in Muggeridge, *Something Beautiful for God*, 60.

36. For Teresa's brief reflections on her childhood home, see Kathryn Spink, *Mother Teresa: An Authorized Biography* (New York: HarperOne, 2011), 3.

37. Ibid., 6.

38. For more on Mother Teresa, including her childhood, one of the best biographies is Spink, *Mother Teresa*. Currently, one of the most widely read (if not the most widely read) biography of the saint is Wyatt North, *Mother Teresa: A Life Inspired* (Boston: Wyatt North Publishing, 2014), but this work is rather scant and quick as compared to others. There are of course elements of Teresa's life that were revealed for the first time in her private writings (*Come Be My Light: The Private Writings of the "Saint of Calcutta,"* ed. Brian Kolodiejchuk [New York: Doubleday, 2007]); but if one were to read just one book on Mother Teresa, I would recommend Muggeridge, *Something Beautiful for God*.

39. For more on killing compassion, in particular, and the conditions for mercy more broadly, see Miguel Romero, "The Call to Mercy: Veritatis Splendor and the Preferential Option for the Poor," *Nove et Vetera* 11, no. 4 (2013): 1205–27.

40. Catherine of Siena, *The Dialogue* (New York: Paulist Press, 1980), 34, 35.

5. Sacrifice and the Joy of Trust

1. For more on the culmination of human freedom in Mary's "yes," see Alfred Delp, *Advent of the Heart: Seasonal Sermons and Prison Writings, 1941–1944* (San Francisco: Ignatius, 2006), especially 28.

2. Radcliffe, *What Is the Point of Being a Christian?* 198.

3. Flannery O'Connor speaks of true art in these terms, including and especially religious art in *Mystery and Manners*, 162–63; cf. DeLorenzo, *Witness*, 48–49.

4. See "Preparatory Document of the XV Ordinary General Assembly of the Synod of Bishops on 'Young People, the Faith and Vocational Discernment,'" January 13, 2017, especially section 3, http://www.vatican.va/roman_curia/synod/documents/rc_synod_doc_20170113_documento-preparatorio-xv_en.html.

5. See again Miller, *Consuming Religion*, especially 126–44.

6. Nancy Jo Sales, "Tinder and the Dawn of the 'Dating Apocalypse,'" *Vanity Fair*, September 2015, http://www.vanityfair.com/culture/2015/08/tinder-hook-up-culture-end-of-dating; cf. Zachary Siegel, "Love in the Time of Tech: Your Brain on Dating Apps," February 1, 2016, http://www.thedailybeast.com/

love-in-the-time-of-tech-your-brain-on-dating-apps; Julie Beck, "The Rise of Dating-App Fatigue," *Atlantic*, October 25, 2016, https://www.theatlantic.com/health/archive/2016/10/the-unbearable-exhaustion-of-dating-apps/505184; Azadeh Aalai, "Are Dating Apps Ruining Your Love Life?" *Psychology Today*, February 28, 2017, https://www.psychologytoday.com/blog/the-first-impression/201702/are-dating-apps-ruining-your-love-life; Sherry Turkle, *Reclaiming Conversation: The Power of Talk in a Digital Age*, reprint edition (New York: Penguin Books, 2016), especially 3–58.

7. On this point, see, for example, Barry Schwartz, *The Paradox of Choice: Why More Is Less* (New York: Ecco, 2016). Furthermore, the articles cited above regarding dating apps either explicitly touch on this point or implicitly assume it.

8. In naming these two disciplines, I am following the lead of Henri Nouwen (see *Making All Things New: An Invitation to the Spiritual Life*, reissue edition [San Francisco: HarperOne, 2009], 65–92), though my presentation of the discipline of community is different in some important respects from Nouwen's own.

9. Ibid., 69. On the importance of believing that God is personally present and active in the world, especially for the spiritual lives of young adults, see Nicolette Manglos-Weber and Christian Smith, "Understanding Former Young Catholics: Findings from a National Study of American Emerging Adults," National Survey of Youth and Religion (Notre Dame, IN: University of Notre Dame: Institute for Church Life and Center for Study of Religion and Society, 2015), 8; cf. DeLorenzo, *Witness*, 6–13.

10. See Thomas Merton, *The Sign of Jonas* (New York: Harvest Books, 2002), 311.

11. As Mother Teresa confessed, "Read the Gospel attentively, and you will see that Jesus sacrificed even charity for prayer," as quoted in Sarah, *The Power of Silence*, 47.

12. In the seventh dwelling place of the *The Interior Castle*, Teresa of Avila writes, "For just as in heaven so in the soul His Majesty must have a room where He dwells alone. Let us call it another heaven" (trans. Kieran Kavanaugh and Otilio Rodriguez [New York: Paulist Press, 1979], 175 [VII.3]).

13. St. Augustine, *The Confessions*, trans. Maria Boulding (New York: Vintage Books, 1998), 6 [I.6].

14. Nouwen, *Making All Things New*, 76.

15. Ibid., 77.

16. St. Thérèse of Lisieux's preparation for receiving Holy Communion is both illustrative and instructive on this point. See *Story of a Soul*, 172.

17. W. H. Vanstone, *The Stature of Waiting* (London: Darton, Longman and Todd, 2001), 56.

18. Rev. Gregory Boyle, "2017 Laetare Address," accessed May 28, 2017, http://news.nd.edu/news/rev-gregory-j-boyle-sj-2017-laetare-address; cf. Boyle, *Tattoos on the Heart*, especially xiv–xv.

19. Robert Bolt, *A Man for All Seasons* (New York: Vintage, 1990), xiii.

20. Ibid., xiv.

21. Ibid., 91 (emphases in original text).

22. Ibid., 121–22 (emphases in original text).

23. "The Trial of Thomas More: July 1, 1535," Center for Thomas More Studies, accessed May 29, 2017, https://thomasmorestudies.org/docs/The%20Trial%20of%20 Thomas%20More.pdf; cf. Bolt, *A Man for All Seasons*, 159.

24. In the play, Bolt himself presented this theme of "standing on" in the juxtaposition of water and dry land. From the beginning of the play, everyone is being carried back and forth by water, especially between More's estate and the king's castle. The water is all the things that are in flux, and everyone is being carried by these currents, this fluidity, this mutability. Along the water is how people move . . . until Thomas More cannot get a boat. The precise moment when this happens is the occasion of the second debate with Norfolk (above), right after More is confronted by Cromwell, his prime adversary. When the winds and the tides shift against him, Thomas More can either go along with the forces of the day or stand on the dry and stable land of his trust in Christ's words. This is the sacrifice of actually standing somewhere and taking responsibility for being *someone* because you trust in *Someone*. More walks home, by land (see Bolt, *A Man for All Seasons*, 120–25). For a stirring meditation on the need for firm ground and the stability of trust in the Lord, especially during times of crisis, see Delp, *Advent of the Heart*, 41–42.

25. See Gordon Charles Zahn, *In Solitary Witness: The Life and Death of Franz Jägerstätter* (Springfield, IL: Templegate, 1986); cf. Franz Jägerstätter, *Franz Jägerstätter: Letters and Writings from Prison*, ed. Erna Putz, trans. Robert Krieg (Maryknoll, NY: Orbis Books, 2009), xxv–xxvii.

26. Jägerstätter, *Franz Jägerstätter*, 152.

27. Ibid., 165; see also 237–40. Elsewhere, Jägerstätter likens catechesis and the study of scripture to the practice of studying a map for a foreign journey, where the signs may not be trustworthy and hardship may befall you. The one who learns how to read the terrain in advance, who knows how to navigate and not just expect to arrive, is capable of making his way and even revise his course when resourcefulness, skill, and firmness of character are required. Franz eventually lives this parable (see 168–69). For consideration of how we have become dependent on ready-at-hand guidance in our modern lives, like GPS negotiating all terrain for us, see Carr, *The Glass Cage*, 205; and David Brooks, "The Outsourced Brain," *New York Times*, October 26, 2007, http://www.nytimes.com/2007/10/26/opinion/26brooks.html.

28. Jägerstätter, *Franz Jägerstätter*, 237; cf. Delp, *Advent of the Heart*, 130.

29. Pietro Molla and Elio Guerriero, *Saint Gianna Molla: Wife, Mother, Doctor*, trans. James Colbert (San Francisco: Ignatius, 2004), 11.

30. Ibid., 90.

31. Ibid., 69; see also Elio Guerriero, ed., *The Journey of Our Love: The Letters of Saint Gianna Beretta and Pietro Molla*, trans. Ann Brown (Boston: Pauline, 2009), 40–44.

32. Molla and Guerriero, *Saint Gianna Molla*, 35, 63–64.

33. Ibid., 68–69.

34. Ibid., 73.

35. Ibid., 75; see also her daily prayer to Jesus on 136; cf. Guerriero, *The Journey of Our Love*, 9.

36. Molla and Guerriero, *Saint Gianna Molla*, 39.

37. Ibid., 60; Guerriero, *The Journey of Our Love*, 19, 41. Charles Péguy reveals that he also entrusted his children to the care of the Blessed Mother, especially when one of his children was quite ill (see *The Portal of the Mystery of Hope*, 27–31).

38. Molla and Guerriero, *Saint Gianna Molla*, 136. Along with this prayer, Gianna also prayed a daily prayer to Jesus, one in which she asks for the grace to entrust herself, of resting securely, of being loved in the same arms of the Father who holds the weakest, sickest, and most needy in tender care. In her prayer to Mary, she is asking Mary to bring her close to the one Mary herself held closest of all: Jesus. (The prayer to Jesus appears on the same page.)

Epilogue: The Ones Who Give Life

1. Sarah, *The Power of Silence*, 92.

Selected Bibliography

Aalai, Azadeh. "Are Dating Apps Ruining Your Love Life?" *Psychology Today*. February 28, 2017. https://www.psychologytoday.com/blog/the-first-impression/201702/are-dating-apps-ruining-your-love-life.

Alter, Adam. *Irresistible: The Rise of Addictive Technology and the Business of Keeping Us Hooked*. New York: Penguin, 2017.

———. "Tech Bigwigs Know How Addictive Their Products Are. Why Don't the Rest of Us?" *WIRED*. Accessed March 29, 2017. https://www.wired.com/2017/03/irresistible-the-rise-of-addictive-technology-and-the-business-of-keeping-us-hooked.

Apple. *Your Verse*. Apple, 2013. https://vimeo.com/85377877.

Arnett, Jeffrey Jensen. *Emerging Adulthood: The Winding Road from the Late Teens through the Twenties*. 2nd edition. New York: Oxford University Press, 2015.

Augustine. *The Confessions*. Translated by Maria Boulding. New York: Vintage Books, 1998.

———. *Teaching Christianity: De Doctrina Christiana*. Translated by Edmund Hill. Hyde Park, NY: New City Press, 1996.

Balthasar, Hans Urs von. *Theo-Drama: Theological Dramatic Theory, Volume V: The Last Act*. Translated by Graham Harrison. San Francisco: Ignatius Press, 1998.

———. "The Timeliness of Lisieux." In *Carmelite Studies: Spiritual Direction*. Washington, DC: ICS Publications, 1980.

Beck, Julie. "The Rise of Dating-App Fatigue." *Atlantic*, October 25, 2016. https://www.theatlantic.com/health/archive/2016/10/the-unbearable-exhaustion-of-dating-apps/505184.

Benedict XVI. *Jesus of Nazareth, Part II: Holy Week: From the Entrance into Jerusalem to the Resurrection*. San Francisco: Ignatius Press, 2011.

Bock, Darrell. *Proclamation from Prophecy and Pattern: Lucan Old Testament Christology*. Sheffield, England: Sheffield Academic Press, 1987.

Bolt, Robert. *A Man for All Seasons*. New York: Vintage, 1990.

Bonaventure. "The Life of Saint Francis (Legenda Maior)." In *Bonaventure*, translated by Ewert Cousins, 177–327. Classics of Western Spirituality. Mahwah, NJ: Paulist, 1978.

Bovon, Francois. *A Commentary on the Gospel of Luke 1:1–9:50*. Edited by Helmut Koester. Translated by Christine Thomas. Minneapolis: Augsburg Fortress, 2002.

Boyle, Gregory. "2017 Laetare Address." Accessed May 28, 2017. http://news.nd.edu/news/rev-gregory-j-boyle-sj-2017-laetare-address.

———. *Tattoos on the Heart: The Power of Boundless Compassion*. New York: Free Press, 2010.

Brooks, Cleanth. *The Well Wrought Urn: Studies in the Structure of Poetry*. Orlando: Mariner, 1956.

Brooks, David. "The Outsourced Brain." *New York Times*, October 26, 2007. http://www.nytimes.com/2007/10/26/opinion/26brooks.html.

———. *The Road to Character*. New York: Random House, 2015.

Brown, Raymond. *The Birth of the Messiah: A Commentary on the Infancy Narratives of Matthew and Luke*. New York: Doubleday, 1993.

Burnham, Rika. "Intense Looks: Solitude, Scholarship, and a Teacher's Transformative Experience." In *Teaching in the Art Museum: Interpretation as Experience*, 67–78. Los Angeles: J. Paul Getty Museum, 2011.

Carr, Nicholas. *The Glass Cage: How Our Computers Are Changing Us*. New York: W. W. Norton and Company, 2014.

———. *The Shallows: What the Internet Is Doing to Our Brains*. New York: W. W. Norton and Company, 2011.

Catherine of Siena. *The Dialogue*. New York: Paulist Press, 1980.

Cavadini, John. "The Sweetness of the Word: Salvation and Rhetoric in Augustine's 'De Doctrina Christiana.'" In *Augustine's De Doctrina Christiana: A Classic of Western Culture*, edited by Duane Arnold and Pamela Bright, 164–81. Notre Dame, IN: University of Notre Dame Press, 1995.

Chávez, Eduardo. *Our Lady of Guadalupe and Saint Juan Diego: The Historical Evidence*. Lanham, MD: Rowman and Littlefield, 2006.

Chesterton, G. K. "Saint Francis of Assisi." In *Saint Thomas Aquinas and Saint Francis of Assisi*, 191–320. San Francisco: Ignatius, 2002.

Coakley, Sarah. "Deepening Practices: Perspectives from Ascetical and Mystical Theology." In *Practicing Theology: Belief and Practices in Christian Life*. Edited by Miroslav Volf and Dorothy Bass, 78–93. Grand Rapids, MI: William B. Eerdmans, 2011.

Coleridge, Mark. *The Birth of the Lukan Narrative: A Commentary on the Infancy Narratives in the Gospels of Matthew and Luke.* Sheffield, England: Sheffield Academic Press, 1993.

Collins, Jim. "Reading, in a Digital Archive of One's Own." *PMLA* 128, no. 1 (January 2013): 207–12.

Cooper, Betsy, Daniel Cox, Rachel Lienesch, and Robert Jones. "Exodus: Why Americans Are Leaving Religion—and Why They're Unlikely to Come Back." *PRRI*. Accessed April 17, 2017. https://www.prri.org/research/prri-rns-poll-nones-atheist-leaving-religion.

Daniélou, Jean. *The Infancy Narratives.* Translated by Rosemary Sheed. New York: Herder and Herder, 1968.

Dante Alighieri. *Inferno.* Edited and translated by Robin Kirkpatrick. New York: Penguin, 2006.

———. *Paradiso.* Edited and translated by Robin Kirkpatrick. New York: Penguin, 2007.

———. *Purgatorio.* Edited and translated by Robin Kirkpatrick. New York: Penguin, 2007.

Day, Dorothy. *By Little and By Little: The Selected Writings of Dorothy Day.* Edited by Robert Ellsberg. New York: Alfred A. Knopf, 1984.

———. *The Long Loneliness.* San Francisco: HarperCollins, 1952.

DeLorenzo, Leonard J. "Blessed Is the Fruit: Canonizing the Parents of the St. Thérèse." *Aleteia.org*, October 16, 2015. http://aleteia.org/2015/10/16/blessed-is-the-fruit-canonizing-the-parents-of-the-st-therese.

———. "Facebook and Christian Time: Some Disturbing and Comforting Aspects." *Oblation: Liturgy and Life.* Accessed May 26, 2017. http://sites.nd.edu/oblation/2014/12/31/facebook-and-christian-time-some-disturbing-and-comforting-aspects.

———. *Witness: Learning to Tell the Stories of Grace That Illumine Our Lives.* Notre Dame, IN: Ave Maria, 2016.

———. *Work of Love: A Theological Reconstruction of the Communion of Saints.* Notre Dame, IN: University of Notre Dame Press, 2017.

Delp, Alfred. *Advent of the Heart: Seasonal Sermons and Prison Writings, 1941–1944.* San Francisco: Ignatius, 2006.

Doctorow, Cory. "Writing in the Age of Distraction." *Locus Online Features*, January 2009. http://www.locusmag.com/Features/2009/01/cory-doctorow-writing-in-age-of.html.

Edwards, Jonathan. *Heaven: A World of Love.* CreateSpace Independent Publishing Platform, 2013.

Fitzmyer, Joseph A. "The Virginal Conception of Jesus in the New Testament." *Theological Studies* 34, no. 4 (1973): 541–75.

Fitzsimmons, William R. "Guidance Office: Answers from Harvard's Dean, Part 1." *The Choice Blog*, September 10, 2009. https://thechoice.blogs.nytimes.com/2009/09/10/harvarddean-part1.

———. "Guidance Office: Answers from Harvard's Dean, Part 2." *The Choice Blog*, September 11, 2009. https://thechoice.blogs.nytimes.com/2009/09/11/harvarddean-part2.

———. "Guidance Office: Answers from Harvard's Dean, Part 3." *The Choice Blog*, September 14, 2009. https://thechoice.blogs.nytimes.com/2009/09/14/harvarddean-part3.

———. "Guidance Office: Answers from Harvard's Dean, Part 4." *The Choice Blog*, September 15, 2009. https://thechoice.blogs.nytimes.com/2009/09/15/harvarddean-part4.

———. "Guidance Office: Answers from Harvard's Dean, Part 5." *The Choice Blog*, September 16, 2009. https://thechoice.blogs.nytimes.com/2009/09/16/harvarddean-part5.

Flannery, Austin, ed. "Dogmatic Constitution on the Church: Lumen Gentium." In *Vatican Council II: Constitutions, Decrees, Declarations.* Revised edition, 1–96. Northport, NY: Costello Publishing Company, 1996.

Forsberg, Geraldine. "Neil Postman and the Judeo-Christian Worldview." *Second Nature*, 2015. https://secondnaturejournal.com/neil-postman-judeo-christian-worldview.

Francis. Apostolic Exhortation on Love in the Family. *Amoris Laetitia* (March 19, 2016). https://w2.vatican.va/content/dam/francesco/pdf/apost_exhortations/documents/papa-francesco_esortazione-ap_20160319_amoris-laetitia_en.pdf.

———. *Evangelii Gaudium: The Joy of the Gospel.* Washington, DC: United States Conference of Catholic Bishops, 2013.

Frank, Robert H., and Philip J. Cook. *The Winner-Take-All Society: Why the Few at the Top Get So Much More Than the Rest of Us.* Reprint edition. New York: Penguin, 1996.

Glass, Ira. "Kid Logic." *This American Life*. Chicago, June 22, 2001. https://www.thisamericanlife.org/radio-archives/episode/188/kid-logic.

Grinspan, Izzy. "7 College Students Talk about Their Instagrams and the Pressure to Seem Happy." *The Cut*. Accessed November 24, 2015. http://nymag.com/thecut/2015/07/college-students-on-the-pressure-to-seem-happy.html.

Guardini, Romano. *The End of the Modern World*. Translated by Elinor Briefs. Wilmington, DE: ISI Books, 1998.

Guerriero, Elio, ed. *The Journey of Our Love: The Letters of Saint Gianna Beretta and Pietro Molla*. Translated by Ann Brown. Boston: Pauline, 2009.

Gula, Richard M. *Reason Informed by Faith: Foundations of Catholic Morality*. New York: Paulist, 1989.

Gutiérrez, Gustavo. *A Theology of Liberation: History, Politics, and Salvation*. Translated by Caridad Inda and John Eagleson. Revised edition. Maryknoll, NY: Orbis Books, 1988.

Hahnenberg, Edward P. *Awakening Vocation: A Theology of Christian Call*. Collegeville, MN: Liturgical Press, 2010.

Heffernan, Lisa, and Jennifer Wallace. "To Get into College, Harvard Report Advocates for Kindness instead of Overachieving." *Washington Post*, January 20, 2016. https://www.washingtonpost.com/news/parenting/wp/2016/01/20/to-get-into-college-harvard-report-advocates-for-kindness-instead-of-overachieving/?tid=a_inl&utm_term=.210bde2c4dd1.

Hoover, Rose. "The Communion of Saints. Lest the Journey Be Too Long." *The Way* 30 (1990): 216–30.

Ingold, Tim. *Being Alive: Essays on Movement, Knowledge and Description*. London: Routledge, 2011.

Isaac, M. E. "Mary in the Lucan Infancy Narrative." *The Way* 25 (1975): 80–95.

Jackson, Maggie. *Distracted: The Erosion of Attention and the Coming Dark Age*. Amherst, NY: Prometheus, 2009.

Jägerstätter, Franz. *Franz Jägerstätter: Letters and Writings from Prison*. Edited by Erna Putz. Translated by Robert Krieg. Maryknoll, NY: Orbis Books, 2009.

Jaschik, Scott. "More Pressure Than Ever: The 2014 Survey of College and University Admissions Directors." *Inside Higher Ed*, September 18, 2014. https://www.insidehighered.com/news/survey/more-pressure-ever-2014-survey-college-and-university-admissions-directors.

Jensen, Lene Arnett, ed. "Emerging Adulthood(s): The Cultural Psychology of a New Life Stage." In *Bridging Cultural and Developmental Approaches to Psychology: New Syntheses in Theory, Research, and Policy*, 255–75. New York: Oxford University Press, 2011.

Johnson, Luke Timothy. *The Gospel of Luke*. Sacra Pagina Series 3. Collegeville, MN: Liturgical Press, 1991.

Kanigel, Robert. *The One Best Way: Frederick Winslow Taylor and the Enigma of Efficiency*. New York: Viking Adult, 1997.

Kelly, Kevin. "Becoming Screen Literate." *New York Times*, November 21, 2008. http://www.nytimes.com/2008/11/23/magazine/23wwln-future-t.html.

Kierkegaard, Soren. *The Concept of Anxiety: A Simple Psychologically Orienting Deliberation on the Dogmatic Issue of Hereditary Sin (Kierkegaard's Writings, VIII)*. Edited by Reidar Thomte. Princeton, NJ: Princeton University Press, 1981.

Kinsella, W. P. *Shoeless Joe*. New York: Mariner Books, 1999.

Kosloski, Philip. "Leonie Martin: St. Therese's 'Difficult Sister' Continues on the Road to Canonization." *Aleteia.org*, January 26, 2017. http://aleteia.org/2017/01/26/leonie-martin-st-thereses-difficult-sister-continues-on-the-road-to-canonization.

Landes, David S. *Revolution in Time: Clocks and the Making of the Modern World*. Cambridge, MA: Harvard University Press, 2000.

Leshed, Gilly, Theresa Velden, Oya Rieger, Blazej Kot, and Phoebe Sengers. "In-Car GPS Navigation: Engagement with and Disengagement from the Environment." Proceedings of the SIGCHI Conference on Human Factors in Computing Systems. New York: ACM, 2008.

Lewis, C. S. *The Great Divorce*. San Francisco: HarperOne, 2000.

Lewis, Madeline. "In a Fog." Stories of Grace: Episode 9. *Church Life Journal*, January 18, 2017. https://churchlife.nd.edu/2017/01/18/stories-of-grace-episode-9.

Lubac, Henri de. *Catholicism: Christ and the Common Destiny of Man*. Translated by Lancelot Sheppard and Elizabeth Englund. San Francisco: Ignatius Press, 1988.

Mandell, Judy. "What College Admissions Officers Say They Want in a Candidate." *Washington Post*, August 30, 2016. https://www.washingtonpost.com/news/parenting/wp/2016/08/30/what-21-college-admissions-officers-say-they-want-in-a-candidate/?utm_term=.0c37314a25dc.

Manglos-Weber, Nicolette, and Christian Smith. "Understanding Former Young Catholics: Findings from a National Study of American Emerging Adults." National Survey of Youth and Religion. Notre Dame, IN: University of Notre Dame: Institute for Church Life and Center for Study of Religion and Society, 2015.

Martin, James. *My Life with the Saints*. Chicago: Loyola, 2007.

Martin, Louis, and Zélie Martin. *Call to a Deeper Love: The Family Correspondence of the Parents of Saint Therese of the Child Jesus*. Edited by Frances Renda. Translated by Ann Connors Hess. New York: Alba House, 2011.

McLuhan, Marshall. *Understanding Media: The Extensions of Man*. Edited by W. Terrence Gordon. Critical edition. Corte Madera, CA: Gingko Press, 2003.

Meier, John P. *A Marginal Jew, Volume I: The Roots of the Problem and the Person*. New York: Doubleday, 1991.

Merton, Thomas. *The Sign of Jonas*. New York: Harvest Books, 2002.

Meyer, Ben F. "'But Mary Kept All These Things . . .' (Lk 2, 19.51)." *Catholic Biblical Quarterly* 26, no. 1 (January 1964): 31–49.

Miller, Joe. "How Facebook's Tentacles Reach Further than You Think." *BBC News.* Accessed May 26, 2017. http://www.bbc.com/news/business-39947942?SThisFB.

Miller, Vincent. *Consuming Religion: Christian Faith and Practice in a Consumer Culture.* New York: Continuum International Publishing Group, 2003.

———. "Online, We Encounter Suffering from Afar: How Do We Respond?" *America Magazine,* October 3, 2016. http://www.americamagazine.org/issue/geography-mercy.

"Miracle Teenager Survives on His Own for Almost 6 Hours with No Wi-Fi." *Waterford Whispers News,* September 23, 2016. http://waterfordwhispersnews.com/2016/09/23/miracle-teenager-survives-on-his-own-for-almost-6-hours-with-no-wi-fi.

Molla, Pietro, and Elio Guerriero. *Saint Gianna Molla: Wife, Mother, Doctor.* Translated by James Colbert. San Francisco: Ignatius, 2004.

Muggeridge, Malcolm. *Something Beautiful for God: The Classic Account of Mother Teresa's Journey into Compassion.* New York: HarperOne, 1971.

Mulhere, Kaitlin. "Lots More College Admissions Officers Are Checking Your Instagram and Facebook." *Time,* January 13, 2016. http://time.com/money/collection-post/4179392/college-applications-social-media.

Mumford, Lewis. *Technics and Civilization.* Reprint edition. Chicago: University of Chicago Press, 2010.

Neighborhood Film Company. *Any Given Day,* 2012. https://vimeo.com/48618719.

Newman, John Henry. "Holiness Necessary for Future Blessedness." In *Selected Sermons, Prayers, and Devotions,* 3–11. New York: Vintage, 1999.

———. "The Orthodoxy of the Body of the Faithful During the Supremacy of Arianism." In *The Arians of the Fourth Century,* 445–68. Eugene, OR: Wipf & Stock Publishers, 1996.

———. "Remembrance of Past Mercies." In *Selected Sermons, Prayers, and Devotions,* 197–206. New York: Vintage, 1999.

North, Wyatt. *Mother Teresa: A Life Inspired.* Boston: Wyatt North Publishing, 2014.

Nouwen, Henri J. M. *Making All Things New: An Invitation to the Spiritual Life.* Reissue edition. San Francisco: HarperOne, 2009.

O'Connor, Flannery. *Mystery and Manners: Occasional Prose.* Edited by Sally Fitzgerald and Robert Fitzgerald. New York: Farrar, Straus, and Giroux, 1969.

———. "A Temple of the Holy Ghost." In *The Complete Stories,* 236–48. New York: Farrar, Straus, and Giroux, 1971.

O'Malley, Timothy P. *Bored Again Catholic: How the Mass Could Save Your Life.* Huntington, IN: Our Sunday Visitor, 2017.

Origen. "Homily 26." In *Homilies on Numbers.* Edited by Christopher A. Hall. Translated by Thomas P. Scheck. Downer's Grove, IL: InterVarsity Press, 2009.

Péguy, Charles. *The Portal of the Mystery of Hope.* Translated by David Louis Schindler Jr. Grand Rapids, MI: William B. Eerdmans, 1996.

Pelikan, Jaroslav. *Credo: Historical and Theological Guide to Creeds and Confessions of Faith in the Christian Tradition.* New Haven, CT: Yale University Press, 2005.

Pelikan, Jaroslav, and Valerie Hotchkiss, eds. *Creeds and Confessions of Faith in the Christian Tradition.* Vol. I. New Haven, CT: Yale University Press, 2003.

Perrin, Andrew. "One-Fifth of Americans Report Going Online 'Almost Constantly.'" *Pew Research Center*, December 8, 2015. http://www.pewresearch.org/fact-tank/2015/12/08/one-fifth-of-americans-report-going-online-almost-constantly.

Piat, Stephane-Joseph. *The Story of a Family: The Home of St. Thérèse of Lisieux.* Translated by A Benedictine of Stanbrook Abbey. Rockford, IL: Tan Books and Publishers, 1994.

Pieper, Josef. *Leisure: The Basics of Culture.* Translated by Alexander Dru. San Francisco: Ignatius, 2009.

———. *The Four Cardinal Virtues.* Notre Dame, IN: University of Notre Dame Press, 2014.

Postman, Neil. *Amusing Ourselves to Death: Public Discourse in the Age of Show Business.* 20th Anniversary Edition. New York: Penguin, 2005.

"Preparatory Document of the XV Ordinary General Assembly of the Synod of Bishops on 'Young People, the Faith and Vocational Discernment,'" January 13, 2017. http://www.vatican.va/roman_curia/synod/documents/rc_synod_doc_20170113_documento-preparatorio-xv_en.html.

Radcliffe, Timothy. *What Is the Point of Being a Christian?* London: Bloomsbury, 2005.

Rahner, Karl. "Being Open to God as Ever Greater." In *Theological Investigations*, translated by Cornelius Ernst et al., 7:25–46. Limerick, Ireland: Mary Immaculate College, 2000.

Ratzinger, Joseph. *The God of Jesus Christ: Meditations on the Triune God.* Translated by Brian McNeil. San Francisco: Ignatius Press, 2008.

Reider, Jon. "Five Qualities That Universities Look for in Students." Tips for Parents. *UniversityParent*. Accessed April 8, 2017. https://www.universityparent.com/topics/tips-for-parents/five-traits-that-matter-in-college-admissions.

Richtel, Matt. "Are Teenagers Replacing Drugs with Smartphones?" *New York Times*, March 13, 2017. https://www.nytimes.com/2017/03/13/health/teenagers-drugs-smartphones.html.

Roberts, Jennifer L. "The Power of Patience: Teaching Students the Value of Deceleration and Immersive Attention." *Harvard Magazine*, 2013. http://harvardmagazine.com/2013/11/the-power-of-patience.

Robinson, Brett T. *Appletopia: Media Technology and the Religious Imagination of Steve Jobs*. Waco, TX: Baylor University Press, 2013.

———. "Recreational Dubs: Constituting Apple's iPod Cult." In *Drugs & Media: New Perspectives on Communication, Consumption, and Consciousness*. Edited by Robert C. MacDougall. New York: Continuum, 2011.

Robinson, Phil Alden. *Field of Dreams*. Universal Pictures, 1989.

Sales, Nancy Jo. "Tinder and the Dawn of the 'Dating Apocalypse.'" *Vanity Fair*, September 2015. http://www.vanityfair.com/culture/2015/08/tinder-hook-up-culture-end-of-dating.

Sarah, Robert. *The Power of Silence: Against the Dictatorship of Noise*. Translated by Michael J. Miller. San Francisco: Ignatius, 2017.

Schwartz, Barry. *The Paradox of Choice: Why More Is Less*. New York: Ecco, 2016.

Shellenbarger, Sue. "Teens Are Still Developing Empathy Skills." *Wall Street Journal*, October 15, 2013, sec. Careers. https://www.wsj.com/articles/teens-are-still-developing-empathy-skills-1381876015.

Shirky, Clay. "Why I Just Asked My Students to Put Their Laptops Away. . . ." *Medium*, September 9, 2014. https://medium.com/@cshirky/why-i-just-asked-my-students-to-put-their-laptops-away-7f5f7c50f368#.c61x3ztnv.

Siegel, Zachary. "Love in the Time of Tech: Your Brain on Dating Apps," February 1, 2016. http://www.thedailybeast.com/love-in-the-time-of-tech-your-brain-on-dating-apps.

Singer, Natasha. "How Google Took Over the Classroom." *New York Times*, May 13, 2017. https://www.nytimes.com/2017/05/13/technology/google-education-chromebooks-schools.html.

Smith, Christian. "Is Moralistic Therapeutic Deism the New Religion of American Youth? Implications for the Challenge of Religious Socialization and Reproduction." In *Passing on the Faith: Transforming Traditions for the Next Generation of Jews, Christians, and Muslims*. Edited by James L. Heft. New York: Fordham University Press, 2006.

Spink, Kathryn. *Mother Teresa: An Authorized Biography*. New York: HarperOne, 2011.

Stenovec, Timothy. "Facebook Is Now Bigger Than the Largest Country on Earth." *Huffington Post*, January 28, 2015, sec. Tech. http://www.huffingtonpost.com/2015/01/28/facebook-biggest-country_n_6565428.html.

Sullivan, Andrew. "I Used to Be a Human Being: My Distraction Sickness—and Yours." *New York Magazine*, September 2016. http://nymag.com/selectall/2016/09/andrew-sullivan-technology-almost-killed-me.html.

Swenson, Gayle. "NIST Launches a New U.S. Time Standard: NIST-F2 Atomic Clock." Text. *NIST*, April 3, 2014. https://www.nist.gov/news-events/news/2014/04/nist-launches-new-us-time-standard-nist-f2-atomic-clock.

Taylor, Frederick Winslow. *The Principles of Scientific Management*. Eastford, CT: Martino Fine Books, 2014.

Teresa of Avila. *The Interior Castle*. Translated by Kieran Kavanaugh and Otilio Rodriguez. New York: Paulist Press, 1979.

———. *The Way of Perfection*. Edited by E. Allison Peers. Mineola, NY: Dover Publications, 2012.

Thérèse of Lisieux. *Story of a Soul*. Translated by John Clarke. Washington, DC: ICS Publications, 1996.

"The Trial of Thomas More: July 1, 1535." Center for Thomas More Studies. Accessed May 29, 2017. https://thomasmorestudies.org/docs/The%20Trial%20of%20Thomas%20More.pdf.

Turkle, Sherry. *Alone Together: Why We Expect More from Technology and Less from Each Other*. New York: Basic Books, 2012.

———. *Reclaiming Conversation: The Power of Talk in a Digital Age*. Reprint edition. New York: Penguin Books, 2016.

"Turning the Tide: Inspiring Concern for Others and the Common Good through College Admissions." Making Caring Common Project. Harvard Graduate School of Education, 2016. http://mcc.gse.harvard.edu/files/gse-mcc/files/20160120_mcc_ttt_execsummary_interactive.pdf?m=1453303460.

University of Notre Dame Enrollment Division. "Admission Statistics." *Undergraduate Admissions*. Accessed April 8, 2017. http://admissions.nd.edu/apply/admission-statistics.

———. "Evaluation Criteria." *Undergraduate Admissions*. Accessed April 8, 2017. http://admissions.nd.edu/apply/evaluation-criteria/.

Vanstone, W. H. *The Stature of Waiting*. London: Darton, Longman and Todd, 2001.

Verdon, Timothy. *Art & Prayer: The Beauty of Turning to God*. Brewster, MA: Mount Tabor, 2016.

————. *The Story of St. Francis of Assisi: In Twenty-Eight Scenes*. Brewster, MA: Mount Tabor, 2015.

Wassink, Stephanie Klein. "What Really Goes on in a College Admissions Office?" *Time*, February 18, 2016. http://time.com/money/collection-post/4227671/what-really-goes-on-in-a-college-admissions-office.

Weddell, Sherry A. *Forming Intentional Disciples: The Path to Knowing and Following Jesus*. Huntington, IN: Our Sunday Visitor, 2012.

Weil, Simone. *Awaiting God: A New Translation of "Attente de Dieu and Lettre a Un Religieux."* Translated by Bradley Jersak. Maywood, CT: Fresh Wind Press, 2013.

Williams, Rowan. *Resurrection: Interpreting the Easter Gospel*. New York: Pilgrim Press, 1984.

Wollheim, Richard. *Painting as an Art: The A. W. Mellon Lectures in the Fine Arts*. Princeton, NJ: Princeton University Press, 1987.

Zahn, Gordon Charles. *In Solitary Witness: The Life and Death of Franz Jägerstätter*. Springfield, IL: Templegate, 1986.

Zuckerberg, Mark. Digital Letter. "Building Global Community." Digital Letter, February 16, 2017. https://www.facebook.com/notes/mark-zuckerberg/building-global-community/10103508221158471.

Leonard J. DeLorenzo works in the McGrath Institute for Church Life and teaches theology at the University of Notre Dame. He is the author of *Witness* and *Work of Love,* and he is the coeditor of *Dante, Mercy, and the Beauty of the Human Person.*

DeLorenzo earned his doctorate in systematic theology from the University of Notre Dame, where he also earned his master's (systematic theology) and bachelor's degrees (theology and philosophy). He has served on the leadership teams for Notre Dame Vision, the Notre Dame Catechist Academy, the Notre Dame Character Project, and the Church Life Internship. He speaks regularly on the saints, biblical catechesis, vocation and discernment, and the theological imagination. His website is leonardjdelorenzo.com.

He and his wife, Lisa, live in South Bend, Indiana, with their children.

Also by Leonard J. DeLorenzo

Witness
Learning to Tell the Stories of Grace That Illumine Our Lives

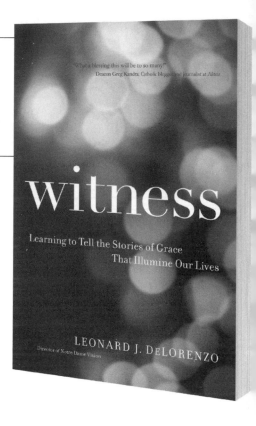

Beginning with the apostles themselves, Christians have practiced the art of telling their stories to bring others to faith. Leonard J. DeLorenzo, theology professor and director of Notre Dame Vision—a program designed to help youth and young adults find their true vocation—presents seven guiding principles to help you share your faith in a genuine way and teach others to do so as well.

"What a blessing this will be to so many!"

Deacon Greg Kandra

Catholic blogger and journalist at *Aleteia*